Studying the Life of Saint Francis of Assisi

Studying the Life of Saint Francis of Assisi

A Beginner's Workbook (2nd Edition)

Coordinated with the new
Francis of Assisi: Early Documents

by William R. Hugo, O.F.M. Cap.

New City Press
Hyde Park, New York

To Art and Betty

Published in the United States by New City Press
202 Comforter Blvd., Hyde Park, NY 12538
www.newcitypress.com

Cover design by Leandro de Leon
Cover art by Dr. Terrence J. Riddell. Used with permission.

Library of Congress Cataloging-in-Publication Data

Hugo, William.
Studying the life of Saint Francis of Assisi : a beginner's workbook / by William Hugo. — 2nd ed.
p. cm.
Includes bibliographical references and index.
ISBN 978-1-56548-397-2 (pbk. : alk. paper) 1. Francis, of Assisi, Saint, 1182-1226—Textbooks.
2. Franciscans—Textbooks. I. Title.
BX3602.3.H84 2011
271'.302—dc23 2011020023

Printed in the United States of America

Contents

Preliminaries

Tools

Work

Abbreviations

The writings of Francis of Assisi

Adm	*The Admonitions* (FA:ED I 128–137)
BlL	*A Blessing for Brother Leo* (FA:ED I 112)
CtExh	*The Canticle of Exhortation for the Ladies of San Damiano* (FA:ED I 115)
CtC	*The Canticle of the Creatures* (FA:ED I 113–114)
ER	*The Earlier Rule* also called the *Regula non bullata* abbreviated RnB (FA:ED I 63–86)
ExhP	*The Exhortation to the Praise of God* (FA:ED I 138)
LtAnt	*A Letter to Brother Anthony of Padua* (FA:ED I 107)
1LtCl	Earlier Edition of *Exhortation to the Clergy* also called *A Letter to the Clergy* (FA:ED I 52–53)
2LtCl	Later Edition of *Exhortation to the Clergy* also called *A Letter to the Clergy* (FA:ED I 54–55)
1LtCus	*The First Letter to the Custodians* (FA:ED I 56–57)
2LtCus	*The Second Letter to the Custodians* (FA:ED I 60)
1LtF	*Earlier Exhortation to the Brothers and Sisters of Penance* also called The First Version of *The Letter to the Faithful* (FA:ED I 41–44)
2LtF	*Later Admonition and Exhortation to the Brothers and Sisters of Penance* also called The Second Version of *The Letter to the Faithful* (FA:ED I 45–51)
LtL	*A Letter to Brother Leo* (FA:ED I 122–123)
LtMin	*A Letter to a Minister* (FA:ED I 97–98)
LtOrd	*A Letter to the Entire Order* (FA:ED I 116–121)
LR	*The Later Rule* also called the *Regula bullata* abbreviated RB (FA:ED I 99–106)
LtR	*A Letter to the Rulers of the People* (FA:ED I 58–59)
OfP	*The Office of the Passion* (FA:ED I 139–157)
PrCr	*The Prayer before the Crucifix* (FA:ED I 40)
PrsG	*The Praises of God* (FA:ED I 108–111)
PrH	*The Praises To Be Said at All the Hours* (FA:ED I 161–162)
PrOF	*A Prayer Inspired by the Our Father* (FA:ED I 158–160)
RH	*A Rule for Hermitages* (FA:ED I 61–62)
SalBV	*A Salutation of the Blessed Virgin Mary* (FA:ED I 163)
SalV	*A Salutation of the Virtues* (FA:ED I 164–165)
Test	*The Testament* (FA:ED I 124–127)
TPJ	*True and Perfect Joy* (FA:ED I 166–167)

First Franciscan century sources

AC *The Assisi Compilation* (This abbreviation refers to the version found in FA:ED II 111–230. In Habig, this work is called *The Legend of Perugia*, abbreviated LP. The numbering system is different in the two editions.)

AP *The Anonymous of Perugia* also called *The Beginning or Founding of the Order and the Deeds of Those Lesser Brothers Who Were the First Companions of Blessed Francis in Religion* by John of Perugia (FA:ED II 29–58)

1C *The Life of St. Francis* also called *The First Life of St. Francis* by Thomas of Celano (FA:ED I 169–308)

2C *The Remembrance of the Desire of a Soul* also called *The Second Life of St. Francis* by Thomas of Celano (FA:ED II 231–393)

3C *The Treatise on the Miracles of St Francis* by Thomas of Celano (FA:ED II 395–468)

DBF *The Deeds of Blessed Francis and His Companions* also called *The Acts of Blessed Francis and His Companions* By Ugolino Boniscambi of Montegiorgio (FA:ED III 427–565)

Eccleston *The Coming of the Friars Minor to England* by Thomas of Eccleston (Chronicles 79–191, selections)

Fior *The Little Flowers of St. Francis* also known as the *Fioretti* (This abbreviation refers to the version found in Habig 1301–1506 that contains *The Considerations of the Sacred Stigmata* at its end and is later than the version LFl in FA:ED III)

Jordan *The Chronicle of Brother Jordan of Giano* (Chronicles 3–77, selections)

L3C *The Legend of the Three Companions* (FA:ED II 59–110)

LegCl *The Legend of Saint Clare* (CA:ED 277–329)

LFl *The Little Flowers of St. Francis* also known as the *Fioretti* (This abbreviation refers to the version found in FA:ED III 566–658 that does not contain *The Considerations of the Sacred Stigmata* at its end and is earlier than the version Fior in Habig)

LJS *The Life of St. Francis* by Julian of Speyer (FA:ED I 361–420)

LMj *The Major Legend of St. Francis* by Bonaventure of Bagnoregio, also known by its Latin name, *Legenda maior* (FA:ED II 525–649. The cited pages are followed by ten chapters of miracles occurring after Francis' death that are never cited in this workbook.)

LMn *The Minor Legend of St. Francis* by Bonaventure of Bagnoregio also known by its Latin name, *Legenda minor* (FA:ED II 684–717)

LP *The Legend of Perugia* (This abbreviation refers to the version found in Habig 977–1091. In FA:ED, this work is called *The Assisi Compilation,* abbreviated AC. The numbering system is different in the two editions.)

1MP *A Mirror of the Perfection*, Rule, *Profession, Life, and True Calling of a Lesser Brother*, also called *The Mirror of Perfection* (Lemmens Edition) (FA:ED III 205–252). Worksheets in this workbook never cite this edition.

2MP *A Mirror of Perfection of the* Status *of a Lesser Brother*, also called *The Mirror of Perfection* (Sabatier Edition) (FA:ED III 253–372). All citations in this workbook are for this edition.

Editions of Franciscan sources

AB Armstrong, Regis J. and Ignatius Brady, trans. and eds. *Francis and Clare: The Complete Works*. The Classics of Western Spirituality. New York: Paulist Press, 1982.

CA:ED *Clare of Assisi: Early Documents*. Ed. and trans. Regis J. Armstrong. Second revised edition. New York: New City Press, 2006. All citations in this workbook are from this edition. The original edition was published by Paulist Press in 1988, and an earlier revised edition was published by the Franciscan Institute Publication in 1993.

Cousins Cousins, Ewert, trans. and ed. *Bonaventure: The Soul's Journey into God, The Tree of Life, The Life of St. Francis*. The Classics of Western Spirituality. New York: Paulist Press, 1978.

Chronicles Hermann, Placid, trans. and ed. *XIIIth Century Chronicles: Jordan of Giano, Thomas of Eccleston, Salimbene degli Adami.* Chicago: Franciscan Herald Press, 1961.

FA:ED *Francis of Assisi: Early Documents*. Eds. Regis J. Armstrong, J. A. Wayne Hellmann, William J. Short. Four volumes. New York: New City Press, 1999, 2000, 2001, and 2002. A Roman numeral after *FA:ED* indicates the volume. Arabic numbers refer to page numbers.

Habig Habig, Marion A., ed. *St. Francis of Assisi: Writings and Early Biographies. English Omnibus of the Sources for the Life of St. Francis*. Chicago: Franciscan Herald Press, 1973.

RA Armstrong, Regis J. *St. Francis of Assisi: Writings for a Gospel Life*. New York: Crossroad, 1994.

Chronology of Francis' Life and Medieval Writings about Him

1181/82	Francis was born
1202, November	Battle of Collestrada in which Assisi lost to Perugia and Francis was taken prisoner
1206	Francis' trial before Bishop Guido of Assisi
1208	Francis heard a gospel that gave his life new direction; Bernard of Quintavalle was the first to join and remain with Francis
1209/1210	Pope Innocent III approved *The Primitive Rule*
1215	The Fourth Lateran Council
1217	Chapters began and the order was divided into provinces
1219, November 5	Battle of Damietta in Egypt
1223, November 29	Pope Honorius III approved *The Later Rule*
1223	Christmas at Greccio
1224, Aug 15–Sept. 29	Francis' religious experience (stigmata) at La Verna
1226, October 3	Francis died
1226, October 4	Francis was buried at San Giorgio in Assisi
1228, July 16	Pope Gregory IX canonized Francis in Assisi
1228–1229	Thomas of Celano's *The Life of St. Francis* (1C)
1230, May 25	Francis' remains were transferred to the Basilica of St. Francis in Assisi
1234–1235	Julian of Speyer's *Life of St. Francis*
1240/41	*The Anonymous of Perugia* by John of Perugia
1244	Franciscan General Minister Crescentius of Jesi asked that new information about Francis be sent to him
1246	The Three Companions wrote *The Greccio Letter* and submitted their reminiscences which became the basis of *The Assisi Compilation*

1246	*The Legend of the Three Companions*
1246–1247	Thomas of Celano's *The Remembrance of the Desire of a Soul* (2C)
1250–1252	Thomas of Celano's *The Treatise on Miracles of Saint Francis* (3C)
1257/58	Thomas of Eccleston's chronicle
1260–1262	Bonaventure of Bagnoregio's *The Major Legend of St. Francis* (*Legenda maior*)
1262	Jordan of Giano's chronicle
1311	The early reminiscences of The Three Companions and other independent texts reached their final form as *The Assisi Compilation* at the hand of an anonymous redactor
1318	*The Mirror of Perfection*
1328–1337	Ugolino of Montegiorgio's *Actus beati Francisci et sociorum eius* (*The Deeds of Blessed Francis and His Companions*)
after 1337	*Fioretti* (*The Little Flowers*), an early Italian translation of *The Deeds* found in FA:ED III. By 1396 a more redacted version including the addition of *The Considerations of the Sacred Stigmata* appeared and is the version found in Habig.

Introduction and Acknowledgments

Much has happened in the world of Franciscan scholarship since the first edition of this workbook in 1996. The advances have been particularly intense in the English-speaking world. Publishing houses devoted to Franciscan or religious titles as well as university and secular presses have produced many and diverse works that often go beyond the expected lines of traditional Franciscan research. The new studies have been original English investigations as well as translations of acclaimed works from around the world. Particularly *Greyfriars Review* has kept the English-speaking Franciscan world abreast of recent research.

The crown jewel of these advances in the English-speaking world can only be *Francis of Assisi: Early Documents* (FA:ED), published in three volumes plus an index from 1999 through 2002 by New City Press. It updates and incredibly expands the resources found in the previous English collection of Franciscan first-century primary sources edited by Marion Habig and affectionately called *The Omnibus* by students of Francis' life. Representing the three branches of the Franciscan First Order, the editors of this new edition—Regis Armstrong (Capuchin), Wayne Hellmann (Conventual), and William Short (Friar Minor)—have garnered an expansive amount of new research and allowed the English-speaking world to benefit from its freshness. They have done in a decade what few could do in a lifetime. Only giants in any field are able to synthesize and interpret such a vast amount of information.

Their achievement challenges teachers and students of Francis of Assisi in new ways. Specifically, this monumental publication demands a new edition of this workbook. FA:ED is the new standard bearer, and this workbook must be user friendly for FA:ED's readers. A summary of FA:ED's characteristics must include:

- Translating many sources into English for the first time
- Bringing together many previously translated sources for the first time
- Applying the research of the last fifty years to all the sources, often providing new answers to old questions about the dating, authorship, and valuation of the sources
- Providing marginalia that refers readers to relevant earlier hagiography, scripture, and Franciscan writings
- Abundant indices
- Colorful and intelligible maps

Since the publication of FA:ED warrants a second edition of this workbook, I took the opportunity to accomplish other goals as well. The various bibliographies found within are considerably updated. New discoveries and theories by Franciscan scholars are reflected in the worksheets. Several worksheets are totally redone. A few worksheets that did not prove valuable in the classroom have been eliminated.

This workbook has been shaped by my students from the beginning. Their difficult experience locating the proper citations of primary sources has caused me to introduce a new way of making those citations. Because many of the works cited in this workbook contain long sections with multiple paragraphs, I have begun to more precisely indicate citations with lower case letters referring to paragraphs. The order of the letter in the English alphabet indicates the number of the paragraph in a given section. For example, "a" refers to the first paragraph, "b" to the second, "c" to the third, etc. Thus the citation AC 3b refers to the second paragraph (b) in the third section (3) of *The Assisi Compilation*. Unless a citation specifically refers to Habig's edition, all citations using lower case letters refer to paragraphs in the FA:ED edition.

Many people deserve my thanks for making both editions of this publication possible. I begin with those who helped craft the book in an interactive way: my students. These include novices, postulants, Secular Franciscans, professed Franciscans, and graduate students at Graduate Theological Union. Their use of these pages brought them to the more advanced stage found here.

Let me list the host of people who helped in one way or another with either or both editions. They know their contributions: TL Michael Auman, Keith Clark, Anthony Ciorra, Edward Foley, Daniel Fox, Alan Gaebel, Wayne Hellmann, John Holly, Sue Hulse, Raphael Iannone, Gerald Kafer, Michael Marigliano, Jack Rathschmidt, Terrence Riddell, Norma Rocklage, Maurice Sheehan, Joanne Schatzlein, Kenneth Smits, and Gandolf Wild.

I thank Gary Brandl of New City Press for his invaluable help in bringing this second edition to fruition.

One person deserves my special thanks. Maurice Sheehan, more than anyone else, shaped the way I approach Franciscan studies while he was my mentor at St. Bonaventure University. I thank him for teaching me about *method*, the most important thing in education, and developing in me an appreciation for accurate history as the basis for good Franciscan spirituality.

PRELIMINARIES

Why and for Whom This Book?

Because it works! The *it* is a method for studying the life and writings of Francis of Assisi (1181/2–1226). Many people either want to learn about Francis or have the responsibility of teaching others about Francis. The purpose of this book is to teach a method for doing either that I have found successful. However, before I tell you why I think it works, let me describe what I think has not worked and why.

For over three decades, I have taught the life and writings of Francis of Assisi to numerous groups of people. Before approaching the first group, I considered a variety of methods to accomplish my task.

It seemed that most Franciscan novice directresses/directors—charged with the same task of teaching the life and writings of Francis—used one of two common approaches. The first was the most popular: the common reading of a popular biography, followed by group discussion. Undoubtedly, the most common book chosen was *Saint Francis of Assisi: a Biography* by Omer Engelbert (1965 & 1979). The second approach was lectures. In the latter case, the presenters usually focused on themes from Franciscan spirituality that they ferreted out of their own study of the Franciscan tradition.

The first method appealed to beleaguered formation directresses/directors who had little background in formal Franciscan studies and for whom Franciscan studies was only one small piece of a much larger and demanding formation program. The second approach allowed those with a more extensive background to spread their wings and to discuss their favorite aspects of the Franciscan story.

I observed a number of common responses to both methods. The predominant response was boredom. This response was too bad and too pervasive. To learn that most novices disliked or loathed their Franciscan studies pained me who had just completed an exciting masters degree in the field. I could not fathom how initiates into Franciscan life would fare later on without an enthusiasm for the foundation and inspiration of their new, chosen life.

Secondly, I was amazed at how uninformed many novices were *after* their "Franciscan education." They had a paltry awareness of the major questions and issues surrounding Francis' life. In fact, many had a meager knowledge of the basic outline of his life! Most did not possess a high confidence in their knowledge about Francis and abhorred the prospect of one day having to do additional Franciscan studies.

However, my third impression was the most devastating. Few left initial Franciscan formation with the tools to do any further study of the life or writings of Francis. Too often, they were left only with the opinions or points of view of their teachers or authors, and these were quickly forgotten! If a new question about Francis or Franciscan life came up, the former student was damned to seeking out the answer from an expert or some old Franciscan book in the house library. Such dependency is debilitating.

Later, I'll tell you more about the method I constructed to address my concerns. For now, let me tell you the three goals I had as I designed it.

First, it had to be engaging. Boredom is the enemy of all learning and to be avoided at all cost. I wanted a method that would challenge my students and spark their curiosity. So, I designed a method that did not provide them with answers, but asked them to discover what we could know about Francis. I also wanted a method in which students would question each other, creating group interaction in a challenging way. I banked on the assumption that more involvement in a discovery process would make the task more interesting.

Second, I wanted my students to complete my course actually knowing quite a bit about Francis. Just making the project interesting would assist toward this. However, I also suspected that students learn more when they have to struggle with the material themselves. Furthermore, if the students were to be well versed in Francis' life and writings, they needed to be exposed to a wide spectrum of material about him.

Finally, I knew from my own studies that, in actuality, we remember very little of what we learn in school. It's a sad but true fact of life. My teaching method had to take this into account. So rather than focus exclusively on teaching information about Francis, I knew my primary goal had to be the teaching of a *method* for studying the life and writings of Francis. That way, any student could relearn an old area of forgotten knowledge or research a new area as new questions arose. I hoped my students would become independent and able to form their own conclusions based on their own quality research.

When I finally developed a method to achieve these goals, I discovered a wonderful fact. Students didn't need me to use the method! Surely, I knew that the presence of a knowledgeable and skilled teacher enhanced the learning process. But the fact remained; students could use this method on their own. I discovered this when I prepared a number of study guides for some brother Capuchins who were planning a one-month pilgrimage to Assisi. I pulled some worksheets from my class notes for novices and shared the wealth. A few months later, I met them in Assisi during the journey. They were ecstatic with the results.

So, the potential audience for this book expanded before my eyes. Originally, I wrote to share my work with other formation directors/directresses who had the same task I did. I knew that they too could lead their postulants, novices or temporary professed through a high-class study of Francis. Later, I realized that any one desirous to learn more about Francis could do so alone or in groups with friends or colleagues. All they needed was a method that would unlock the riches of the sources for Francis' life and writings. This might include veteran religious who have been Franciscans all of their adult lives but who never received Franciscan input, members of the Secular Franciscans, students of the history of religious life or spirituality, or people interested in the lives of the saints.

Technical considerations

Obviously, I have not targeted the scholarly community with this book. However, I do hope to bring the fruit of their scholarship to this enterprise. I assume most of my readers are people in the trenches of life who look to Francis for inspiration and guidance. Therefore, I have striven to keep oblique scholarly apparatus to a minimum. I have stricken footnotes from my manuscript. When a citation needs to be acknowledged, I do so in the text itself. Some parenthetical remarks refer you to bibliography at the end of a chapter. If an explanation is important enough to include for your consideration, I have made it part of the text.

Periodically, I offer you suggestions for further reading on a particular topic. In a few chapters, I offer a more extensive analysis than normal and, therefore, want to provide you with a short bibliography on the topic. In these cases, I generally restrict myself to English publications. In a few cases, I cite foreign language publications because of their importance in Franciscan studies or because no English source is able to document the point I feel is important.

My intent is to provide you with sources that are usable and helpful. If you have more scholarly needs, you should be able to find additional foreign language bibliography in the English sources I cite.

Before you move on, you might want to reflect on your own experiences of Franciscan studies and discern what made them successful and enjoyable or not.

Know Your Biases; Know My Biases

A hallmark of my approach to studying Francis of Assisi is to gather as much objective data about him as possible. I wish to know the historical Francis as well as possible. All other images of him (theological, spiritual, symbolic) should be based on good history.

Despite this goal, I am powerfully aware of how biased all of us are. *Bias* carries many connotations I wish to clarify. Certainly, the word can imply a negative prejudice that might even lead to sin. Racial bias can be the unjust basis for racial discrimination. Sexism, ageism, and racism are all evils grounded upon biases.

People are also biased in favor of certain things. When watching a NFL football game that doesn't involve my favorite team, I usually root for the underdog. That reflects a bias.

Our lives are full of biases, most of which we are unaware. They are frequently subconscious and usually unreflected upon. We don't have the mental or emotional energy to deal with all our biases. Yet at certain times it becomes critical to expend some energy to become aware of our biases and to reflect upon them.

Biases shape perspective. Perspective helps us to recognize some realities and ignore others. Getting in touch with your biases gets you in touch with your partiality, preferences and prejudices. You become aware of your attitudes about how you think life is and, just as importantly, how you think life *should* be. What you think makes the world go 'round is partly the result of your biases. Is it love, money, power, or some other force in life?

Biases influence the way people approach big and small tasks. I know a religious whose ministries have involved prison and inner city work in part because he is biased in favor of social underdogs. He decries every political, social and economic event that does not specifically help the poor. A lot of his bias has to do with the fact that he considers himself an underdog in life. He is welcomed to his opinions and actions, but others in his religious community will evaluate his proposals for their common life in light of his bias and whether or not they share it.

People of faith, theologians, popes, atheists and historians are all people with biases. They and we are no different from the rest of our race. I draw out this point because many people hold the bias that some people *are not biased*. This is a difficult bias to dispel, especially if the bias involves religious belief. For example, some people believe popes are not biased because they are inspired by God's spirit. However, popes are people; they are biased. Some think saints could do no wrong. Otherwise they wouldn't be saints. Since bias is too often construed as a weakness or imperfection, they often consider saints to have been unbiased. However, saints were people; they were biased. Others view scholars as people devoted to objective truth. Since bias is not objective, scholars, at least good scholars, cannot be biased. But scholars are people; they are biased. Teresa of Calcutta, John Paul II, the Dalai Lama, and Aristotle all were biased. They were human beings.

That is important for our study of Francis of Assisi; he too was biased. In fact, his bias should be an object of our study of Francis.

More importantly, I am biased, and so are you. If we are to benefit from this study of Francis' life, it is critical that we are aware of our own and each other's biases. This needs to be further explored.

Teachers possess tremendous power. If they are well trained, they know more about the topic being discussed than most others in the room. They often can hide their uncertainty or incompetence from the eyes of their students. Teachers are selective in the material they present and the way they present it. I remember being resentful when in graduate school I came to realize there were more than one approach to sociology. My undergraduate sociology teacher only exposed me to one of the approaches, i.e., his approach. I was intellectually held hostage.

Many teachers are unaware of their biases. Too often they confuse their biases with objective truth. First, teachers need to become aware of their biases if they are to be good teachers. I obviously don't mean all their biases. I suspect that is an impossible task. But they need to constantly discover more of their biases so they are aware of how these biases influence their own thought and teaching. Awareness will also allow teachers to examine and reconsider their biases. This can only make them better and more honest teachers.

Just as significant, teachers should reveal their important biases to their students. This is only fair. It's a little like truth in lending. People should know up front what they are getting into, whether the commodity is financial or intellectual. The real importance of this practice is that it leaves the students *free*. They should be free to decide for themselves, to evaluate the soundness of their arguments, and to know how their teachers' biases might shape their approach to the information they share.

When teachers share their biases, students are forced to examine their own. That's more than half of education. It's beautiful when it happens. Let me share examples from my life that have an impact on my teaching the life of Francis.

One of my biases is that institutions are essential to preserving values. Partially because of this, I don't share a different bias held by many others that Franciscan and church leaders after Francis subverted his charism to the point of unfaithfulness. This bias I have will influence the way I evaluate some of the Franciscan sources as reliable historical accounts. So, it's important for me to disclose it to my students. Another of my biases is that I believe too many people think the saints were more perfect human beings than they really were. Because of this bias, I tend to ask a lot of questions about their limitations. When discussing matters involving these or other important biases, I often tell my students, "This is my bias," or "It's my opinion that …" I usually follow up my revelation with, "What do you think?"

I believe this approach is important, respectful and freeing. But that's my bias!

Which biases are the important ones to reveal? The answer is different for each of us. Different biases influence each person's ideas and approaches more than others. The biases that critically shape your thinking are the important ones to become aware of, understand, examine, and reveal. It's a process that never stops.

Frankly, it's a process that excites me. This self-discovery is as important as the information we learn through study. In the end, it will help us learn about Francis of Assisi as much as reading medieval stories.

My Lens: History

As long as we are talking about biases, I need to reveal another of mine. I prefer to study Francis of Assisi from a historical perspective.

Scholars study Francis using the lenses of a variety of disciplines. Church people tend to use the disciplines of theology, philosophy, spirituality, and history (usually church history) to study Francis. Others have studied him through art history. A surprising number of secular scholars study Francis' writings and biographies as pieces of literature.

For my purposes, I take a mostly historical approach. I have several reasons for this choice.

My first reason lies in the nature of hagiography, which I will discuss in a few chapters. Hagiography is writing that has a heavy emphasis on *interpreting* the saints. As we will see, this image or interpretation of the saint is more important than the facts about the saint.

There is nothing wrong with simply studying these interpretations if one is willing to accept medieval interpretations as adequate for today. I don't. So I strive to uncover as much historically reliable information about Francis as I can. Once I have done that, I need to interpret Francis again, hopefully in meaningful terms for us living 800 years after Francis' birth.

Medieval hagiography mythologized Francis. (I use *mythologize* in a positive way.) Some describe the process of stripping away that mythology as *demythologizing*. If we want to continue with the pattern, the final step might be called *remythologizing*. All this myth-talk highlights an important factor: the myth or interpretation of Francis is just as important as the history of Francis.

We seldom know historical figures as they really were (historically). We more commonly know them through images, a few characteristics, or a solitary action for which she or he is famous. Actually, the same is true about modern people we know only through the media. Consider how the "handlers" of a presidential candidate work to shape our image of the candidate. In a sense, their job is to create a favorable myth or interpretation of their candidate to help win votes. The truth is not as important as what people believe is true. Of course there are limits to the handlers' abilities. Sometimes a candidate's record is so obvious that the desired image will not stick. Also, handlers work to create negative images of their opponents, often with tremendous success. The result is often competing images in conflict. Nonetheless, the truth is that we come to know these people through their images.

Another fact is that these myths or interpretations change with time and circumstances. When I was a child, Christopher Columbus was an indisputable hero. My childhood classmates and I viewed the advent of the

European as a blessing for America. However by 1992, the 500th anniversary of his arrival in the western hemisphere, many judged his halo to be significantly tarnished. We were much more aware of the suffering caused to Native Americans as a result of advancing European "civilization." What happened? The myth changed, not the facts. Historians and the public simply put the already known facts together in a different way that led to a different interpretation or myth. Further, we should expect Columbus' myth to change again as new concerns shape our perspective.

However, unless we know the facts, adequate reinterpretations have difficulty emerging. That is why my preferred approach to Francis of Assisi is through history. My hope is that our myths or interpretations will be informed by accurate history: the facts as best we can know them. We don't need to feel sinister about this process. The medievals already did it for themselves. While we can learn from their interpretations, we are not obliged to accept them hook, line and sinker. In fact, we are wise to examine their interpretations closely. What was adequate for Anglo school children in the 1960's to believe about Columbus was not adequate for the children of 1992. Nor should we think what was adequate for medievals to believe about Francis is adequate for us today.

Undoubtedly, we will experience disagreements about the historical Francis. That's OK. Professionals in every field disagree about major issues in their disciplines. However, awareness of our differences will sensitize us and make us more cautious. More importantly, we will be surprised at how much we agree on.

There is another level for agreement and disagreement that this book will not focus on: What can we say about the shape of Franciscan life today? However, I wrote this book to help you answer that very question. The fact is I cannot answer it for you because there is no one correct answer. We will further explore this area in my final chapter. Until then, suffice it to say that unless we get our history down, it is futile to talk about the meaning of Franciscan life today.

Suggested reading

- Sheldrake, Philip. *Spirituality & History: Questions of Interpretation and Method.* New York: Crossroad, 1992. An excellent, readable summary of recent changes in approaches to history (chapter one), the history of spirituality (chapter two), the disciplinary interchange between history and spirituality (chapters three and four), case studies containing Franciscan subject matter (chapters five and six), and hermeneutics or the theory of interpreting texts (chapter seven).

Work with the Tools and Ask Questions!

I have one more preliminary topic to discuss: How will we accomplish our learning task?

In my opening section, I alluded to my teaching style: help the student discover the material. I don't believe discovery comes easily. It usually involves a great deal of work and a little luck. I can do little to increase your luck. However, I can give you the tools to do first class work.

So, there are two major parts to this book. In the first, I give you the tools you need to do the job. We must develop a critical attitude in the best sense of the word. A critical attitude is the most important tool. Without it, our work will suffer. With it, we can make up for a lot of other deficiencies. We also want to understand medieval hagiography, the form or genre of most sources for Francis' life. Finally, we want to learn about each of the sources, discovering their biases and perspectives.

It's my job to impart most of this information to you. Study it well. Read and reread each section. Make notes comparing one source to the others. Come back to this section even after you have begun your own work in the following section. Relearn what you have already forgotten. This is important material! If you are a group leader, you may want to learn this material beforehand and present it in lecture style. Always allow your group to ask questions and compare the various sources.

The next section belongs to you. This section systematically goes through the life of Francis. I don't tell you the story; you have to discover it. My part is to provide you with the sources, the places to find your information. You must read, examine, analyze, and compare them. Use all the tools you received in the previous section. Become critical and produce your best effort to discover something about the historical Francis.

Questions are so important to the process. That's why I believe this process is best done in groups. More minds think of more questions. No one of us can ask all the questions to get all the angles on a topic we study. The group enriches the process. Don't be afraid to have others question your assumptions or work. Furthermore, don't be afraid to question the assumptions and work of others in your group. If we don't ask questions of each other, we might as well disband as a study group. An important resource (each other's critical approach) will be squandered in our timidity. I might also add, questions are what make the process more interesting.

So, roll-up your sleeves. We're ready to get working.

Tools

Begin with a Question: What Don't I Like about Francis of Assisi?

I know it's an unusual place to begin. After all, we're studying the life of someone I presume you admire. Actually, that's where the problem lies.

- "Love is blind." That's why jurors have difficulty believing the testimony of the accused's spouse.
- Children frequently think they are responsible for their parents' divorce. They have difficulty understanding that their parents are responsible.
- Every four years we hear campaign managers for presidential candidates tell us how their nominee slaughtered the other during a televised debate. None of us expects them to be honest. Nevertheless, we must go through the ritual of asking them.

Admiration makes it difficult for human beings to be objective and honest in their judgments. We expect objectivity and honesty in others, but find it difficult to cultivate them in ourselves. Yet, I believe our study of Francis will promise valuable results only in proportion to our objectivity and honesty.

I don't believe people can like everything about any other person. Maybe people will say they do for that early moment of infatuation between people newly in love. But we know that people who don't move beyond that blind infatuation are destined for trouble in their relationship. The unacknowledged dislikes about each other are sure to surface eventually with destructive power.

Francis of Assisi was a human being. There have to be things about him that we don't like or turn us off.

That's why I am amazed year after year when I ask my students to think quietly for two minutes and then tell us "What don't you like about Francis of Assisi?" About half of my students are unable to give an answer. A few announce, "Nothing!" Others are confused by my question and sheepishly confess, "I don't know." Still others answer a different question. "I couldn't live as poor as he did." "I don't understand why he wanted to die as a martyr." "It must have hurt him to abandon his family."

Actually, my question is designed to invite students to say something negative about Francis. Perhaps it is something they dislike about him. However, it might amount to acknowledging a personal limitation in him. Maybe their response will be a criticism of something he did. A few students might share the judgment that Francis was really off base in some area.

Why are such negative recognitions important? Because Francis of Assisi is a canonized saint of the Roman Church! Too often, people put saints on a pedestal level with God. Most will deny that is what they are doing, but that attitude seeps out in the way they talk about their saints. If anything negative can be said, it usually is about the person before conversion, when limitations and sinfulness make for a more dramatic conversion to holiness. It's the "playboy to priest" syndrome. It makes for a great story.

It's also an illusion. If we want to meet the historical Francis, we have to meet his limitations. If we don't, we will preoccupy ourselves with something that is not human and of doubtful help in our own lives. I never could identify with the indestructible hero, the flawless leader, or the sinless saint. I'm none of those things and never will be.

Aside from the unhelpfulness of the *perfect* model, it simply isn't a historical portrayal of Francis or any human being. When we can say something negative about Francis, we have broken through a mental barrier, which allows us to be as objective and honest as we possibly can.

"I think Francis abused his body with his physical penances." "I don't believe Francis understood his father or gave him a fair chance." "I suspect Francis was part of a dysfunctional family." "Francis was not tolerant of people who opposed him in the order."

Whether or not these judgments are true is not that important at this early stage. We can test their accuracy later. However, those students who were able to say them jumped one more hurdle, which allowed them to study Francis from new perspectives. I am also happy to say that their boldness helped the others to eventually admit to their own reservations about the man.

Another of my biases is emerging: when saints are seen as human beings they become understandable, imitable, and, most importantly, approachable.

Take some time to answer the question for yourself: What don't you like about Francis of Assisi?

Positive Criticism

Yes, criticism can be positive! In fact, God save us from people who cannot give positive criticism of others or themselves. Without the presence of positive criticism, going to doctors, riding space shuttles, acting on investment advice from your stock broker, and being on trial before a judge are all dangerous enterprises. To people in these situations, I say, Good luck!, because luck is all you will be able to lean on.

In many situations, we use *critical* to describe negative attitudes, contrary opinions, faultfinding people, or unfavorable judgments. This is not the type of criticism I propose for doing Franciscan studies. *Critical* can also mean doing the best job possible, using the finest tools and methods available, or making informed and discriminating judgments. This is the positive criticism I suggest we absolutely need for a helpful and modern study of Francis' life and writings.

Any study of Francis of Assisi must begin with some very old sources, in fact *medieval* sources. Believe me, medieval folks had very different thoughts and values than we have. The rules for public writing were different from our own. If we want to understand the historical Francis, we need to understand the world and thoughts of the medievals who wrote about him and created the first images that interpreted his importance.

The alternative is to read those medieval documents according to our assumptions for modern writing. This would be *uncritical*; we would not be using the finest tools and methods available for us to make informed judgments about what Francis was really like.

The use of positive criticism is not new to scholars in the church. Perhaps the most familiar church use of positive criticism is in scripture studies. Bible scholars have used a variety of techniques aimed at understanding various aspects of the ancient writings that compose our Bible. They call these techniques criticisms, and use of the techniques helps scholars understand the various levels of interpretation going on in the text.

Form criticism seeks to understand the genre of a document. Once a genre can be determined, the scholar can use the rules of composition for the genre to better understand what the author might be trying to say. The novel is a genre. One of its basic rules is that it is fiction. On the other hand, biographies are supposed to be historically accurate. If readers unfamiliar with *Moby Dick* believe it is a biography, they most likely would end up thinking that Captain Ahab who pursued Moby Dick was a historical person. People from another time and unfamiliar with the TV sit-com genre from the 1970's, might view an episode of *All in the Family* and wonder if all American families in that period were characterized by misunderstanding, bigotry, and little appreciation for the arts. On the other hand, if the same viewers experienced other sit-coms and were able to compare that genre to the 1980 TV documentary, they would understand the entertaining quality of the sit-com's exaggeration and mockery. People who understand the difference in the genres are critical; those who don't understand are uncritical.

Scripture scholars identify the forms or genres of liturgical rituals, royal coronations, proverbs and creation stories in the scriptures. Identifying and understanding the genres help understand the meaning of the text. Most of the medieval writings about Francis of Assisi were legends or florilegia. The more general genre that includes both legends and florilegia is hagiography. If we want to understand Francis of Assisi, we have to understand these genres through which his story and meaning are transmitted to our age. This is being critical, and we will examine these genres later in a section on hagiography.

There are numerous types of criticism made famous by scripture scholars. Redaction criticism looks at the goals and biases of the person who gave a writing with a long tradition its final form. A particular book or section of the scripture may have developed over centuries, accumulating the thoughts of many authors along the way. The final editor or redactor had the advantage of selecting and rejecting the accumulated material. She could shape the material to reflect her point of view and discredit others. Stories about Francis of Assisi likewise have an organic life. They grew with time. We are lucky to possess copies of many stories at several points in their development so we can discover the biases and goals of their redactors. This is being critical.

All literature is created in a historical environment: political, social, economic, military, religious, etc. Knowledge of that environment reveals the subtleties of literature. Applying that knowledge to a piece of literature is called historical criticism. It attempts to determine what really happened.

Knowing something about ancient Egypt helps to understand the Book of Exodus. Understanding industrializing England helps one enjoy the novels of Charles Dickens. The stories about Francis of Assisi all make more sense if we know something about medieval feudalism, the meaning of money, the existing forms of religious life, the Islamic threat to Christianity and the Christian threat to Islam.

My first point is this: positive criticism helps us to understand the text as it was meant to be understood. It reveals the truth hidden from us by our ignorance of another time and place. Criticism prevents us from being fooled by the tricks and slyness of the time-span that separates us from the text we are reading.

My second point follows: criticism is a friend not to be avoided. It requires us to be questioning, suspicious, and astute. But it can also open up a world of wonder, warmth, conviction and spirit. Most importantly, it strives to understand the truth. What we do with the truth we discover is quite another question.

Don't be afraid of positive criticism. If you want to meet the historical Francis, learn the tools of criticism well and practice them. Make criticism an attitude when you pick up the stories about this remarkable man. You will discover a lot, and what you learn will be interesting and enlightening.

It is difficult to find a short yet helpful book on critical tools for studying medieval hagiography. Our best sources may be books about biblical criticism. Not all of their tools may apply, but an understanding of biblical techniques will take us a long way in developing the critical attitude that can help us discover the historical Francis. If you want to pursue this topic more, pick up any good and recent book on biblical criticism.

Hagiography

The worst part of mastering this section is learning how to pronounce the word, especially the first "g." *Webster's* indicates four acceptable ways to pronounce the first syllable. I prefer to pronounce the first "g" like the "j" in *John* and the first "a" long as in *day*. Consult your dictionary for other acceptable pronunciations.

Most people think hagiography is biography of saints. The most accurate part of that definition is that the object of hagiography is a saint—or someone an author hopes will be declared or considered a saint. *Biography* is a more complicated matter.

Modern Westerners expect biographies to be objectively true. Well, maybe we hedge a bit. Bill Clinton's autobiography might contain subjective interpretations from Clinton's perspective, but we still expect his *facts* to be reliable. If they are not, critics, colleagues, and historians will trash it as *untrue*.

Hagiography technically carries a meaning that does not presuppose *truth* in the same way. Hippolyte Delehaye wrote what I still consider the best easy-to-read book on hagiography available in English. He defines it as "writings inspired by devotion to the saints and intended to increase that devotion" (3 in Fordham edition).

The motive of the hagiographer is the key to understanding the difference between hagiography and modern biography. Delehaye says it is to "increase … devotion" to the subject, the saint. He breaks that down to five elements: to *edify* the reader, to *verify* the subject's sanctity, to *increase* the reader's devotion to the saint, to *move* the reader to moral change, and to *please* the reader by the writer's description and style.

Edification is a curious activity. The word's basic meaning is *to teach*. However, we usually reserve the word for those times when basic values are at stake. Through their writings about saints, hagiographers hope to teach readers what it means to be a Christian. The focus of attention is the ideal Christian life.

Moderns generally want to verify facts; medievals wanted to verify holiness. Relating events involving the saint is the undisputed way medievals did that. However, they did not hesitate to hedge the facts to achieve their final goal: to convince the reader that the subject was holy, i.e., a saint.

Devotion begins with holding someone in high esteem. It expresses itself by talking about the person, fussing over her or him, and trying to extend the devotion to others. When involving saints, devotees read the life and writings of their saints, try to live out the saints' values, and often pray privately or publicly to them. This prayer and devotion is called the cult of the saint.

The religious salvation of readers was the goal of every good medieval hagiographer. Gospel living was the means of receiving that salvation. Unless readers learned from the saint's story and changed their behaviors accordingly, the medieval hagiographer was a failure.

Modern people enjoy a well crafted story. So did medievals. Boredom is the curse of education in all ages and situations. Without an interesting writing style, a hagiographer's work might not be read or circulated in the medieval world. If people don't read the saint's story, they cannot learn from it, believe the saint was holy, become a saint's devotee, or change their lives. Don't be fooled by hagiographers' declarations of humble writing ability. They knew their goals depended on interesting writing, and not a few of them were proud of their literary accomplishments!

Edification, verification of holiness, increasing devotion, moral change, and interesting writing styles were the goals of good hagiographers. None of these goals demand that a hagiographer hedge on the truth, much less out-and-out lie. However, objective truth about historical facts in a person's life was not a medieval value, even though hagiographers go out of their way to claim objectivity and trustworthiness. They were products of an era with different values and notions of truth. When we fully understand their goals, it is easier to understand their techniques, which often offend modern readers. Let's explore some of the more common techniques.

Plagiarism

Plagiarism may be too strong a word, but medievals felt no shame when incorporating the work of a previous author into his or her own work. In a sense, "borrowing" was a form of flattery. No one considered it immoral, and certainly there were no laws making it illegal! Verbatim transfers of texts were not uncommon. Use of similar organization was routine. Often a story was reproduced in a later work with subtle changes that served the new author's particular purposes. In all these cases, don't expect a footnote from the medieval writer citing the source! If the reader could figure out the source, the author was thought to be well read. If not, the reader would be all the more amazed by the story in hand.

Saintly models

Saintly models were burned into medievals' minds. Medieval people measured new saints against the models depicted in older and better-known saints. Hagiographers used the established models of holiness to convince their readers that the subjects of their current works were also saints.

The martyr model probably had the earliest beginnings. In it, the martyr always endured hounding persecution, an obnoxious trial, and unimaginable torture. During the trial, the martyr usually delivered an incredibly eloquent testimony to his or her faith, in a forum we know seldom provided the opportunity for such soliloquies. The tortures should have resulted in numerous deaths, but the physical resilience of the martyrs testified to their holiness. A common way of ending the ordeal was beheading, a fate impossible to survive. But even that was overcome by the early bishop of Paris, St. Denis, who picked up his severed head and walked through the countryside until he dropped it where stands still today an incredible gothic church in his honor.

It is worthwhile to quote Delehaye's summary of the martyrdom of Ss. Agathangelus and Clement of Ancyra. This superhuman story makes its superhuman point.

> To start with, Clement is hung up, his flesh torn with iron combs, and his lips and cheeks battered with stones; he is bound to a wheel, beaten with sticks, and horribly slashed with knives; spikes are thrust into his face, his jaws broken and his teeth pulled out, and his feet are crushed in iron shackles. Then both martyrs are scourged and suspended from a beam; their bodies are scorched with burning torches and they are thrown to wild beasts. Red-hot prongs are forced under their nails, and then they are covered with quick-lime and left thus for two days; afterwards strips are torn from their skin and they are whipped again. They are laid on iron grids heated white-hot, and then cast into a fiery furnace where they remain for a day and a night. Once more they are rasped with metal hooks; then a sort of harrow is set up and they are thrown against its tines. Agathangelus in addition has molten lead poured over his head; he is dragged about the town with a millstone round his neck, and stoned. Clement alone has his ears pierced with red-hot needles, then is burned again with torches, and beaten over the head with a stick. At last, having for several days running received fifty lashes from a whip, he is beheaded, and Agathangelus with him. (71–72)

Any prospective saint who died for the faith would be plugged into this martyr model. Why? It proved they were saints. How? By following the pattern (model) of previous martyrs.

There were other models as well. The *founding monk or nun* created a lifestyle of holiness associated with a monastery or a group of monasteries. The *angelic* model portrayed saints who like angels were more spirit than flesh. They denied themselves human pleasure and inflicted suffering on themselves. They bi- or tri-located (being in more than one place at a time), levitated (rising off the ground), had visions, talked to and were understood by animals and nature, read people's thoughts, and fought devils. *Missionary bishops* left their homelands to evangelize distant heathen people. They endured suffering for the glory of God and managed to establish a new people of faith. Their lives often ended in martyrdom, and, thus, their stories often follow the martyr model as well.

The point is this: fitting a model helped prove a person's holiness and thus saintliness, one of the five goals of the hagiographer. It was difficult to convince a reader of the subject's holiness if he or she did not conform to the common models of holiness that were familiar at the time.

Saintly replacements

Pressure to portray a holy person within a predefined model or role also created strings of saints whose lives seemed strikingly similar. Sometimes two saints might only have shared a particular event in common; at other times, their entire lives may have appeared as reruns. Through this phenomenon, saints tended to replace one another in the history of hagiography.

Many of these similarities can be seen in the lives of Martin of Tours (c. 316–c. 397) and Francis of Assisi. A significant event in Martin's conversion was meeting a beggar; Francis' conversion included an important meeting with a leper. Both men thought of military careers, only to choose something else. Robbers plundered the two of them. Francis sought advice from Bishop Guido of Assisi (c. 1204–1228); Martin, from Bishop Hilary of Poitiers (d. 367). When their parents fumed about their choices in life, both took refuge in churches. Martin displayed his growing conviction by splitting his cloak and giving half to the poor; Francis gave all his clothes back to his father. Each man's legend includes a story of struggle with a devil. And, of course, both saints changed other people by their example.

I do not mean to suggest that none of these events occurred in Francis' life simply because parallels can be found in Martin's life. Many of these stories are natural parts of people's lives. However, if the stories about Martin had any resemblance to those about Francis, a good hagiographer would be sure to exploit the resemblance to forward his goal of proving Francis' holiness. The story might be cast in such a way that the medieval person would be sure to make the connection. The later saint might go just a step further than the earlier saint, showing the newer subject to be *holier* than the older saint.

Stock incidences

While hagiographers often employed models to portray holiness, they also used stock incidences to make their points. Stock incidences are different from models in that they are special stories which can be cut-and-pasted from any saint's story to another's, even if the two saints follow different models. Stock incidences abound in hagiographic material. If one saint is portrayed by a stock incidence, a thousand others are as well. And that's the point. If so many proven saints did a particular action, what better way to prove your saint's holiness than to portray her or him with the same behaviors!

Many of the animal stories about Francis of Assisi are stock incidences: talking to animals, silencing animals, overcoming a dangerous animal (the wolf of Gubbio), and having animals become personal friends. Legends about Francis' follower, Anthony of Padua (c. 1195–1231), also contain similar animal stories. Saving a ship at sea during a storm, as Francis did, is a common story about saints. Finally, many saints have religious experiences before crucifixes as Francis did in the chapel of San Damiano. While no statues talked to Francis as they often did for other saints, later versions of the San Damiano crucifix story portrayed the crucified Christ as speaking to Francis.

Exaggeration

Exaggeration in hagiography is like salt in a stew; it spices things up and brings out the flavors that are already there. We, in our century, criticize exaggeration in historical writing. From our perspective, it distorts the truth. However, from the medieval hagiographer's perspective, exaggeration promoted the truth. It helped them illustrate the saint's holiness and moved readers to astonishment and the desire to change their lives. Medievals would think of exaggeration in hagiography more as embellishment than deception.

Exaggeration can shape hagiography in many ways. It can simply take a historical story in the life of a saint and build upon that bit of truth, making it more dramatic. It can take a story from one saint's life and embellish it for use in another's story.

One of the more interesting uses of exaggeration or embellishment is in the developing tradition of stories about a single saint. Later on, I will discuss Francis' meeting with a leper during his conversion, an event I believe was historically based. In the earlier accounts of this event, the meeting was very simple, though emotional. Francis unexpectedly met a leper, one with a disease he tremendously feared. Francis overcame that fear and embraced the leper. Even by Francis' own reckoning, it was an important event in his conversion. However, later versions of the same story tell us that after Francis mounted his horse to leave the scene, the leper was nowhere to be seen. What a powerful way to depict the leper as an angel, a messenger from God, or Jesus himself! Nonetheless, it is clearly an embellishment of a historical story to make claims beyond history.

Fill-ins

We are lucky to have numerous medieval biographies about Francis. This allows us to compare and critique each of them. In doing this, we discover many additions, subtractions, and changes to stories, as we see in the leper story above. When making these comparisons, we can clearly see many fill-ins throughout the stories. Most of them are incidental and have little bearing on the story; others are remarkably important. The incidental occurrences simply make for a better story, filling in details to complete the picture. The remarkable additions can change the very purpose of the story or even refute its original intent! The leper meeting is an example in Francis' life. The original story sought to portray his ongoing conversion. The later versions focused more on God's testing of that conversion, thus proving Francis' holiness. Some fill-ins are *interpolations*, i.e., added by others after the main text was composed. For example Thomas of Celano's *Life of St. Francis* 25 states that Giles of Assisi lived a long life. Giles died in 1262, some thirty-three years after Celano's Life was completed in 1229!

Hearsay

Hearsay is inadmissible as proof in today's courtrooms. In medieval days, it could be as good as eyewitness testimony. Hagiographers used any material that supported their cause, even hearsay.

False eyewitness claims

The previous points do not mean medievals did not differentiate between levels of reliable sources. Many hagiographers went out of their way to establish a fact as coming from an eyewitness. This bolstered their argument. And occasionally it may have been true. But don't automatically assume that claims to receive information from eyewitnesses were always true. Making false claims that a source was an eyewitness was a common medieval technique. Who could argue with an eyewitness? This was a technique especially employed when talking about miraculous occurrences that would normally be doubted. It may seem perverted to us, but such a tactic was completely honorable to medievals.

False attribution to friends

A similar practice was to ascribe certain information to known close friends of the saint. This not only lent credibility to reported activities of the saint, but also gave credibility to the author's interpretation of the inner motivation of the saint. This technique played an important role among the medieval works about Francis as they struggled to have their sometimes-conflicting images of Francis accepted by the reading public.

Universalizations

Some years ago, I was part of a change in the phone system where I ministered. One irate caller, unhappy about the change, informed me that *nobody* liked the change! She really meant to say that *she* didn't like the change.

This incident is an example of a universalization. Universalizations are a type of exaggeration, but deserve their own mention because they are so common in hagiography. Universalizations give the reader an impression of unanimity. Because of that, hagiographers found them useful to convince a reader of some point. Examples abound in the conclusion of many preaching and miracle stories: "Everyone was amazed!" The technique lent support to the truthfulness of the story and modeled the change that the author hoped would occur in the reader. But don't be fooled. Even though a saint may have been very popular, there usually were some skeptics who questioned her or his saintliness.

Forgery

Forgery was a common medieval writing technique in general and specifically in hagiography. Today, we usually think of forgery as signing someone else's name on a check. In essence, one person deceives another about her or his real identity. In the case of check forgery, the goal is to defraud others of money. Forgery in historical or hagiographic writing was often meant to defraud others of their reputation and authority for one's own benefit.

A classic forgery in Western history was the Donation of Constantine. According to this document, after legalizing Christianity in the Roman Empire, Emperor Constantine (311–337) gave the bishop of Rome many privileges and territory in what today is Central Italy. The document was actually written in the medieval period and provided a historical justification for the existence of the Papal States and secular papal authority. Historians began to doubt the document's authenticity by the 15th century. After the document was established as a forgery, many continued to consider it historical. This example shows that undetected forgeries can have tremendous political as well as economic, social, cultural, and religious impact.

Another classic example is the *Letter to the Hebrews*. I grew up as a child believing Paul of Tarsus authored this letter. Today, I know of no credible scripture scholar who does. Nonetheless, attributing the work to Paul certainly helped the letter attain notoriety and acceptance in the Christian world. We will study a couple of similar situations among the Franciscan sources.

Miracles

Miracles were indispensable in the portrayal of a person as a saint in medieval times. Many people continue to believe that even today.

No period in history has a completely unanimous idea of holiness. There are always elements in a society or church that oppose the exultation of certain people either as heroes or saints. Relating miracles involving the person attempts to put the debate to rest. Once God demonstrates favor toward humans by performing super-human feats through them, opponents are left at a loss for a credible argument. This was and is especially true in cultures or periods that lend easy acceptance to unexplained events as miracles.

The medieval period was intensely taken up by the miraculous. Their prescientific mentality not only easily accepted alleged miracles but also sought to see them wherever possible. In their worldview, God was constantly sending them messages through incredible signs and wonders.

It is no wonder that medievals could not conceive people being saints who never performed miracles. After all, they reasoned, if they were indeed saints, God would have made that clear through miraculous events during and after their lives. Anselm of Canterbury (c. 1033–1109) is a notable victim of this scenario. Despite being a virtuous man, eminent bishop, and important church figure, Anselm had difficulty receiving *official* canonization from his church. One probable reason is that his hagiographer, Eadmer of Canterbury (c. 1060–c. 1130) wrote more like a modern biographer and neglected to include many miracles.

No medieval could be canonized or develop a serious cult without being portrayed as a miracle worker. The most important technique of medieval hagiographers was a generous dose of miracles. Nothing else could take their place.

Inaccurate chronology

The final technique I wish to discuss is really the *lack* of a technique. Medievals had little concern for dates or accurate chronology. Accuracy in these matters can be a fetish for our period. It was the last concern of medieval hagiographers. This lack of attention to detail is very evident in the written tradition about Francis. The best chronology we have of his life involves his early conversion period and the last two years of his life. We don't know his birth date and even dispute his year of birth (1181 or 1182).

Perhaps this fact is not that important. What is important is that we learn not to trust a particular date or chronology simply because it is written somewhere. Chances are another version of the same story will contain a different chronology or anchor the event at a different point in Francis' life. We'll read plenty of examples in the life of Francis.

That's enough techniques for the moment. I hope you are getting the idea that hagiography is not the same as biography and operates under a different set of goals, presumptions, and rules. We now need to examine how this difference affects our study of Francis.

My personal assumption is that spirituality changes from place to place and time to time. Modern Christians share a great deal with medieval Christians. We also are very different. We know a lot more than they did, and have very different values. Our notions of truth are unique to our periods. Our worldviews are far apart. What we take for granted, they could not conceive, and vice versa.

Medieval hagiographers constructed images of Francis that met the spiritual needs of their day. Frankly, they were very successful; they accomplished their goals. However, if we continue to read the same medieval stories with the same medieval eyes, we will not end up with an adequate Franciscan spirituality for the vigorous demands of our own day. We will become anachronistic: living in a time and place other than our own. We need to access the stories of Francis and appropriate from them what will help us today.

How can we do this? Certainly not by applying our modern notions of historical accuracy to medieval hagiography. The medievals started with the historical Francis they experienced and built up an interpretation of his importance with their hagiography.

We have to do the same. Our difficulty is that we cannot experience the historical Francis. He is dead. So how do we do it? We are left to ask our historical questions of documents which never intended to provide us historical answers. Impossible? Perhaps. Many scholars doubt we can be sure of even the most basic facts of most early and medieval saints. However, we have no other options.

Historians have had to deal with this limitation for centuries. My goal in this section is to help readers learn from those historians and to develop a new *attitude* about an *approach* to hagiography. The attitude is suspicion; the approach is to question, question, and question. Once we know the goals and techniques of the medievals, we can use that knowledge to peel off the layers of hagiography that cover the historical Francis. In the end, we will be left with less knowledge about Francis. However, what we have will be more reliable for our modern minds.

That part of the process is the primary goal of this book and the easier of the two parts. The second part is more difficult and beyond the scope of this book: reconstructing an image of Francis that interprets his importance for today. I will make a few attempts to begin that reinterpretation. But I must confess that these attempts are only a beginning. The modern meaning of a classic figure like Francis of Assisi goes beyond my personal biases and suspicions. His meaning for today must be ferreted out in a group process that often will not be conscious or directed. Many individuals will have to share their ideas. Groups will need to make decisions about their common life. In the end, a consensus will emerge that will adequately interpret Francis for our time and place.

It's not a short or harmonious process. The primary medieval documents about Francis took over 100 years to shape his medieval image. And even then, church and political leaders as well as Franciscans themselves continued their fights to impose their image of Francis on the others. We are currently struggling with the same thing today. Someday, another generation will need to free itself of our interpretation and construct its own.

Suggested reading

The most important work for you to read about hagiography is Hippolyte Delehaye's *The Legends of the Saints.* It has been out of print for some time, but is frequently found on the shelves of used bookstores. I also suspect you will find a copy in the well-stocked library of an area Catholic college or religious community. There are two editions in English. Citations in this section from Delehaye's book are from the Attwater translation.

- Dalarun Jacques. "The Death of Holy Founders from Martin to Francis." Trans. Edward Hagman. *Greyfriars Review* 14.1 (2000) 1–19. In Dalarun's consistently brilliant manner, he shows how the hagiographic descriptions of Francis' death demonstrate Francis' holiness by following the established patterns of saints' deaths.
- Delehaye, Hippolyte. *The Legends of the Saints.* Trans. V. M. Crawford. Notre Dame: University of Notre Dame Press, 1961.
- ____. *The Legends of the Saints.* Trans. Donald Attwater. New York: Fordham University Press, 1962. (This is the version I quote in this section.)
- Dolciami, Francesco. "Francis of Assisi in Devotion, Cult and Liturgy." Trans. Edward Hagman. *Greyfriars Review* 18.1 (2004) 75–115. While Dolciami's interest is the devotion of St. Francis and how that expressed itself in his cult, especially his liturgy, he spends considerable time explaining a new model of holiness emerging through Francis' canonization process and subsequent hagiography.
- Paciocco, Roberto. "Miracles and Canonized Sanctity in the 'First Life of St. Francis.'" Trans. Patrick Colbourne and Edward Hagman. *Greyfriars Review* 5.2 (1991) 251–274. A discussion of the role of miracles in establishing the sanctity of saints in the early 13th century.
- Paul, Jacques. "The Image of St. Francis in the *Treatise on the Miracles* by Thomas of Celano." Trans. Edward Hagman. *Greyfriars Review* 14.3 (2000) 257–276. Paul argues that miracles had a limited appeal in the cult and hagiography of Francis of Assisi and that Francis' virtues

were considered of greater value. Still, certain sectors demanded that miracles be included more abundantly and explicitly in the written record.

- Prinzivalli, Emanuela. "A Saint to be Read: Francis of Assisi in the Hagiographic Sources." Trans. Edward Hagman. *Greyfriars Review* 15.3 (2001) 253–298. Prinzivalli's study illustrates how many techniques of hagiography influenced the medieval literature about Francis of Assisi.
- Short, William. "Hagiographical Method in Reading Franciscan Sources: Stories of Francis and Creatures in Thomas of Celano's *First Life* (58–61)." *Greyfriars Review* 4.3 (1990) 63–89. Short illustrates many of the techniques studied in this chapter through a very focused topic.
- Ward, Benedicta. *Miracles and the Medieval Mind: Theory, Record, and Event, 1000–1215.* Philadelphia: University of Pennsylvania Press, 1982.

Early Franciscan Primary Sources and Their Editions

I liked history courses in high school. Remembering names and movements for a test might have been difficult, but writing term papers was a breeze. As long as I had access to the library's encyclopedias or a "great-find" book on the subject, I was in business. Few people were as good as I at weaving a string of quotes together to make my point. I also quickly learned that a footnote from *Encyclopedia Britannica* made a much greater impression than one from *Worldbook Encyclopedia.*

So you can imagine my surprise when I received a "D" on my first history paper in college. I had written it just like my high school papers and couldn't figure out where I had gone wrong. After meeting with the teacher, I learned that my tried and true high school method for writing was, in fact, the problem. I was about to learn the difference between a primary source and a secondary source.

I liked using encyclopedias or other helpful books in high school because their authors did all the work for me. *They* gathered all the information, put it together in a helpful order, and usually added some insightful analysis. I was simply in the habit of summarizing, distilling, combining, and quoting. Wasn't that doing good history?

Actually, no. There's no other way to say it. The other authors were doing history; I was simply summarizing, distilling, combining, and quoting. If I wanted to write history I, like them, needed to begin with the primary sources.

Primary sources are those things from the time or near the time of an event that give us the clues about what really happened. For example, the *Declaration of Independence* is a primary source for the American Revolution. It is part of the raw data from the revolution. Likewise, the *Bill of Rights* is a primary source for the early history of the United States. It reveals what early Americans valued and found lacking in their constitution. The writings of James Madison are a primary source for interpreting the *Bill of Rights*. After all, Madison was one of the shakers and movers among those who adopted them. Primary sources are evidence *from* and *about* the past. They were there. They were part of it. That's why historians rank them first among sources and call them "primary sources."

Those wonderful encyclopedias that got me through high school are *secondary sources.* They were all written significantly later than the events they describe. Consequently, they are less reliable, and more prone to the bias of hindsight. Don't misunderstand. I do not mean to imply that primary sources are unbiased. *All* sources are biased, primary and secondary. But secondary sources have the added bias of looking at people and events after the fact and without having been an eyewitness.

Most casual readers of history read secondary sources. They don't have time to sort through the primary sources themselves. They want historians to review the primary sources for them and to write reliable and interesting accounts of what happened. Enlightening analyses are also desirable.

When I wrote term papers using secondary sources as my sources, my writing was already a third level removed from the event. Even though historians seldom distinguish sources beyond primary and secondary, I like to call these compositions *tertiary sources*. They are so far removed from the events that they are of questionable value unless their purpose is to put technical historical writing in a popular format.

By now you have probably guessed that my method asks you to use primary sources for your study of the life of Francis of Assisi. You could pick up any number of secondary source biographies, but I have several reasons for asking you to go back to the primary sources. Here is a list of some of them. Many modern biographies of Francis are boring. Too many secondary sources miss the main emphases of Francis and focus on tangential topics like Francis talking to animals. There are strong opinions and feelings about how Franciscans should live today; followers of Francis should go to the sources themselves and not have to rely on the biases of their teachers. The work of studying the primary sources makes for a more interesting experience, and we usually learn more when we are interested.

In the end, we should be able to substantiate any claim we make about Francis with support from the primary sources. Just as important, if we know the primary sources, we will be able to evaluate the claims others make about Francis and decide for ourselves if we believe they're true.

In the next few chapters, I will discuss each of the primary sources for the life of Francis. Here I simply want to list where you can find good editions of them for use in your own study with this workbook.

Essential sources

- *Francis of Assisi: Early Documents*. Eds. Regis J. Armstrong, J. A. Wayne Hellmann, and William J. Short. New York: New City Press. Vol. 1: The Saint, 1999. Vol. 2: The Founder, 2000. Vol. 3: The Prophet, 2001. Vol. 4: Indices, 2002. Abbreviated FA:ED followed by a Roman numeral indicating the volume.

  The first edition of this workbook looked forward to the day when we would have a new edition of primary Franciscan sources in English.

It is finally complete. This is the preferred edition for working with this workbook. With only a few exceptions (notably the chroniclers Thomas of Eccleston and Jordan of Giano) most of the citations in this workbook can be found in FA:ED. Its translations are the most recent, and its introductions will provide valuable additional information.

- *St. Francis of Assisi: Writings and Early Biographies, English Omnibus of the Sources for the Life of St. Francis.* Ed. Marion A. Habig. Chicago: Franciscan Herald Press, 1972. Recently available in a two-volume paperback edition. Abbreviated Habig.

  Before FA:ED, Habig was the "bible" of students of Francis of Assisi. It realized a tremendous achievement when it collected most primary sources in English and translated valuable introductions from other languages' collections. While still usable today, its introductions are now dated, and it does not contain as many primary documents as FA:ED. Like FA:ED, it lacks the chroniclers mentioned above, *The Deeds*, and *The Anonymous of Perugia*, which at publication was not recognized as valuable. All these sources must be found elsewhere.

  However, the writings of Francis contained in Habig should not be used any longer. That edition of the writings came from the still older collection by Benen Fahy. Though this translation is convenient because it is included in Habig, it was published before Esser's critical edition and, therefore, does not have the value of *Francis and Clare: The Complete Works*, which I generally recommend be used in conjunction with Habig.

- *Francis and Clare: The Complete Works.* Eds. Regis Armstrong and Ignatius Brady. The Classics of Western Spirituality. New York: Paulist Press, 1982. Those using FA:ED will not need this edition because FA:ED includes an updated version of this translation by the same Regis Armstrong.

Recommended publications

- *XIIIth Century Chronicles.* Trans. Placid Hermann. Chicago: Franciscan Herald Press, 1961. This is the only English volume that contains *selections* from the important thirteenth century chroniclers Thomas of Eccleston and Jordan of Giano. All citations in my worksheets refer to this edition. Users of FA:ED and Habig will need a copy.
- Fortini, Arnaldo. *Francis of Assisi.* Trans. Helen Moak. New York: Crossroad, 1980 and 1992 in paper.

Fortini's work requires special comments. First, I place his work in this list of primary sources with great hesitation because his is not a primary source. Nonetheless, I include it because Fortini, as mayor of Assisi in the middle of the last century, had access to documents in the archives of Assisi that are not available in English. Those resources are primary sources. Fortini's translated work is the only place where much of this archival information is available in English.

Many readers of Fortini comment that they have never felt they knew Francis as well after reading any other biography. I believe that is primarily because Fortini, more than other biographers of Francis, describes life in Assisi in great detail. The result is as much a biography of Assisi during the late 12th and early 13th centuries as a biography of Francis.

While I recommend Fortini's book because of its entrée into Assisian life, I also must caution you. This is a secondary source and carries with it the additional bias of one who was not present, but is looking back. The key to good utilization of the book is to cautiously distinguish between Fortini's description of what he found in Assisi's archives and his interpretations of what that means. If you do this, you should be able to avoid assigning more value to Fortini's book than it deserves.

- Armstrong, Regis J. *St. Francis of Assisi: Writings for a Gospel Life.* New York: Crossroad, 1994. (abbreviated RA)

Before the publication of FA:ED I in 1999, Armstrong updated his translation in this edition, which also provides more commentary about the writings than AB. However, RA does not include all the writings of Francis, number sections of the writings, provide the extensive footnoting or indexing found in AB or FA:ED I, nor make it easy to find specific writings of Francis. Because my worksheets refer you to specific parts of numerous writings, I always use references to FA:ED I. I recommend the Crossroad edition (RA) to those who also seek a more explicit reflection on the spirituality of Francis' writings. Some worksheets will refer you to RA for further reading.

Who Wrote Francis' Writings?

The obvious answer is Francis. However, there are other pens visible in the layers of composition found in Francis' writings. Without a doubt, Francis, at various times, had secretaries writing down his spoken words, correcting and improving his written words, and collecting and organizing the ideas of groups of friars before committing them to paper. Here is some of the evidence for making these claims.

Perhaps the most important evidence is written claims that other friars worked as secretaries for Francis. *The Assisi Compilation* is the source for three of these references. The compilation narrates that both Leo of Assisi and Bonizzo of Bologna were present on Fonte Colombo when Francis wrote his *Later Rule* for the Friars Minor (AC 113). It describes Leo writing down the rule as Francis dictated it. Since *The Later Rule* has a learned style unlike Francis', we assume Leo had a strong role in determining the style of the rule. How much he influenced the content is uncertain.

Bonizzo's role is more uncertain. The legend says nothing about what Bonizzo did on the mountain with Francis and Leo. Many assume Bonizzo was a canon lawyer for three reasons. First, Bologna had one of the most famous medieval law schools in Europe. Second, we know from other sources that the order and church had numerous legal concerns about the rule of the Friars Minor. Third, *The Later Rule* displays a more legal approach than *The Earlier Rule*. Add these circumstances together, and many suspect Bonizzo, too, had a hand in shaping *The Later Rule*.

The third secretary of Francis was Benedict of Piaroco. The compilation describes a scene where Francis was close to death, and the friars wanted him to leave a testament. Francis called for Benedict and asked him to write down what came to be called the *Siena Testament and Blessing* (AC 17).

Finally, Jordan of Giano, in his chronicles, states that Caesar of Speyer was asked to embellish *The Earlier Rule* with scripture passages (Jordan 15). The majority of scriptures found in *The Earlier Rule* were eliminated in *The Later Rule.*

If there are strong witnesses to four secretaries writing for Francis, we have to wonder how many more secretaries there were. The sources establish a pattern, and there is no reason to assume there were only these four.

Another reason to assume Francis had help writing his compositions is the vast stylistic differences found in his writings. Francis' *The Letter to the Faithful* has two versions. The first is short, simple, and in document form. The second version is longer, addresses more concerns borne out of experience, and is modified into letter form. *The Earlier Rule* rambles and repeats itself. *The Later Rule* is concise. Speaking of the rule, we will study its development later in this book. That study will reveal how many people were part of a process resulting in the multiple versions of the rule over a fifteen-year period.

The Prayer before the Crucifix also shows development in its manuscript tradition. The oldest versions are simple and in early Italian. Later versions are more developed and in Latin.

Finally, several sources testify that while Francis was more educated than average medievals, he was not a great writer. Bonaventure of Bagnoregio says Francis had a *slight* knowledge of reading and writing (LMj I 1). Eccleston reports Francis had a *falsum* or poor Latin. Further, Francis' education at San Giorgio in Assisi would have been rudimentary: basic reading, writing and arithmetic. Many of his writings contain run on sentences, grammar mistakes, and Italian idioms literally translated into Latin. Such a person does not seem capable of the more polished writing attributed to Francis.

By now, you are probably wondering what exactly we can say Francis did write. Don't become glib on this matter. My purpose is not to argue that these writings do not reflect Francis' thought. I believe they do reflect his thought and are the best sources for studying Francis. However, my goal is to help you understand the nature of Francis' writings and the role of individual friars and chapters (official gatherings of friars) in shaping his writings, and the development in his writings. This is not an unusual phenomenon for medieval times. Notes of students listening to their teacher's lectures comprise the modern editions of many works of great medieval philosophers and theologians.

While this has been the standard portrait of Francis' education for several decades, new studies are increasingly discovering a more literate Francis. Studies of Francis' writings are disclosing his use of complex literary tools, like the medieval cursus (using rhyme and rhythm), that a "simpleton" simply could not have produced. Fumagalli and Paolazzi's articles listed below argue in this direction. Robert Karris' book on *The Admonitions* also shows a Francis very well versed in the monastic spirituality of Europe's past. It's difficult to believe Francis was not "well educated" in light of these studies, regardless of how he received that education.

Perhaps the final judgment on the nature of Francis' education is not yet in.

Suggested reading

- Fumagalli, Edoardo. "Saint Francis, The *Canticle*, The *Our Father*." *Greyfriars Review* 19. Supplement (2005) 1–87.
- Karris, Robert J. *The Admonitions of St. Francis: Sources and Meanings*. St. Bonaventure NY: The Franciscan Institute, 1999. See

especially his introduction on pages 1–16. However, Karris documents Francis' mastery of ancient sources throughout his study.

- Matura, Thaddée. *Francis of Assisi: The Message in His Writings*. Trans. Paul Barrett. St. Bonaventure NY: Franciscan Institute Publications, 1997. Rather than treat individual writings by Francis, this book summarizes the spiritual message found in his writings. A readable publication by a veteran Franciscan scholar.
- ____. "The 'Language' of Francis in His Writings." Trans. Edward Hagman. *Greyfriars Review* 16.1 (2002) 29–35.
- Miccoli, Giovanni. "The Writings of Francis." Trans. Edward Hagman. *Greyfriars Review* 15.2 (2001) 135–170. A general overview.
- Nguyên-Van-Khanh, Norbert. *The Teacher of His Heart: Jesus Christ in the Thought and Writings of St. Francis*. Trans. Ed Hagman. Eds. Louise Hembrecht and Bernard Creighton. Franciscan Pathways. St. Bonaventure NY: The Franciscan Institute, 1994. A spectacular explanation of the Christology in Francis' writings.
- Paolazzi, Carlo. "Francis and His Use of Scribes: A Puzzle to be Solved." *Greyfriars Review* 18.3 (2004) 323–341.
- Van den Goorbergh, Edith and Theodore Zweerman. *Respectfully Yours: Signed and Sealed, Francis of Assisi: Aspects of His Authorship and Focuses of His Spirituality*. Eds. Elise Saggau and Paul Sansone. St. Bonaventure NY: The Franciscan Institute, 2001. For the advanced student.

Thomas of Celano's *The Life of St. Francis*

With this chapter, I begin an exploration of various medieval primary sources for the life of St. Francis. It is important to learn this information well, as it allows us to evaluate the data coming from these sources for each of the stories about Francis' life.

Date

In his papal bull *Recolentes,* dated April 29, 1228, Pope Gregory IX (1227–1241) commissioned Celano to write this first legend about Francis of Assisi (1C). Celano completed the assignment by February 25, 1229, when Gregory officially accepted the work.

Information about Thomas of Celano

Thomas of Celano (Chay-LAN-oh) is often referred to by the place of his origin, Celano. We are unsure of his birth date, though he probably was born between 1185–1190. He died in 1260.

Celano probably joined the Friars Minor between 1213 and 1216. In paragraph 56 of his first work, Celano describes an attempted trip to Morocco by Francis and some companions (sometime between 1213–1215). He talks of God turning Francis back with an illness in Spain and being "mindful of *me* and of many others." In number 57, Celano says many educated men joined Francis shortly after he returned to Assisi. These references suggest the spread during which Celano probably joined the Order.

Jordan of Giano testifies in his chronicles that Celano was among the first Franciscans to go to modern Germany in 1221 (Jordan 19). He chronicles the many difficulties this first group of friars experienced in Germany. By then, the Franciscans were dividing themselves into territories called provinces. The province of Germany was divided into four custodies. Between 1222 and 1223, Celano served as custos or custodian (leader of a custody) for the custodies of Mainz, Worms, Cologne, and Speyer (Jordan 30). By 1223 he was provincial vicar (second in charge) of the German province (Jordan 31).

Celano was probably present at the canonization of Francis in Assisi on July 16, 1228 by Pope Gregory IX (formerly Cardinal Hugolino), the old friend of Francis and protector of the order. Earlier that year, Gregory asked Celano to write a legend of Francis to which Gregory gave his official confirmation on February 25, 1229 (1C). Around 1230, Celano wrote a shorter legend for use during Liturgy of the Hours called *Legenda ad usum chori* (The Legend for Use in the Choir).

Between 1246 and 1247, the Franciscan general minister, Crescentius of Jesi (1244–1247), commissioned a second major work on Francis from Celano, *The Remembrance of the Desire of a Soul* (2C). Later, the general minister, John of Parma (1247–1257), probably asked for an additional treatise on miracles associated with Francis. Celano completed this *Treatise on the Miracles* in 1252 (3C).

Many previously thought Pope Alexander IV (1254–1261) commissioned Celano to write a legend on Clare of Assisi (1193–1253), but scholars are increasingly unwilling to assert Celano as the author (see CA:ED 184–187). Various devotional prayers, including the *Dies irae*, have been ascribed to Celano's authorship over the years. However, little certain evidence exists to confirm these assertions.

In 1260, Thomas died in Tagliacozzo where he was chaplain to the Poor Clares. In 1516, his bones were transferred from the abandoned Poor Clare convent to the friars' church in the same city.

Looking at the writings we are certain Celano wrote, we see evidence of a well-educated medieval individual. He was steeped in the literary tradition of the West: the classics, Fathers of the church, and hagiography. Celano knew the scriptures well and was aware of numerous writings of Francis.

The nature of Celano's acquaintance with Francis is a mystery. In the prologue to his first work, Celano says one of his sources was Francis' words, which he himself heard. Whether Celano personally met Francis or simply heard him speak at a chapter is uncertain. If in fact Celano accompanied Francis during his attempted trip to Morocco, the two men obviously shared significant face-to-face time.

Origin and purpose of Celano's first life

Francis' old supporter, Cardinal Hugolino, became bishop of Rome (Pope Gregory IX) shortly after Francis' death and quickly canonized him. Undoubtedly, he was eager to confirm Francis' sanctity before the masses of Christendom and spread devotion to him. So, Gregory IX commissioned Celano to write this first legend about Francis. There was no known legend about Francis before Celano's work. This scenario conforms to one of Delehaye's purposes for hagiography: verification of holiness (see previous section entitled *Hagiography*). The purpose of this legend was to present Francis as a saint and to secure general acceptance in the church of Gregory's canonization of Francis. Perhaps the clearest enunciation of that goal is Celano's words, "Who would be so dull-witted and senseless as not to realize the obvious truth? He is a saint!" (1C 113). This is an important factor to remember later when we evaluate the worth of Celano's work.

This origin of Celano's life about Francis also introduces us to the first of three hagiographic traditions about Francis. Because the bishop of Rome commissioned Celano's work, I call it an *official* biography. As such, it represents the interests and biases of the institutional church. At the time of composition, that official church interest was to demonstrate that Francis was a saint.

Organization

Celano himself has divided his first work into three "books." The first (paragraph numbers 1–87) deals with Francis' early life and concentrates on his conversion. It includes the famous Christmas story at Greccio in 1223. This first book is chronological up to the end of Francis' conversion and visit to Pope Innocent III (1198–1216) in 1209/10. Then the book becomes chronologically confusing and is sporadic in its treatment of Francis' life through 1224.

The second book (numbers 88–118) treats the final two years of Francis' life and his death. This section returns to a clear chronological order.

The third book (numbers 119–150) is an eyewitness description of Francis' canonization on July 16, 1228 by Gregory IX and a listing of numerous miracles associated with Francis. The FA:ED edition of 1C separates the miracles from the third book. There are also a brief prologue and epilogue to the work.

Celano's first life has been divided into chapters and paragraphs. The chapter numbers begin anew in each of the three "books" and the concluding section containing miracles. Since the paragraph numbers are continuous across all the chapters, we seldom cite the chapter numbers. In making references to Celano's first life, it is only necessary to cite the paragraph number. Thus we refer to 1C 58, not 1C XXI 58, when we want to cite paragraph 58 which also happens to be in chapter 21 of the first "book."

Celano's sources

We know of at least four different sources available to Celano as he wrote his life of Francis.

Personal experience

We believe that Celano probably was present for the canonization of Francis in 1228 in Assisi. However, we also suppose that he was present for one or more of the various chapters held at least annually near Assisi beginning in 1217. One of them, the Chapter of Mats, was considered a gathering of all the friars, about 5,000 men. We also suspect he attended the chapter in 1221 which sent friars to modern Germany. Finally, since we suspect Celano joined the order no later than 1216 and was part of the leadership of the order, we suppose he experienced a great deal during the period just after the founding of the Franciscans. Celano reveals that he personally heard from Francis some of what he recorded in his first work (1C prologue, 1).

Reliable witnesses

Celano was among the leaders of the early order. He was well educated and commissioned by the pope to write the first life of Francis. He was present for the canonization and a member of the order for no less than twelve years when he began to write. All these facts indicate that Celano would have had access to any number of witnesses to the beginnings of the order and stories about Francis' conversion.

Among those with whom we suppose Celano talked were Francis' close friends and companions. With Celano writing only two years after Francis' death, many intimates of Francis were still alive. It is not unreasonable to assume Celano even may have spoken with the famous "Three Companions": Leo, Rufino (d. 1270–1271), and Angelo (d. 1258). These three often accompanied Francis on his travels and spent time with him in hermitages.

Elias Buonbarone of Assisi (also called Elias of Cortona, d. 1253) was Francis' vicar from 1221 to 1227. He functioned as general minister of the order at Francis' death until a chapter was held in Assisi in 1227 at which he may have resigned to devote his time to the building of the Basilica of St. Francis in Assisi. He again was elected general in 1232 and served until 1239.

John Parenti (1227–32) was the general minister while Celano was writing. With the support of the pope behind his composition, Celano surely would have had access to John Parenti and his resources.

Pope Honorius III appointed Cardinal Hugolino (later Gregory IX) cardinal protector of the Franciscans in 1220 at Francis' request. Obviously, Francis requested Hugolino because of their previous relationship. Since it was Hugolino who canonized Francis, wanted to promote devotion to Francis, and commissioned this first life, he undoubtedly shared his knowledge of Francis' life with Celano. Gregory and Francis' close relationship is described in 1C 73–75.

Guido II, bishop of Assisi from Francis' conversion through his death, was constantly interacting with Francis and his followers. It is difficult to imagine that Celano would not have consulted with him for this legend, if he could before the bishop died on July 30, 1228.

Finally, Clare of Assisi grew up in Assisi, just a few years behind Francis. She obviously knew him before joining him in 1212, and Francis is recorded as consulting her several times about the direction of his life. Their relationship was important enough for the friars to bring Francis' corpse to San Damiano so that Clare and her companions could view his body. Since Clare lived just outside Assisi, Celano had easy access to this valuable witness.

Francis' writings

Celano accurately quotes five of Francis' writings: *The Earlier Rule* (1221), *The Later Rule* (1223), *The Testament* (1226), *The Admonitions* (undated), and *The Canticle of the Creatures* (1225–1226). We assume that Celano would also have been familiar with some of Francis' letters and prayers that had wide circulation among the friars and in some cases the general public.

The Bull and *Acta of Canonization*

It was common practice at the time for the pope to write a bull of canonization. The term bull comes from the Latin word *bulla*, which referred to the lead seal on papal documents indicating their authenticity. It was also common to write the proceedings of the canonization, which typically included a reading of the miracles ascribed to the saint. This work is called the Acta of Canonization. The Acta in Francis' case has been lost. Its recovery would be a great event for Franciscan scholars. However, we assume that Celano, who attended the canonization, would have had the prepared bull of canonization titled *Mira circa nos* (FA:ED I 565–569).

Model of hagiography

In the previous section on hagiography, I talked about the use of models. By comparing a prospective saint to already established saints, an author bettered her or his chances of convincing the readers of the subject's sanctity.

Many of those established models couldn't be applied to Francis of Assisi. Since he was not a bishop, his hagiographers could not use the missionary bishop model. He did not die as a martyr and therefore didn't fit that model. Neither was Francis the founder of a group of monks whose monastery became famous for a form of monastic life (though the model could have been adapted to Francis' situation).

While I was studying at the Franciscan Institute of St. Bonaventure University, an unpublished translation of a paper by Sophronius Clasen was circulating among faculty and students. In that paper, Clasen suggested that Celano used the angelic model to convince his readers that Francis was a saint. In this model, the saint was portrayed as living outside her or his body, living in communion with other angels, and having special abilities to act outside time and space. Using this model, Celano portrayed Francis as engaging in many ascetical practices, having relationships with animals, being visited by angels, doing combat with demons, and bilocating.

This model may make Francis appear nonhuman and difficult to relate to. However, for the medieval, this superhuman image would be very convincing that Francis was indeed a saint. In part this was due to the fact that the medievals often had superhuman images of holiness.

Evaluation

1. Celano's life of Francis is the earliest legend we have. It was commissioned only two years after his death and completed within the next year or two. I generally have a prejudice in favor of earlier hagiographic works. I believe that the shorter the time between the person's life and the time the hagiography was written, the better the chances that the work has not been tampered with in either the oral or written traditions. While this is not an absolute principle, it is an important consideration.
2. The officialness of Celano's works has always presented a problem in determining their value. There has been a group of scholars who have held that Celano's objectivity was significantly compromised when he agreed to write for the institutional church. These critics include the French historian Paul Sabatier at the turn of the last century. However, modern scholars increasingly write about these concerns.

   The "officialness" critics essentially believe that the institutional church and order subverted the original inspiration and intention of Francis in order to serve their own purposes to maintain stability in the order. In particular, they believe these institutions supplanted Francis' radical poverty with a poverty more palatable to the institution. In so doing, they assert the most basic element of Francis' vision was lost. They also frequently assert that the "officialness" of Celano's writings caused him to veil Francis' conflicts with popes, cardinals, bishops, and leaders and educated members of his growing community. The *Leonine* tradition (*The Assisi Compilation* and *The Mirror of Perfection*) is often portrayed as offering an alternate vision. We will examine this tradition more closely later.
3. Other people have different concerns about Celano's official role. They believe his goal to establish Francis as a saint for the universal church led him to employ hagiographic techniques (most notable, the use of miracles) to prove Francis' holiness. In this view, the overt pressures of hagiographic expectations so tampered with the stories about Francis that few of them can be trusted to be historically accurate. This is a general criticism of most medieval hagiographic works.

   However, some point to 1C 70, in which Celano professes not to be concerned with miracles, as proof that he was not unduly influenced by the hagiographic penchant to narrate miracles. Yet, Celano's announcement itself immediately follows his account of numerous miracles occurring during Francis' life. It would seem 1C 70 reflects contemporary papal policy to discount miracles occurring during a person's life as proof of sanctity. However, the contradictory inclusion of such miracles would seem to satisfy the continuing popular demand for them, despite the new papal policy (see Paciocco).

My assessment is this. Celano recounted fewer miracles in 1C than was common at the time. However, he does recount them. This reflects the changing expectations for hagiography at the time but does not remove 1C from the criticism that its interest in miracles affected its historical accuracy. This critical analysis is accurate of many early sources for Francis' life. What makes some stories in these sources unusual and of value is their near abandonment of miraculous material. In the end, a comparison of a story's versions in the various sources may be the best way to discover reliable truth.

The continued importance of miracles to the success of 1C is made clear when Celano chose not to repeat them in his second major work (2C). The friars responded negatively to excluding the miracles, and the general minister, John of Parma, had to ask him to compose another work of just miracles (3C)!

What's an honest, critical historian to do? I prefer to err on the conservative side than to draw conclusions that might later prove questionable. This may mean I believe to know less information about Francis than others believe to know. But I'd rather doubt some characteristic of Francis than believe something that had no basis in reality.

4. Celano's first life gives us the basic chronology for the life of Francis. While it is not complete, it is the most complete. Scholars base their critique of the chronologies in other biographies on that of Celano. In the long run, his chronology, where present, is pretty reliable.

5. This work has the tone of a success story. It avoids negative things about Francis. Celano probably would have had a hard time answering my question in an earlier chapter, "What don't you like about Francis?" While this tone means Celano may not be presenting the entire story of Francis, it does not imply what he does report is false. Again, we need to be prudent and critical in forming our conclusions.

In my own perspective, this earliest biography of Francis is a mixed bag. Its early composition holds positive importance for me, just as its employment of miracles holds negative importance. After you have worked with the various sources for the life of Francis, these considerations will take on more obvious importance for you. I suspect you will begin to shape more definite opinions on the matter. And, as always, your biases will shape your conclusions as much as mine have shaped my conclusions.

Suggested reading and sources cited

- Armstrong, Regis, trans. and ed. *Clare of Assisi: Early Documents.* Second revised edition. New York: New City Press, 2006. Originally published in New York by Paulist Press, 1988. Also found in the first revised and expanded edition by Franciscan Institute Publications in St. Bonaventure NY, 1993. In the New City Press edition, the citation referring to doubts about Celano's authorship of Clare's legend is found on pages 272–275.
- ____. "'Mira circa nos': Gregory IX's View of Saint Francis of Assisi." *Laurentianum* 25 (1984) 385–414. Also published in *Greyfriars Review* 4.1 (1990) 75–100.
- Clasen, Sophronius. "Vom Franziskus der Legende zum Franziskus der Geschichte." *Wissenschaft und Weisheit* 29 (1966) 15–29. I am unaware of any published English translation or treatment of Clasen's work applying the "angelic model" of holiness to Celano's hagiographic portrayal of Francis. Those who can read German will find his ideas in this article.
- Dalarun, Jacques. *The Misadventure of Francis of Assisi: Toward a Historical Use of the Franciscan Legends.* Trans. Edward Hagman. Saint Bonaventure NY: Franciscan Institute Publications, 2002. Dalarun represents a new generation of scholars who are not Franciscans themselves. *The Misadventure* is a challenging book for beginners, but perhaps the best updated comprehensive review of "The Franciscan Question," i.e., the debate over the dating, authorship, and consequent value of the various medieval sources for the life of Francis. Prinzivalli's article listed below would be shorter and dependent in part on Dalarun.
- Grau, Engelbert. "Thomas of Celano: Life and Work." Trans. Xavier John Seubert. *Greyfriars Review* 8.2 (1994) 177–200.
- Gregory IX. *Mira circa nos* (FA:ED I 565–569).
- Menestò, Enrico. "The Franciscan Question as a Philological Problem." Trans. Edward Hagman. *Greyfriars Review* 16.1 (2002) 1–28. A very scholarly article that explores the importance of the "Franciscan Question," which seeks to understand the importance of medieval hagiography about Francis by studying each work's authorship, dating, and biases. This article includes an extensive bibliography of mostly foreign language studies of the issue.
- Paciocco, Roberto. "Miracles and Canonized Sanctity in the 'First Life of St. Francis.'" Trans. Patrick Colbourne and Edward Hagman.

Greyfriars Review 5.2 (1991) 251–274. This article documents the changing role of miracles in relationship to establishing sanctity during the early 13th century. Papal policy at the time distrusted miracles during a persons' life as proof of her or his sanctity. Still, popular culture required them. While Celano seems aware of the papal policy and obviously needs to acquiesce to it since the pope commissioned this first life, he still managed to include such miracles to confirm Francis' sanctity (See 1C 70).

- Prinzivalli, Emanuela. "A Saint to be Read: Francis of Assisi in the Hagiographic Sources." Trans. Edward Hagman. *Greyfriars Review* 15.3 (2001) 253–298. Prinzivalli's study illustrates how many techniques of hagiography influenced the medieval literature about Francis of Assisi. She provides a penetrating analysis of the uniqueness of each primary source from the document of Francis' canonization (*Mira circa nos*) to *The Assisi Compilation*. Shorter than Dalarun listed above, which is book-length.
- Short, William J. "Francis, the 'New' Saint in the Tradition of Christian Hagiography: Thomas of Celano's Life of Saint Francis." *Francis of Assisi: History, Hagiography and Hermeneutics in the Early Documents*. Ed. Jay M. Hammond. Hyde Park NY: New City Press, 2004. 153–163.

Julian of Speyer's
The Life of Saint Francis

Date

Most scholars have narrowed the date of Julian's *The Life of Saint Francis* (LJS) to 1234–1235.

Information about Julian of Speyer

Julian of Speyer's birth date is unknown, although we know that he was born at the end of the 12th century. It is fascinating that Julian's professional life revolved around music. Before joining the Friars Minor, Julian studied music in Paris and eventually served as master of song at the French court of Philip II (1180–1223) and/or Louis VIII (1223–1226). These responsibilities at an important place testify to his considerable musical accomplishment.

Julian had to have entered the Friars Minor before October 1227, when he attended the general chapter in Assisi. He spent a short time thereafter in Germany, no doubt using his German origins to aid the order's second attempt to establish itself there after a disastrous earlier attempt. Many believe that Julian's detailed account of the moving of Francis' body on May 25, 1230 indicates that Julian was present (LJS 76). Later in 1230, he returned to Paris where he was involved in the Franciscan center of studies at the University of Paris until his death in 1250. Most likely, Julian taught music and trained new friars in the liturgical aspects of Franciscan life as it was developing. This means that, among other important early Franciscans, Julian would have been involved in the training of the great Bonaventure of Bagnoregio who later became general minister and authored his own life of Francis.

We have certain knowledge of several literary works by Julian of Speyer. They demonstrate his literary and musical abilities, and his liturgical interests. The general minister Haymo of Faversham popularized Julian's office of Francis, which caused it to be known early by virtually all Franciscans. Thus, the theological images Julian used to portray Francis influenced the way friars understood him and later wrote about him. It is important to identify a few later additions to Julian's Office of Francis by other ecclesial officials. These are clearly identified in FA:ED I. His known Franciscan writings include:

The Divine Office of St. Francis (1232–1235)
The Divine Office of St. Anthony (of Padua) (1232–1241, probably mid-30s)
The Life of St. Francis (1234/1235)
The Life of St. Anthony (1232–1241, probably mid-30s and after *The Divine Office of St. Anthony*)

Purpose and difference from Celano's First Life

In his prologue, Julian offers three reasons for writing LJS: (1) to praise God who authored Francis' conversion, (2) that the humility of the innocent be increased, and (3) that those fallen from grace might receive hope. These can be considered standard hagiographic goals for the time. He then indicates that he will achieve these goals by highlighting the differences between the weaknesses of Francis' early life and his final manner of life.

Julian's goals are not that different from Celano's. What is evident from the text itself is that Julian intended to write a much shorter work than 1C. He indicates this as a goal no fewer than 26 times in the text (see Miskuly 110) and more than halved the length found in 1C. These comments highlight his belief that no amount of words could totally capture Francis' life, that lengthier treatments would tire some readers, and that further verbiage would add nothing. In fact, 1C's length seems to be Julian's only difficulty with it. Interestingly, Julian barely changes any of Celano's content (Miskuly 112), and adds few and brief new elements, often of a more interpretive than factual nature. LJS primarily seems to be a condensation of 1C (Miskuly 113). Obviously, what is of interest is what Julian chose not to include, achieving his desired brevity. Here is a brief list of some of the changes from 1C that Julian makes.

- Julian omits many of Celano's editorial interjections, which tend to interpret Francis (compare 1C 1–7 with LJS 1–5). Often the removed material is homiletic, idealistic, romantic, quixotic, or exaggerated. Sometimes Julian supplants his own commentary that is always shorter and more humanly understandable. His comment in LJS 1 reflects this edgy attitude when noting that more could be said about Francis' youth, but "Why say any more?"
- He rearranges elements in 1C that seem out of sequence (compare LJS 24–26 with 1C 41–44, and compare LJS 73–75 to the various texts in 1C 73–75, 88,109, 123–126, which Julian organized into a more concise and logical presentation).
- He omits information about people other than Francis, e.g., Clare (1C 18–20) and Pope Gregory IX (1C 73–75)).
- Julian excises most of 1C's book three (119–151) about Francis' canonization and many miracles.
- He likewise omits Celano's section on the early friars' virtues (1C 39–41).
- Only a summary of 1C's description of Francis' first companions (24–25) is provided by Julian.

- While Julian mentions Francis' stigmata more than 1C, he does omit 1C's lengthy interpretation (114–115).

Part of a work's purpose is uncovered in its intended audience. Since LJS' text does not list an audience, we must use conjecture to uncover it. In Julian's case, it seems quite reliable to assert that the students at the *studium generale,* the Franciscan house of studies in Paris, were his primary audience. Julian's entire known life from shortly before he composed the LJS until his death concerns the students at that *studium.* When joining this information to our analysis of the text's relationship to 1C, it seems clear that Julian's purpose had more to do with the form of the text, especially its length, than its content.

I typically categorize the medieval legends and florilegiums about Francis in one of three "traditions": official, Egidian, or Leonine. Because LJS appears to have been written for the training of new friars and because its primary source is the official 1C, I place LJS in the official tradition.

Sources

There is no evidence that Julian ever met Francis of Assisi. Furthermore, while he certainly visited Assisi, he never lived there or anywhere in the Italian peninsula for any great length of time. Julian spent most of his life in the German and Parisian provinces.

This situation suggests that Julian's sources for his life of Francis would be indirect, i.e., not from direct conversation with the eyewitnesses of the story. The text of LJS supports this probability. Miskuly's introduction amply demonstrates Julian's heavy dependence on 1C as his primary and most important source. Julian's insertion of new facts not found in 1C about Francis' life are few and, thus, of limited importance (Miskuly 112). Most additions seem to have come from Celano's *Legend for Use in the Choir*. Some would say that Julian's *The Divine Office of St. Francis* (1232–1235) was also a source since some of its syntax is reproduced in LJS. While this is true, it seems odd to list it as a *source* for a later work *by the same author*. Usually, *sources* refer to outside conduits of information, not previous works by the same person.

Value

When I was beginning my Franciscan studies in 1973, most teachers virtually ignored Julian's life of Francis. Undoubtedly, one reason was that the text was not published in English until Miskuly published it in 1989 in *Franciscan Studies*. However, even that publication had little impact at the popular level of Franciscan studies because few people at that level were aware of the publication. Furthermore, before its publication, many instructors explained the lack of an easily available translation by describing it as simply an unimportant abridged version of 1C. They reasoned that there was little reason for modern students to pay attention to a work that offered so little new information.

If one were only looking for new information about Francis, these critics probably were correct. However, the rhetorical and esthetic differences resulting from the abridgement create an interesting effect on the reader, now and in the 13th century. Julian's work shows that he and his Parisian audience valued 1C's information about Francis while having no problem placing its interpretations and tangential information to the side. This allows modern readers to have access to a medieval primary source without many of the typical medieval hagiographic accoutrements.

In the process, this stripped down presentation actually becomes a new and different interpretation. The stories as presented by Julian replace 1C's more ambivalent interpretive language with blunter expressions. These make his presentation clearer and more concrete, which also makes it more humanly believable. Thus, Julian's razor cutting changes the tone of his work when compared to 1C.

In the first edition of this workbook published in 1996, I did not include references to LJS. The work was not readily available in translation, and its information seemed merely repetitive. However, its inclusion in FA:ED changes the situation, and, after working for years with the hagiography about Francis, my reassessment of the work finds value in comparisons with its tone and interpretations. Comparing Julian's stories to their parallels in 1C offers very different receptions for the reader. In fact, I believe that LJS is more retrievable by our modern generation because, while it is still medieval and hagiographic in nature, its language is more direct and, thus, immediately understandable. For this reason, I have integrated more material from LJS into this revision of the workbook than any other new material provided to the English-speaking world in FA:ED.

Suggested reading

- Miskuly, Jason. "Julian of Speyer: Life of St. Francis." *Franciscan Studies* 49 (1989) 93–117. Miskuly's introduction documents in detail the differences between LJS and its source, 1C.

The Anonymous of Perugia

Title

Following the lead of the manuscript, the editors of FA:ED entitle this work *The Beginning or Founding of the Order and the Deeds of Those Lesser Brothers Who Were the First Companions of Blessed Francis in Religion.* While it is an accurate title, I suspect it is too long and will not be used popularly to describe this work. In the absence of alternatives, I expect that *The Anonymous of Perugia* will last as the commonly used title, even though it is not an accurate title or description.

Date

For most of the last century, scholars thought this source was written during the 1260's, toward the end of the life of Giles of Assisi. Most believed it was a crude condensation of *The Legend of the Three Companions*, which was also thought to have been composed in the 1260's. However, more recent studies suggest that both works were actually written in the 1240's and that *The Anonymous of Perugia* was the first, whose structure was adopted by the later *Legend of the Three Companions.*

The arguments are rather technical, and it is difficult for the non-professional historian to decide for him or herself. I personally am persuaded by the arguments that *The Anonymous of Perugia* came first and date the work between 1240 and 1241.

Authorship

As its name suggests, scholars had long been unable to discover the author of this work. Recently, John of Perugia (d. c. 1270) has gained more and more acceptance as the author. Unfortunately, we know precious little about the man. The one thing we believe to know is that John was a companion of Giles of Assisi (1190–1262) and Bernard of Quintavalle (d. c. 1242), both early companions of Francis. Bernard was his first companion to remain. The principle source for this belief is a reference in the so-called *Greccio Letter* (published within L3C by the editors of FA:ED II 66–68).

If John was the author, the importance of The *Anonymous of Perugia* increases tremendously since he would have heard stories about Francis and the early days of the order directly from those who were there.

Origin and purpose

Neither *The Anonymous of Perugia* nor references to it give any details of the work's origin and purpose. Our only clues come from reading the text and understanding its point of view. It seems to be the writings of a companion to Francis' first followers who realized that they were getting old and soon to die. The author probably felt it important to preserve the memories of such important witnesses to the early Franciscan experiment. This would seem to make sense given that *The Anonymous of Perugia* was probably written fourteen to fifteen years after the death of Francis when increasingly fewer living people knew him personally. Also, this is possibly the reason why the work focuses so warmly on people and events associated with the commune of Assisi.

Organization

There is no structural organization to *The Anonymous of Perugia* like the three books of Celano's first life. However, the author does discuss four broad periods with a large gap of information between the third and fourth:

1. Francis' conversion
2. The coming of the first friar companions
3. The growth, spread and formal establishment of the order
   (gap of information)
4. Francis' death

The work begins with a brief prologue establishing its purpose and the credentials of the author. It concludes with a brief epilogue urging readers to reflect on and to change their lives.

Other characteristics

One of the more fascinating aspects of *The Anonymous of Perugia* is that, compared to the other medieval sources, it uses few hagiographic techniques. This does not mean there are no traces of the hagiographic genre. The work includes a number of miracles, which were necessary for any hagiographic work to be taken seriously. However, surprisingly, even miracles are kept to a minimum. It simply doesn't play up to the expectations of medievals for their saints.

The difference is so impressive, I sometimes wonder if *The Anonymous of Perugia* should be classified as hagiography. More than any of the other medieval sources, it seems to reflect many of our expectations for modern biography. Most of the text is humanly understandable. There is a minimum of obvious polemics (fighting or political positioning). One might imagine that the author heard many stories around a campfire and decided to write them down for no reason other than to save them.

Before Francis of Assisi, standard hagiography tended to keep its characters flat, uninteresting and similar to previous heroes or saints. The hagiography about Francis begins a more intimate model that strives to show a feeling and engaged individual. This new approach is especially achieved in *The Anonymous of Perugia* by its use of personal conversation between Francis and his early followers. It portrays Francis as a man who struggled with life, not one who had it all put together from the very beginning. Finally, by minimizing miracles, it leads the reader to focus more on the inner workings of Francis.

The general lack of polemics in *The Anonymous of Perugia* is of special interest to us. Many commentators criticize one or the other source as biased because of the author's vested interests. For example, some criticize Celano because he wrote on behalf of the institutional church and order. They argue this caused him to portray Francis in ways that supported their institutional agendas. Others criticize *The Assisi Compilation* for infusing the later Spirituals' agenda into its image of Francis. That image is very concerned with poverty, the eremitical life and asceticism. It is difficult to see any agenda in *The Anonymous of Perugia* other than to save the stories about a man who was very important to the author.

Sources

Amusingly, we doubt the two assertions in the title *The Anonymous of Perugia*. It was thus named because researchers first found it in a Perugian library and did not know its author. Today, many believe John of Perugia wrote the work and that it largely reflects experiences of friars living in and around Assisi. Because of *The Greccio Letter* (see next chapter), we believe two of John's sources were Giles of Assisi and Bernard of Quintavalle, Francis' early followers. We suspect other early companions also were sources. FA:ED asserts that 60% of *The Anonymous of Perugia* is new material (II 32). While the remaining 40% comes largely from 1C, *The Anonymous of Perugia* often reports that material with a different point of view. Because Giles was a source for *The Anonymous of Perugia*, I describe it as the oldest of the Egidian (from the Latin name for Giles) sources.

Evaluation

1. While the author gives no indication he knew Francis personally, his access to the earliest companions of Francis gives his work importance.
2. The lack of polemics in the text moderates concern about the vested interests of the author that might influence the story. The only vested

interest of John that I can discern is the desire to preserve stories of the aging early companions about their beloved Francis. The stories presented in *The Anonymous of Perugia* are more believable because they show little tampering. This trustworthiness gives the work a great deal of credibility.

3. As a piece of literature, *The Anonymous of Perugia* has little value. It displays a very simple and often crude literary style. However, that simplicity and crudeness also suggest to me that the text is in a very early stage of its development. In other words, others had little opportunity to change the developing text in the manuscripts to address their own interests. Again, this makes the text historically valuable.
4. Despite these high marks for *The Anonymous of Perugia*, there is one glaring limitation: it is exceptionally brief. Many important stories found in the other sources are missing here, including stories about San Damiano and the stigmata. So while we may have a very reliable source in *The Anonymous of Perugia*, what it has to offer is quite limited.

The Dilemma of *The Greccio Letter*

In 1244, the general minister, Crescentius of Jesi, asked people who knew stories about Francis to send them to him so a new official biography could be written. Obviously, Crescentius was anxious to receive reports from people who knew Francis personally or from eyewitnesses.

Among those to respond were three early and dear companions of Francis: Leo, Rufino, and Angelo. Because of their early and close relationship with Francis, their witness is very important for any attempt to write a life of Francis.

The three companions responded to Crescentius' call with material accompanied by a letter dated August 11, 1246. The letter clearly states that the attached material was their response to Crescentius' request. Then, they give a description of their goals:

1. They did not want merely to report miracles associated with Francis since they did not view miracles as the cause of his sanctity.
2. They wanted to relate notable facts about Francis for those who would follow later.
3. They did not intend to write a *legend*, that is a chronological account of Francis' life. Instead, they were writing a *florilegium*. That's a Latin word meaning a collection of flowers—in other words, a collection of short stories about Francis. Medieval *florilegia* were seldom organized chronologically. Frequently the stories were organized by topic.
4. They announced they would not relate events already available from previous authors.

All of this seems straight forward enough. And the fact that every known manuscript version of this letter prefaces the same work about Francis caused scholars to name that work *The Legend of the Three Companions*.

With such a strong manuscript link between the letter and the work, it is not surprising that people would originally think the three actually wrote the attached work. However, it is very surprising that the name stuck so long given numerous problems reconciling the content of the letter with the following composition. Here is a list of some of the problems:

1. Perhaps most important is that *The Legend of the Three Companions* is a *legend*, not a *florilegium*.
2. Another work, which today we call *The Assisi Compilation* and formerly has been called *The Legend of Perugia*, is not really a *legend*, but a *florilegium*. In fact, its new name highlights the work as a *compilation* of stories and sources. It seems to be the kind of work *The Greccio Letter* describes.

3. *The Assisi Compilation* frequently includes the Latin phrase *nos qui cum eo fuimus* (we who were with him), which has been linked to Leo's writings.
4. However, what today we call *The Assisi Compilation* has never been directly linked with *The Greccio Letter* in any of the manuscripts.
5. *The Legend of the Three Companions* does include material already included in Celano's first biography, thus contradicting *The Greccio Letter*.
6. Finally, *The Legend of the Three Companions* is organized very much like *The Anonymous of Perugia*. With increasing numbers of scholars accepting an early date for *The Anonymous of Perugia* (1240–1241), they also believe it was a source for *The Legend of the Three Companions*. This would mean the latter falls more into the Egidian tradition (works traced back to Brother Giles; see the previous section) than the Leonine tradition (works traced back to Brother Leo of Assisi).

While there is debate over exactly how this unusual arrangement of writings in the manuscripts occurred, there is significant opinion that Leo and the others were not influential in composing what today we call *The Legend of the Three Companions*. A French Friar Minor named Théophile Desbonnets has theorized that Leo and his friends wrote their recollections and their cover letter, and then proceeded to include other source material (including *The Legend of the Three Companions*) with their material. Somewhere in the process of delivery, the pages were jostled (perhaps by a person gathering the materials). In the end, he postulates that *The Legend of Three Companions* ended up immediately following their cover letter, an order that was then copied in all subsequent manuscripts. Desbonnets' theory is explained in his translated introduction to *The Legend of the Three Companions* in Habig (855–880, esp. 863–872).

Obviously, variations on Desbonnets' theory are possible. For instance, Leo and his friends may have only submitted their own recollections with their letter. After delivering them to Crescentius, a clerk in his office could well have mixed them with other material. While Desbonnets' theory may not be accurate in all its details, I believe his core idea has merit.

The Greccio Letter is important for a number of reasons. As we saw in the previous section, some use it to link John of Perugia to *The Anonymous of Perugia* and claim him as its author. The letter also gave *The Legend of the Three Companions* its name because of their ties in the manuscript tradition. However, the content of the letter now leads us to believe it was not intended to introduce that work, but rather a collection of writings by Leo, Rufino, and Angelo.

Suggested reading

Read *The Greccio Letter* for yourself. It is printed twice in FA:ED. The first instance is in FA:ED I 28 note 9, and the second is in FA:ED II 66–68. Habig printed the letter on pages 887–888. Try to find those parts of the letter discussed in this chapter.

The Legend of the Three Companions

We have already discussed the difficult relationship between *The Legend of the Three Companions* and *The Greccio Letter* in the last chapter. This chapter summarizes other important information about *The Legend of the Three Companions.*

Title

One of the hardest points for beginners to remember is that the name of this primary source is an inaccurate description of its authorship. The title comes from the manuscript tradition in which *The Greccio Letter*, which is signed by Leo, Rufino, and Angelo, three of Francis' early companions, usually precedes this legend. However, this legend does not have the characteristics described in that letter, making authorship by the three companions doubtful at least. Still, there is little doubt that this confusing title will continue to be used. Students need to constantly remind themselves that the title is not an accurate description.

Date

Over the years, scholars have assigned many different dates between 1246 and 1320 to *The Legend of the Three Companions*. Recently, scholars are favoring an early dating of 1246 for two reasons. First, the close manuscript links between the legend and *The Greccio Letter*, which we clearly date in 1246, suggest a similar date for the legend. Second, recent scholarship indicates *The Anonymous of Perugia* was a source for this legend. As scholars moved the dating of *The Anonymous of Perugia* up to 1240 or 1241, they were also inclined to move up the dating for *The Legend of the Three Companions*.

An obstacle to this early dating was that material in the last six sections (chapters 17 and 18) appears to be dependent on other later sources. *The Major Legend* by Bonaventure of Bagnoregio and Celano's *The Remembrance* seem likely sources for this conclusion. Since Bonaventure finished his legend in 1262, scholars assumed *The Legend of the Three Companions* had to be written sometime after then. However, many scholars today believe those sections were added to the original work of *The Legend of the Three Companions* at a later date because the original legend included so little about Francis' later life and death. Once scholars were willing to view the final six sections as a later addition, they paved the way for an earlier dating (1246) of the original work.

Authorship

As noted in the previous chapter, Leo, Rufino, and Angelo were previously thought to be the authors of this work because of its manuscript links with *The Greccio Letter*. Today, fewer scholars believe this. Some scholars have asserted that one of the three authored *The Legend of the Three Companions*. However, no one as of yet has offered any convincing evidence as to who the author might be. This makes it difficult to assess the value of this work.

Since *The Legend of the Three Companions* displays a much improved literary style from *The Anonymous of Perugia*, we might believe that its author enjoyed more education than the common medieval. That's all I feel comfortable saying about the author.

Origin and purpose

Likewise, we know very little about the origin and purpose of the work. Its strong manuscript link to *The Greccio Letter* suggests it too was material prepared in response to Crescentius of Jesi's call in 1244 for information about Francis. Because of its close similarities in organization and content to *The Anonymous of Perugia*, *The Legend of the Three Companions* may have been someone's reworking of *The Anonymous of Perugia* so that it would be submitted to Crescentius in better literary form. Because other source material was also used, it seems the author also hoped to offer an expanded legend compared to *The Anonymous of Perugia.*

Organization

The Legend of the Three Companions closely follows the organization of *The Anonymous of Perugia.*

1. Francis' early life, especially his conversion.
2. The coming of the first friar companions.
3. The growth, spread and formal establishment of the order.
   (a chronological gap of information)
4. Francis' death.

Other characteristics

Like *The Anonymous of Perugia, The Legend of the Three Companions* displays fewer hagiographic techniques than many other medieval sources. While it contains some accounts of miracles, it minimizes them. There is an uncommon amount of personal conversation in contrast to the flat, role-filling dialogue common in most hagiographic works. Excluding the late additions at the end, this work focuses on the early Francis in the process of conversion.

Like *The Anonymous of Perugia* it shows Francis as a person who struggled with his decisions.

It is also important that *The Legend of the Three Companions*, like *The Anonymous of Perugia*, lacks the polemical characteristics of many other medieval works. Perhaps because of its connection to *The Anonymous of Perugia*, it too reflects a warm attitude toward the commune of Assisi.

Sources

Recent studies of the literary connection between L3C and its sources suggest that one-third of its material came from *The Anonymous of Perugia*, one-third from Celano's life, and one-third from another or other source(s). However, I still believe that the primary source for *The Legend of the Three Companions* has to be *The Anonymous of Perugia. The Legend of the Three Companions* has taken on the basic organization of *The Anonymous of Perugia* and reports many events in near identical order. Because of this dependency, I consider *The Legend of the Three Companions* to be part of the Egidian tradition with *The Anonymous of Perugia.*

However, many stories found in *The Legend of the Three Companions* appear to come from Celano's *Life of St. Francis*. Further, as I have already pointed out, the last six sections of our modern version come from later sources, possibly *The Major Legend* of Bonaventure, dated almost two decades later, and Celano's *The Remembrance*. These additions might imply dissatisfaction with *The Legend of the Three Companions* by its contemporaries. Its incompleteness appears to be one area of dissatisfaction.

Evaluation

1. Because sources for *The Legend of the Three Companions* go back to early companions of Francis, the work would appear to be of high value. However, this assessment needs to be tempered. As a development of primarily *The Anonymous of Perugia*, we would first hope to go there to find the original written witness of these early companions. Likewise additions from Celano's *The Remembrance* and Bonaventure's *Major Legend* can be evaluated in those original works.

2. Changes in the stories from their original form in *The Anonymous of Perugia* or Celano's life need to be compared with the same stories in those medieval sources. These comparisons of similar stories across different sources can shed tremendous light on how hagiographic forces shaped the stories over time.

3. Like *The Anonymous of Perugia*, *The Legend of the Three Companions* deserves close consideration because of its lack of polemics. Even

though it contains additions we may not be able to trace, the lack of evident polemical motivation in making those additions is important. The addition of some miraculous material needs to be evaluated in light of the ever-present medieval tendency to look for the miraculous in the lives of saints.

4. Finally, *The Legend of the Three Companions* represents a vast improvement in the literary style of *The Anonymous of Perugia*. While this may make its reading more enjoyable in Latin, it has little impact on our historical investigations.

The Assisi Compilation and Its Problems

Determining the date and authorship of *The Assisi Compilation* is one of the most complicated tasks of mastering the medieval sources for the life of Francis of Assisi. These complications also make it difficult to evaluate its historical value. Needless to say, scholars are often divided over this source. The differences are visible in a comparison of this work and its introductions in the older Habig edition with the newer collection of primary sources (FA:ED II 111–230).

The knotty problems begin to reveal themselves in the various names used to entitle the work: *Legend Antiqua* (The Earliest or Oldest Legend), *I fiori dei tre compagni* (The Flowers or Collection of Stories of the Three Companions), *Scripta Leonis, Rufini et Angeli sociorium S. Francisci* (The Writings of Leo, Rufino and Angelo, Companions of St. Francis), *Legenda Perugina* (The Legend of Perugia), and *Compilatio Assisiensis* (The Assisi Compilation). The last two names are the most popular and familiar in English. The older Habig edition called it *The Legend of Perugia*, a popular name at the time. Its translation followed various editions that eliminated what was considered repetitive, and used an order that did not follow the oldest known manuscript.

Problems with this name intensified as time passed. They include tying it to Perugia mostly because the first known manuscript of the work was found in that city. Today, scholars believe the text reflects the perspectives of Assisian authors. Calling the work a *legend* is also problematic, as that name implies a literary genre that is chronological in nature, something not true of this work. The selective and collective nature of the work is reflected in the editions that title it *I fiori*... or a florilegium. Literally, this name might best be translated as a bouquet of flowers. As a medieval genre of literature the name refers to works that are collections of independent stories, often organized by theme but seldom by chronology.

This final characteristic alone might justify naming the work *The Assisi Compilation*. However, more recent studies are beginning to view the text found in the earliest manuscript (dated 1311) as a compilation of several whole and independent works, not only a compilation of stories. FA:ED favors this view. Increasingly, these components are being identified as including the following preexisting works:

- Two sections shared with *The Remembrance of the Desire of a Soul* (2C) by Thomas of Celano (AC 1–3, 23–49);
- The *Verba Sancti Francisci* (The Words of Saint Francis) often attributed to Leo of Assisi (AC 15–20);

- Two sections of remembrances of early companions of Francis who frequently use the phrase *nos qui cum eo fuimus* (we who were with him) and often thought to include Leo of Assisi and probably Angelo of Tancredi and Rufino di Offreduccio (AC 50–100, 107–120);
- The *Intentio regulae* (The Intention of the Rule) often attributed to Leo of Assisi (AC 101–106);
- Two sections of unknown origin (AC 4–14, 21–22).

This approach marks a subtle but important departure from the approach I took in the first edition of this workbook. In 1996, I preferred to characterize this work as originating with a *single* seed of information provided in the reminiscences of Leo, Angelo, and Rufino, probably written in response to Crescentius' call for information in 1244 and completed by 1246. The Greccio Letter, which describes itself as introducing a work much like AC, probably introduced it, but became physically separated from it in the manuscript tradition. That *single* deposit of stories appeared to undergo significant and prolonged *development*, until it reached its final form in a redaction known to us in a manuscript dated 1311. This view suggests significant difficulty in dating any piece of information from the text any more precisely than between 1244 and 1311 and, consequently, affected any evaluation of how useful that information might be.

The newer emerging approach views the sections listed above as having independent lives before being brought together by a *compiler*, a subtly different designation than a *redactor*, i.e., one who shapes the final text and not simply reproduces the various texts in a continuous succession. This approach would seem to allow some sections to be more highly valued if they were earlier. Manselli's study of the *nos qui cum eo fuimus* section operates out of this assumption. This approach also allows scholars to more easily consider a smaller window for dating the text. Now, for example, FA:ED can suggest that the original compilation was completed by 1260.

Despite the apparent progress in understanding this text, I remain cautious in my assessment and conclusions. Observations that raise numerous unanswered questions remain. Why are some supposedly independent and *whole* segments physically separated in the manuscript? Are the *Verba* and the *Intentio* truly independent segments or parts of a larger single text? Is *The Assisi Compilation* or *The Remembrance of the Desire of a Soul* (2C) the source for the other's stories that are so similar (AC 1–3, 23–49)? (FA:ED II 114 and 118 note b assert 2C is the source.) Or, could there be a third text that is the source of these stories in both AC and 2C? Why does the phrase *nos qui cum eo fuimus* occur in sections not identified as part of the original reminiscences of Leo, Angelo, and Rufino (e.g., AC 14b)?

Further, it remains a difficult but important task to account for the polemical tone of AC. For some time, scholars have supposed that this tone comes from redactors and editors in the latter part of the 13th or the early 14th century, perhaps from a group of Franciscan rigorists called the Spirituals who favored a stricter poverty, vigorous asceticism, the contemplative lifestyle in rural hermitages, the avoidance of large Franciscan houses, and suspicion about studies. Asserting an earlier date (i.e., 1244–1260) leaves this harsh tone less easily explained.

Coupled with questions about AC's tone is the question of whether these texts developed after their initial composition. Manselli's constant assumption is that the form of the stories in the *nos qui cum eo fuimus* section is early. One story from that section places this assumption in question. This marvelous story depicts a new brother crying out in the middle of the night that he is dying of hunger. Though 2C 22 and AC 50 (LP 1) tell the story in different words, the outline of the story and its purpose are remarkably similar. Francis and the others eat with the starving friar out of charity. The incident spawns a short homily from Francis on discernment of what each individual is able to do regarding ascetical practices.

Both versions present this act of charity and the desired discernment in virtuous terms. However AC 50h (LP 1f) adjusts the point of the story by adding a short new conclusion that puts into Francis' mouth, "But I tell you, in the future I do not wish to act this way because *it wouldn't be religious or decent"* (emphasis added). Why wouldn't Francis act again in such a charitable and discerning manner if it were so virtuous? The most reasonable explanation would seem that the redactors of the later version of the story had some reason to adjust it so that it better met their hagiographic goals. While charity and discernment of one's true capability might be virtuous, a story depicting Francis as breaking his fast might also be an embarrassment to a redactor who is trying to hold up Francis as a dedicated ascetic. Since the addition clearly modifies the point of the rest of the story, it makes most sense to believe that the story as we have it in AC represents a later redaction. This also places in question the assumption that the stories in the *nos qui cum eo fuimus* section or any of the other sections represent the earliest version with no subsequent development.

The 1276 directive of the Franciscan General Minister Jerome of Ascoli that stories about Francis and his companions be sent to him further supports the probability of later and ongoing development. While we cannot be sure what Jerome received, we have ample evidence in the subsequent numerous works that much more was written. It is difficult to imagine that *The Assisi Compilation*—a work compiled from many independent documents, with a harsh tone indicative of later sentiments, and whose oldest manuscript is dated 1311—could not have been influenced by the new writing unleashed by Jerome's request.

After this long introduction, it is time to draw some conclusions.

Date and authorship

I prefer a more conservative dating of *The Assisi Compilation*. I believe it originated as the early reminiscences of early companions of Francis, probably written by Leo, Angelo, and Rufino after Crescentius' call for information in 1244 and completed by 1246, the date of the Greccio Letter. Because of this, I categorize the work as a Leonine source. Those reminiscences were used by Thomas of Celano to compose his *The Remembrance of the Desire of a Soul* (2C). However, the original reminiscences also had a life of their own.

Since the authors and the content of their reminiscences would appeal to friars with more rigorist tendencies, and since the text shows some indications of alteration, it remains reasonable to believe that one or more redactors, perhaps spirituals, further developed the text to meet the desires of other rigorists. It is difficult to determine when this might have stopped before the date of the earliest manuscript—1311. So, it seems reasonable to conservatively remain open to possible changes until that date.

Origin and purpose

My comments on the dating and authorship of *The Assisi Compilation* already address the origin and purpose of the work. Let me summarize these points by saying the work does not have a single origin or purpose. It is a development. Later redactors, probably interested in advancing their ideas about Franciscan life in their own time and well after the death of Francis, appear to have taken a core of writings by genuinely early companions of Francis and shaped them into a document that supported their vision.

The original material seems to be the honest reminiscences and reflections of those who knew Francis very well. Their goal seems to have been an honest response to Crescentius' call for material and the sincere desire to share stories about the Francis they knew and loved.

But once these reminiscences were identified as a testimony to primitive Franciscan life, those who mourned the waning of that primitive life added to the reminiscences in ways that supported their view of Franciscan life and were critical of those who held more accommodating perspectives. As such, a large part of its purpose is polemical in nature. There is an always-present struggle hovering just below the surface of this text. This struggle is strong enough to change the original teaching or purpose of stories about Francis.

Organization

The Assisi Compilation is a florilegium, which by definition has no chronological order, but rather organizes material by theme. Many scholars also believe the order of these thematic stories reflects the shape of previously existing independent works listed above. It focuses on the hermitage experience of the order and thus emphasizes stories about contemplative prayer, poverty, and asceticism. All of the stories involve the adult Francis. Nothing is said of his youth or conversion period. Many stories focus on the sick and older Francis. *The Assisi Compilation* fits the description of what the Three Companions said they were writing in *The Greccio Letter.*

Sources and other characteristics

As I have already mentioned, the core of *The Assisi Compilation* is writings believed to be the reminiscences of the Three Companions: Leo, Angelo, and Rufino. Other early companions of Francis may have had input. However, just as importantly, the manuscript as we have it today is the result of tremendous compilation, additions and adaptations, some probably by members of the Spiritual Movement in the Franciscan Order up until 1311.

It is nearly impossible to accurately ferret out who is responsible for what parts of the work. A comparison of texts is very necessary to help make these determinations, and that task involves comparing the stories in various stages of development. (Manselli begins this.) All of this makes the task of deciding who wrote what very difficult for us amateurs.

However, there is little doubt that the work in its final form reflects the concerns of rigorists, probably of the Spiritual Movement and, as such, emphasizes the internal affairs of the order rather than its ministry in the universal church.

Evaluation

1. The fact that Leo and other early companions of Francis are the primary sources for this work makes it potentially very valuable. Many of these sources were eyewitnesses.
2. However, the fact that there has been much adaptation of the original work by Spirituals embroiled in battle over the nature of Franciscan life leaves this valuable pearl lost in a vast ocean. This problem is somewhat diminished now that scholars are beginning to identify independent parts within the whole. However, the probability of later development in any or all parts still leaves us with the problem. It's similar to an important book put on the wrong shelf of a huge library. If you can't find the book, you might as well not own it.
3. Finally, taking the final redaction (completed in 1311) as a whole, its often polemical tone can make it of uncertain value. Comparison with earlier versions of similar stories is required.

Unique mechanics about The Assisi Compilation

Many of the complicating features about *The Assisi Compilation* make it necessary to create unique notation systems to make distinctions and to help students find a designated text.

1. In this workbook (revised edition), I will call this medieval work *The Assisi Compilation (AC)*, not *The Legend of Perugia (LP)*.
2. When making references to this work in FA:ED, I will use the abbreviation *AC*. When making references to the edition in Habig, I will use the abbreviation *LP*. In my worksheets, I generally site passages only from FA:ED since that is the source increasingly used by students. References will be made to the Habig edition when it serves an important purpose.
3. Note that, in its edition of AC, FA:ED II makes cross-references to 2C followed by an upward-pointing arrow (↑) in the inner margins. This is done because FA:ED asserts that 2C is a source for these stories, thus predating AC.
4. My students have found it helpful to make long colored lines in the outer margins indicating which of the possible independent sources listed above are on each page of AC. (Each independent source has its unique color.) This keeps them alert to possible insights and trends in the texts.
5. FA:ED II has cross-referenced stories in AC with those found in Habig's earlier *Omnibus* by citing LP (*Legend of Perugia*) in the inner margin.

Suggested reading

- Burr, David. *The Spiritual Franciscans: From Protest to Persecution in the Century after Saint Francis*. University Park PA: The Pennsylvania State University Press, 2001.
- Menestò, Enrico. "The Franciscan Question as a Philological Problem." Trans. Edward Hagman. *Greyfriars Review* 16.1 (2002) 1–28. A very scholarly article that explores the importance of the "Franciscan Question," which seeks to understand the importance of medieval hagiography about Francis by studying each work's authorship, dating, and biases. This article includes an extensive bibliography of mostly foreign language studies of the issue. A section of this article uses a small and technical example from *The Assisi Compilation* and *The Mirror of Perfection* to illustrate new methods for resolving the Franciscan Question.
- Manselli, Raoul. "We Who Were with Him: A Contribution to the Franciscan Question." Trans. Edward Hagman. Eds. Regis J. Armstrong and Ingrid Peterson. *Greyfriars Review* 14.supplement (2000) 1–196.

Thomas of Celano's *The Remembrance of the Desire of a Soul* Often Called His *Second Life of St. Francis*

Title

Until the publication of FA:ED, the near universal title used for this work had been *The Second Life of St. Francis* or *The Second Legend of St. Francis* by Thomas of Celano. Thus, the title was and is generally abbreviated 2C (as in FA:ED) or 2Cel. The editors of FA:ED have chosen to use the title Thomas himself used, the less familiar *The Remembrance of the Desire of a Soul*. Besides being the historically more correct title, it also is a better description of the work. 2C is not a legend or a life in the more general sense of indicating a chronological life of its subject. Rather, it is more akin to the florilegium genre that typically groups stories by themes or topics.

No doubt, it will take the English-speaking world some time to adjust to the new title. I suspect the new short reference for the work will be simply *The Remembrance.* In many ways, the older common names and abbreviations for this work are deceptive. While students may still want to use the common nickname *Two Celano*, a variant of that title could prove confusing, i.e., *The Second Life*. Also, the abbreviations could prove confusing because we certainly know that *The Remembrance* is not Celano's second literary work. We are certain that Thomas of Celano wrote his *The Legend for Use in the Choir* shortly after completing 1C, making *The Remembrance* at least his third literary work. No doubt *2C* or *2Cel* will continue to be used to refer to *The Remembrance*; that cannot be resisted. However, students will want to think of its number as indicating the second *major* literary work of Celano about Francis.

Date and authorship

There is no doubt that Thomas of Celano is the author of this, his second major work about Francis of Assisi, and that it is dated 1247. He could have begun composition anytime after August 11, 1246, the date of *The Greccio Letter*, which accompanied the material Crescentius had gathered and handed over to Celano. Information on Thomas of Celano can be found in the earlier section on his life of Francis.

Origin and purpose

As I previously discussed, the Franciscan general minister, Crescentius of Jesi, issued a request for information about Francis in 1244. Crescentius handed that collection of stories to Thomas of Celano sometime after *The Greccio Letter* and its accompanying manuscripts arrived in 1246.

Like his original legend, Celano's second work has an *official* quality to it. While the first was commissioned by a pope to confirm Francis' sanctity for the universal church, the second was commissioned by a minister general of the order to preserve the friars' memories of Francis for future generations.

This was especially important as the last remaining witnesses to Francis were fast approaching their own deaths. Furthermore, it seems to have succeeded as early companions like Leo, Angelo, and Rufino, and associates of other early friars like Giles of Assisi and Bernard of Quintavalle (whose memories were recorded in *The Anonymous of Perugia*) presented their recollections.

Organization

This second major work by Celano is divided into two books. The first encompasses only paragraphs 3–25 which largely deal with Francis' conversion. Furthermore, these paragraphs emphasize new material not previously recorded in 1C. What little chronology Celano incorporates in the work is found here.

The second book spans paragraphs 26–220. The only chronology to be found is in paragraphs 210–220 which discuss Francis' death. The rest of the material is organized as a *florilegium*, that medieval literary genre called a collection or bouquet of flowers. In other words, this section collects chronologically disjointed stories and organizes them according to various themes. This thematic organization follows an outline of virtues demonstrating Francis' holiness. The various stories collected in each section illustrate one particular virtue. Celano frequently concludes a section of individual stories with morals that admonish the reader to assimilate the same virtue.

The work begins with a two-paragraph prologue that is a prayer to Francis from his early companions for whom Celano purports to write. Celano's use of the first person plural has prompted many scholars to wonder for whom Celano wrote. It seems plausible to assume at the least that Celano felt he was the final editor or redactor of all the material collected by Crescentius, writing for all those early companions who submitted stories.

Other characteristics

The Remembrance has some important differences in tone from Celano's first work. In comparison, 2C is harsher than 1C. It also develops previous material with miraculous or symbolic dimensions.

For example, while 1C's portrayal of Assisi is rather neutral, 2C depicts the city as a vile place, highlighting the holiness in Francis that overcame its evil. This relates to a change in depicting Francis' conversion. In 1C, Francis' conversion is depicted as gradual. In 2C, Francis' goodness is forcefully present from his birth. In the story of Francis meeting the leper, 2C includes new material that implies that the leper was Christ. In its account of Francis' birth, his baptismal name (John) connects him to the role of John the Baptist. Finally, the Portiuncula assumes a more important place in 2C as a symbol of the Franciscans' mission.

This last point highlights the stricter ascetical tone of 2C. It tends to portray Francis as a pattern of virtue, emphasizing his self-denial. As such, 2C moves toward depicting Francis as another Christ and often recalls the self-emptying (*kenosis*) championed by Paul of Tarsus when he describes in his letters the saving role of Jesus. This results in more attention to poverty and a generally otherworldly spirituality.

Sources

Obviously, Celano had all the same sources available to him when he wrote 1C. For 2C, he also had the sources included in the materials gathered by Crescentius of Jesi. Those certainly included the early writings of Leo and the other companions, *The Legend of the Three Companions, The Greccio Letter*, and possibly *The Anonymous of Perugia*. If other materials were available in the packet, we are unable to isolate them. This is unfortunate, for Engelbert Grau estimates that a full 95 episodes in 2C have no evident connection to other known sources (Grau 193). We can only assume many of these episodes were included in Crescentius' collected material.

Evaluation

1. Official biographies have always made some Franciscan scholars nervous. Their constant fear is that the concerns of institutional authority, whether of the universal church or the Franciscan Order, compromised the original inspiration of Francis in favor of institutional concerns for order and control. Furthermore, they fear that stories that did not reflect well on the institution would be suppressed or changed. However, strangely enough, 2C has a rather stern tone despite this. It *does not* try to soften or hide the tension and struggle in the order in stories it includes. Many of the stories champion views that later would be identified with the Spiritual Tradition, which was often at odds with the institutional church and order.
2. Even though individual stories may show hagiographic development in 2C, the primary story line conforms to that in previous biographies. This

suggests modern readers can usually rely on the broad strokes of *The Remembrance*, but should critically examine details of the stories. This is most easily done when stories in 2C can be compared to the same stories in earlier versions.

3. Celano completed *The Remembrance* twenty-one years after Francis died. That may not seem too long a time. However, it is long enough to allow tremendous growth in the stories of his life.

In the end, I find 2C generally to be a reliable source. We simply need to use a critical approach in studying it. Stories need to be compared to earlier versions. Miraculous happenings should be rigorously narrowed to only the most necessary elements. Readers need to understand the interpretive power of symbols and editorial selectiveness. If these cautions are kept in mind, 2C can be a valuable source for the life of Francis.

A sequel of miracles

Students often doubt my strong words about hagiographic forces shaping portraits of the saints and, particularly, the irresistible medieval penchant for miracles. Well, here is a true story that demonstrates cause for my apprehension.

While the authorities of the order accepted 2C as a valuable addition to the hagiography about Francis, it was found deficient in one important area: *it lacked sufficient miracles*. It stands to reason that Celano would not include many miracles his second time around. His first work contained a fair number of miracles, and he declared his intent not to repeat material found in previous biographies.

However, this did not mollify his readers who simply would not value a hagiographic work devoid of miracles. Within this predicament, a later general minister of the Franciscans, John of Parma, probably commissioned Thomas of Celano to write an appendix-like work called *The Treatise on the Miracles of St. Francis*. Celano obliged John, and the General Chapter of Metz probably approved the work in 1254 after Celano completed the work in 1252. The abbreviation signifying this work is *3C*.

The treatise is actually of little historical or literary value. Most of the work is a recapitulation of stories found in earlier works. Marion Habig found the work to be of such little value that in his edition of the Franciscan omnibus he only included those stories not found in an earlier work. These stories only account for a few pages of printed text. Engelbert Grau, however, disputes this assessment, finding in its pages a testimony to the ways people revered Francis (Grau 199).

Perhaps the greatest value of the treatise for modern readers is its demonstration of the importance of miracles in medieval hagiographic works.

No one could become a medieval saint unless she or he could be connected to miraculous occurrences. The medieval concept of holiness was so tied to miraculous stories that many real life struggles and delights were lost in the hype. Grau implies that Celano himself was concerned that including reports of miracles could overshadow a portrayal of Francis' virtuous life, which truly made him holy (Grau 196, including note 55).

Sources cited and suggested reading

- Grau, Engelbert. "Thomas of Celano: Life and Work." Trans. Xavier John Seubert. *Greyfriars Review* 8.2 (1994) 177–200.
- Paciocco, Roberto. "Miracles and Canonized Sanctity in the 'First Life of St. Francis.'" Trans. Patrick Colbourne and Edward Hagman. *Greyfriars Review* 5.2 (1991) 251–274.
- Paul, Jacques. "The Image of St. Francis in the *Treatise on the Miracles* by Thomas of Celano." Trans. Edward Hagman. *Greyfriars Review* 14.3 (2000) 257–276. Paul argues that miracles had a limited appeal in the cult and hagiography of Francis of Assisi and that Francis' virtues were considered of greater value. Still, certain sectors demanded that miracles be included more abundantly and explicitly in the written record.
- Ward, Benedicta. *Miracles and the Medieval Mind: Theory, Record and Event, 1000–1215.* Philadelphia: University of Pennsylvania Press, 1982.

The Major Legend of St. Francis by Bonaventure of Bagnoregio

Date and authorship

There is no doubt about the dating or authorship of *The Major Legend of St. Francis* ("*Legenda maior*"). The Franciscan General Chapter in Narbonne commissioned its general minister, Bonaventure of Bagnoregio, to write the work in 1260. Bonaventure completed it in 1262. Another general chapter accepted and approved his composition in 1263.

Bonaventure of Bagnoregio is the object of intense historical interest not only because he authored this popular life of Francis of Assisi. Bonaventure was the foremost Franciscan scholar of his day, a teacher at the prestigious University of Paris, and the author of an incredible number of works that fill nine volumes we call his *Opera omnia*. His writings cover three broad areas of interest: theology and philosophy, spirituality, and works related to the Franciscan Order he led.

Bonaventure was born sometime between 1217 and 1221 in the Latian village of Bagnoregio northwest of Rome. A promising scholar, Bonaventure won acceptance at the University of Paris where he worked toward what today we would call his doctorate. He joined the Franciscans in 1243 while studying in Paris. During the 1250's, Bonaventure became embroiled in what we call the *Mendicant Controversy*. This was a heated and prolonged debate whose issues were most commonly argued at the University of Paris. The debate focused on the poverty of Jesus and his disciples. It was of contemporary interest because many felt the Franciscans with their simple lifestyle were more Christ-like than other religious or ministers, including the hierarchy. At different points, some tried to suppress the Franciscans, and Bonaventure was one of the Franciscans' most articulate defenders. The controversy is worth further investigation by those with an interest in it.

The Franciscan General Chapter of 1257 elected Bonaventure the Franciscan general minister, a position he held until he became cardinal bishop of Albano in 1273, a year before dying. Bonaventure's election was particularly amazing because he was not even attending the general chapter! The chapter had the onerous task of electing a successor to the very popular John of Parma whom Rome was forcing out of office for political and theological reasons. Holding John in high esteem, members of the chapter asked John whom he thought they should elect as his successor. In a dramatic announcement, John reported that there was one Franciscan he knew from his travels who could guide the order through its difficult days: Bonaventure of Bagnoregio. The chapter dispatched messengers to tell Bonaventure of his election. Bonaventure accepted and hurried to Italy.

Pope Gregory X (1271–76) appointed Bonaventure a cardinal of the church in 1273. He died in 1274 while attending the Second Council of Lyon where he played a major role in defending the mendicant orders, many of which were suppressed by the council.

His most popular works among Franciscans in general are his spiritual and order-related writings. The Franciscan Institute at St. Bonaventure University in New York State has reestablished an important series of translations of these valuable works.

Origins and purpose

The story leading up to and following the composition of *The Major Legend* is the source of great controversy concerning the value of this work. As you know, several medieval hagiographic works about Francis already existed by 1260. The Franciscan General Chapter of that year commissioned its minister general, Bonaventure of Bagnoregio, to write a *good* biography based on the others. Bonaventure completed his work before the next chapter in 1263 that officially accepted the work. Three years later, the chapter of 1266 ordered that all other lives of Francis be destroyed.

This final point fueled Franciscan infighting right down to our own day. The motivation(s) for both the commissioning of a new biography and the order to destroy the other compositions is (are) not known. None of the known documents about these two events give reasons for these decisions. Some of the possible motivations could be:

1. There was simply a desire for one biography that would have official approbation and be complete.
2. There was a desire to interpret Francis in a consistent manner (i.e., eliminate discrepancies in fact or interpretation found in other hagiographic works).
3. The institutional order was trying to suppress the ideological support system of the Spirituals who favored a more rigorous interpretation of Francis and to contain laxists. In other words, with this biography, officials in the order hoped to bring Franciscan practice to the middle of the ideological spectrum. Some have seen the ultimate goal of this legend to make peace within the order and with the larger church.

People interested in the primitive Franciscan life commonly accepted this third interpretation as the genuine motivation. While I am not certain about the true motivation, I can easily see that many groups in the order were fighting for its ideological soul. The concerns of institutional leaders in the order were seen as centrist. Both groups identified in interpretation #3 above (Spirituals and laxists) were viewed to be on opposite extremes within the order. Both were seen to be a source of tension. Certainly, both were irritating to the other and those on the middle ground.

I caution you from assuming that the middle ground was consequently the most reasonable or desirable ground. Being to the left, right, or center is a relative comparison that changes with time and place. A centrist with the early Franciscans in 1212 would be an extremist in 1260.

Most differences focused on notions of evangelical poverty. The ancestors of the Spirituals held it as an uncompromisable value. Their notions of poverty were absolute and primitive. It excluded the possession of books, which required libraries, which necessitated buildings. Their interpretation of poverty also led to a more mendicant lifestyle of begging and traveling, i.e., not having a house to call home. They favored an eremitical lifestyle. Storehouses for food or other goods were prohibited. The help of lay financial agents was anathema.

The laxists were those who demonstrated little concern for poverty in any form according to the norms of the day. Others perceived them as interested only in creating greater security and luxury in life.

The centrists, whose point of view Bonaventure expressed, spoke highly of poverty as integral to Franciscan living, but accepted accommodations they believed were required by the tremendous growth in the order and the requests by the church to engage in more and more ministry.

There also were outside groups applying pressure to these Franciscan family feuds. Many church leaders and thinkers reacted negatively to what they considered exaggerated attention paid to poverty by many of the mendicant orders, including the Franciscans, who were springing up during the 12th and 13th centuries. Some Franciscans were very critical of diocesan clergy and the hierarchy who may have enjoyed more luxurious lives. Also, diocesan leaders often resented the clerical exemption of many mendicants. Their new form of religious life exempted them from much of the diocesan authority structure and made them accountable to authorities within their orders. Eventually, some of these diocesan leaders would seek to suppress the mendicant orders at the Second Council of Lyon in 1274.

Given these tensions and pressures, it is very plausible that the Franciscan general chapters of 1260, 1263, and 1266 wanted to moderate the extremes within the order. This would obviously create a sense of panic in those at the edges of the Franciscan Spiritual Movement. Many of them believed that the order had already abandoned the true charism of Francis. Their struggle was over truth and integrity. The suppression of works that supported their interpretation of Francis and Franciscan life was unthinkable. Certainly, the writings of Leo and the other companions were the *bible* of the Spirituals. But Celano's second biography also supported many core values of the Spirituals.

The debate is far from over, whether its focus is the motivation to destroy older works or how Franciscans should live today based on the history. Thankfully, the destruction of older works was hardly effective, and all the works we have already discussed managed to survive. One has to wonder if there were other works that didn't survive the chapter decision to destroy them or if there are surviving but lost works waiting to be rediscovered!

Organization

Some scholars describe *The Major Legend* as a theological legend. Using this label, they wish to emphasize the structured way Bonaventure used the life of Francis to illustrate theological and spiritual truths.

Perhaps the most ambitious and explicit explanation of this notion is found in Regis Armstrong's doctoral dissertation from Fordham University. It is also affirmed by Ewert Cousins in his introduction to *Bonaventure.* Regis begins with connections between *The Major Legend* and earlier spiritual works by Bonaventure which present a three-tiered spirituality in terms very common in medieval times. It talks of the spiritual journey as encompassing a purgative, illuminative and unitive way. This spiritual theory deserves intense study, but goes beyond my scope here. In brief, the purgative way involved emptying oneself of all that is sinful, evil, and opposed to God. Think of a dirty sponge that is wrung until almost all of the dirty water is forced out.

The illuminative way is a process in which people fill themselves up with Christ and his love. The Latin root of this word, *lumens*, means light and alludes to the new understanding made possible in people's lives. Through this process, people become *enlightened.* To continue with the sponge analogy, during the illuminative process people are like sponges soaking up new clear liquid.

While God is always present in both of these processes, the human person is active in them as well. People interested in the spiritual journey are coached in ways to facilitate these two actions.

The final process, the unitive way, is totally the action of God. The only thing humans can do is to be open; God does the rest. As its title suggests, this process is one in which a human is intimately united to God. It is so deep and personal that it is difficult to describe. Most authors are reduced to poetic imagery when discussing it.

Actually, each of these three processes contains three sub-processes. As a result, Bonaventure's work portrays a trilogy of trilogies, three steps of three steps each.

Armstrong's thesis and Cousins' introduction hold that Bonaventure illustrated his spiritual theology through his legend of Francis of Assisi. Bonaventure did this by structuring his biography along the same lines as his spiritual theology.

The Major Legend is composed of fifteen chapters. Armstrong holds that beginning with chapter five, Bonaventure wrote a total of nine chapters (5–13) paralleling the nine (3 x 3) steps found in his spiritual theology.

Chapters five through seven deal with austerity, humility, obedience and poverty in Francis' life. These themes fit well into Bonaventure's first steps in the spiritual journey he calls the purgative way. Chapters eight through ten parallel the illuminative way, where Francis fills himself with the things of God through his affectionate piety, fervent charity, desire for martyrdom and zeal for prayer.

The culmination of the spiritual journey, the unitive way, is embodied in chapters eleven through thirteen which describe his understanding of the scriptures, spirit of prophecy, efficacious preaching and healing. The pinnacle of the journey is represented in the account of Francis' stigmata in chapter thirteen. There could not be a more perfect way to symbolize the union of Francis with God than to show Francis bearing the very wounds of the crucified Christ. Here Francis is shown to be as selfless as the savior himself. Chapter thirteen is the pinnacle of Bonaventure's work about Francis.

The remainder of his work is like the denouement or conclusion of a suspenseful novel. From here on, there are no more surprises in the story, and things are brought to a close. The first four chapters are an introduction relating Francis' life before his conversion.

Bonaventure's *The Major Legend* is numbered by chapter and section. The sections do not run continuously as in all the other medieval sources. Because of this, both chapter and section must be cited. I cite Bonaventure's chapters with Roman numerals and his sections with Arabic numerals. Thus, *LMj XIII 3* would designate section three of chapter thirteen in *The Major Legend*. I also wish to point out that *The Major Legend* has two parts. The first is a formal presentation of Francis' life. This is the section to which my citations refer. The second section reports miracles from the life of Francis. Students sometimes become confused because the numeration of part two begins again at chapter one, section one (I 1). I receive several phone calls a year from students who insist my citations are wrong. Actually, they are in the wrong section. I never give a citation to the second part of Bonaventure's work in this book.

Sources and characteristics

Bonaventure adds little new material to the growing traditions narrating Francis' life. His novelty is in having taken material from nearly all the sources previously discussed and shaping the material to serve his spiritual, political, and theological purposes. Because a general chapter commissioned the work, I categorize it as an official source, as I do all of Celano's works.

Evaluation

The Major Legend is a literary masterpiece and splendid example of medieval hagiography and spirituality. However, it provides little new historical material about the life of Francis. Thus while it is basically reliable from a historical point of view, it is preferable to cite material from earlier sources when possible.

On the other hand, Bonaventure's work is very important for understanding the developing spirituality of the followers of Francis in the 1260's and beyond. In particular, it shows us how those early followers were developing in their understanding of the man who founded their movement. While that makes the work valuable in a study of the early history of the Franciscan movement, that value should not be confused with a high rating as a source for the historical life of Francis.

These statements make many Franciscan scholars nervous. Many will disagree with my assessment. I suspect this is mostly because *The Major Legend* is such an incredible masterpiece of medieval hagiography and spirituality. Furthermore, it was the biography most commonly used in the training of new Franciscans through the 1950's. In pre-Vatican II days, it was the preferred tool for teaching the life of Francis, I'm sure in part because of its high spiritual interpretation of Francis.

In the end, I generally trust Bonaventure's history, though I prefer to go to earlier sources when possible, which is most of the time.

A word about The Minor Legend of St. Francis

While *The Major Legend* ("*Legenda maior*") is composed of fifteen chapters and a prologue, *The Minor Legend of St. Francis* ("*Legenda minor*") is composed of seven chapters each with nine paragraphs. It is a masterful condensation of *The Major Legend* 's story line and theology. Bonaventure crafted *The Minor Legend* to be read during the Liturgy of Hours during the octave of Francis' feast day. It too seems to have been completed before the General Chapter of 1263.

Because *The Minor Legend* is a condensation, it is of little historical value for studying the life of Francis. I include occasional references to it in the following worksheets to expose you to the work so that you might become familiar with its structure.

Sources cited and suggested reading

- Armstrong, Regis. *The Spiritual Theology of the* Legenda major *of Saint Bonaventure.* Diss. Fordham University, 1978. Ann Arbor: University Microfilms International, 1978. 7814881.
- _____. "Towards an Unfolding of the Structure of St. Bonaventure's *Legenda Major.*" *The Cord* 39 (1989) 3–17.
- Bonaventure of Bagnoregio. *Bonaventure: The Soul's Journey into God, The Tree of Life, The Life of St. Francis.* Trans. and ed. Ewert Cousins. The Classics of Western Spirituality. New York: Paulist Press, 1978.
- _____. Works of Saint Bonaventure. St. Bonaventure NY: The Franciscan Institute. An ongoing series of the writings of St. Bonaventure in English Translation.

  Vol. 1: *On the Reduction of the Arts to Theology.* Prepared by Zachary Hayes. 1996.

  Vol. 2: *Itinerarium Mentis in Deum.* Ed. Philotheus Boehner. Trans. Zachary Hayes. 2002.

  Vol. 3: *Disputed Questions on the Mystery of the Trinity.* Trans. Zachary Hayes. 2000.

  Vol. 4: *Disputed Questions on the Knowledge of Christ.* Trans. Zachary Hayes. 1992.

  Vol. 5: *Writings Concerning the Franciscan Order.* Trans. Dominic Monti. 1994.

  Vol. 6: *Collations on the Ten Commandments.* Trans. Paul Spaeth. 1995.

  Vol. 7: *Bonaventure's Commentary on Ecclesiastes.* Trans. Campion Murray and Robert Karris. 2004.

  Vol. 8: *St. Bonaventure's Commentary on the Gospel of Luke.* 3 parts. Trans. Robert Karris. 2001–2004.

  Vol. 9: *Breviloquium.* Trans. Dominic Monti. 2005.

  Vol. 10: *Writings on the Spiritual Life.* Intro. F. Edward Coughlin. Trans. Gerry Etzkorn 2006.

  Vol. 11: *Bonaventure's Commentary on the Gospel of John.* Trans. Robert Karris. 2007.

  Vol. 12: *The Sunday Sermons of St. Bonaventure.* Trans. Timothy Johnson. 2008.

  Vol. 13: *Disputed Questions on Evangelical Perfection.* Trans. Thomas Reist and Robert Karris. 2008.

  Vol. 14: *Collations on the Seven Gifts of the Holy Spirit* Trans. Zachary Hayes. 2008.

Vol. 15: *Defense of the Mendicants.* Intro. and notes Robert Karris. Trans. José de Vinck and Robert Karris. 2010.

- Bonnefoy, Jean François. "The Triple Way: A Bonaventurian Summa of Mystical Theology." Trans. Edward Hagman. *Greyfriars Review* 16.supplement (2002) 1–129.
- Burr, David. *The Spiritual Franciscans: From Protest to Persecution in the Century after Saint Francis*. University Park PA: The Pennsylvania State University Press, 2001.
- Carpenter, Charles. *Theology as the Road to Holiness in St. Bonaventure*. Theological Inquiries Series. New York: Paulist, 1999. For the advanced student.
- Delio, Ilia. *Crucified Love: Bonaventure's Mysticism of the Crucified Christ*. Studies in Franciscanism Series. Quincy IL: Franciscan Press, 1998. Difficult for the beginner, but rewarding.
- _____. *Simply Bonaventure: An Introduction to His Life, Thought, and Writings*. Hyde Park NY: New City Press, 2001. An outstanding introduction to the thought and spirituality of Bonaventure that goes beyond his legend of Francis of Assisi.
- _____. *The Humility of God: A Franciscan Perspective.* Cincinnati: St. Anthony Messenger Press, 2005. While this work by Delio has a general *Franciscan* scope, its principle Franciscan sources are the writings of Francis of Assisi and Bonaventure. Thus, it is a valuable bridge between the two men, showing how the spiritual intuitions of Francis achieve a grander theological expression in Bonaventure.
- Hayes, Zachary. *Bonaventure: Mystical Writings*. Spiritual Legacy Series. New York: Crossroad, 1999.
- _____. The Hidden Center: Spirituality and Speculative Christology in St. Bonaventure. New York: Paulist, 1981. Demands at least an intermediate skill level. Very helpful and insightful.
- Johnson, Timothy. *Bonaventure: Mystic of God's Word.* Hyde Park NY: New City Press, 1999. Describes Bonaventure's spiritual theology without using his legend about Francis of Assisi.
- _____. *The Soul in Ascent: Bonaventure on Poverty, Prayer, and Union with God.* Quincy IL: Franciscan Press, 2000.
- Nguyên Van Si, Ambroise. "The Theology of the Imitation of Christ According to St. Bonaventure." *Greyfriars Review* 11.supplement (1997) i–181.

The Mirror of Perfection

Date

In 1898, the French historian who showed such great interest in Francis of Assisi, Paul Sabatier, found the first manuscript of *The Mirror of Perfection* discovered in modern times. His manuscript was dated with the Roman numerals MCCXXVIII, which is 1228.

Sabatier was ecstatic with the discovery. The date on the manuscript indicated that this work about Francis was completed a year before Thomas of Celano completed his legend, making *The Mirror of Perfection* the earliest known writing about Francis. This designation as the oldest life of Francis caused Sabatier to refer to it as the *Legenda antiqua*, or the "oldest life."

Of course, Sabatier realized that the oldest writings about Francis would enjoy unrivaled credibility within the historical community. Being completed only two years after Francis' death, the stories in this work would most probably have the least amount of tampering by the hagiographic process of the day. This mantle of reliability was especially precious to Sabatier since *The Mirror of Perfection* favored the lifestyle of the early Franciscan community with all its rigor and lack of institutionalization.

With time, more copies of the work were discovered in Europe. Many of these manuscripts were dated with different letters. Before long, most scholars accepted this other date of MCCCXVIII, which is 1318. Apparently, a copyist simply replaced the last "c" with an "x." Others copying from the incorrect manuscript multiplied the mistake. It was not until many manuscripts could be compared that the mistake would be corrected.

What a difference that mistake made. Suddenly what was once thought to be the most reliable source became a very late document of suspicious value.

Authorship, sources, origin, and purpose

We have no idea who might have written this work. It has many similarities to other works by Leo of Assisi, the close companion of Francis. However, Leo had long been dead by the time of its composition.

The similarity to Leo's work may best be explained by the fact that the majority of material included in *The Mirror of Perfection* comes directly from *The Assisi Compilation* which grew out of the reminiscences of Leo, Angelo and Rufino. For this reason, I place *The Mirror of Perfection* in the Leonine tradition of sources. The next most prominent source was Celano's *The Remembrance*. Even though these are two distinct sources, they both share an interest in the primitive life of the Franciscans, emphasizing poverty, asceticism and the eremitical life. The presentation of such a list of virtues in MP's twelve chapters is reminiscent of the twelve chapters of Francis' *The Later Rule* and suggests that the redactor might have considered this work and *The Later Rule* as similar guides to perfection for the friars. Finally, a short section seems to come from Celano's legend, and two chapters (2MP 84 and 85) are original material which are a poem describing the ideal Franciscan.

So it makes sense to talk more of the redactor or editor of this work than the author. The redactor barely changed the stories he or she borrowed from other sources. The only significant change is the way the stories are arranged together. It is the placement of the stories that amplifies the polemical tone that was originally found in *The Assisi Compilation.*

It is very plausible that the author was an adherent to the Spiritual Movement, which reached its climax right about the time of composition. The "Spirituals," as they were called, were an unorganized group of friars who harkened back to the early days of Francis' conversion. Their writings tended to be polemical in nature to make their point against the more institutionalized interpretation of Francis as found in Bonaventure's *The Major Legend* .

Organization

Like Celano's *The Remembrance* and *The Assisi Compilation*, *The Mirror of Perfection* is a florilegium, not a chronological legend. Thus, its stories are grouped together by topic to impress upon the reader the values of each section.

Two Parallel Editions

Four years after Sabatier's first edition of this work, Leonard Lemmens published an edition of a related but different manuscript version. Lemmens' version was shorter, organized differently, and more directly related to its visible sources (AC and 2C) without the editorial comments of Sabatier's version. Lemmens' entire version, except its last number, is found in the Sabatier version. Habig published only Sabatier's version in English translation. FA:ED provides both versions, including the first accessible English translation of Lemmens' version.

Despite the fact that there are differences in the tone of the two versions, I have chosen in this workbook to deal exclusively with Sabatier's version. As I explained earlier, I have found that using too many primary sources confuses and discourages beginners in their study of Francis' life. Second, Sabatier's version contains Lemmens' entire version except for one chapter. The reverse is not true. Finally, since Sabatier's version is the only version published in Habig, its usage in this workbook allows students using either Habig or FA:ED to more successfully use this workbook.

The first edition of this workbook used the abbreviation *MP* to designate this work, since only the Sabatier version was available in the older Habig. In order to conform to the abbreviations found in FA:ED, this revised edition of the workbook will use *2MP* to designate the Sabatier version in either FA:ED or Habig. FA:ED uses *1MP* to refer to the Lemmens' version. However, no citation in this workbook will refer to that version. Perhaps more advanced students will want to do studies that compare these two versions after they have completed their initial study of the life of Francis with this workbook.

Evaluation

1. The late date of this work (1318) bodes badly for its value. There is simply too much time that allowed for hagiographic changes to the stories between its composition and Francis' death (1226).
2. Like that of *The Assisi Compilation*, the strong polemical nature of *The Mirror of Perfection* causes us to question its objectivity. It is preoccupied with presenting one view of Francis in opposition to others.
3. Since almost all of 2MP's material comes from earlier sources, it is always better to cite the material from those sources.

In the end, I find *The Mirror of Perfection* to be of little historical value, and encourage students to refer back to its earlier sources.

Suggested reading

- Burr, David. *The Spiritual Franciscans: From Protest to Persecution in the Century after Saint Francis*. University Park PA: The Pennsylvania State University Press, 2001.
- Michaels, Daniel T. "*Speculum*: Form and Function in the *Mirror of Perfection*." *Francis of Assisi: History, Hagiography and Hermeneutics in the Early Documents*. Ed. Jay M. Hammond. Hyde Park NY: New City Press, 2004. 250–263.

The Deeds and *The Little Flowers*: Are They Sources?

Of course they are, but sources for what? The answer can only be discovered after looking at their origin.

Origin

The Little Flowers is an Italian translation, edition and development of an earlier Latin work called *Actus beati Francisci et sociorum eius* (The Acts of Blessed Francis and His Companions). For short, we usually refer to the latter simply as the *Actus, The Acts,* or *The Deeds*. In this workbook, I will usually use *The Deeds*. Traditionally, scholars attribute its authorship to Ugolino Boniscambi of Montegiorgio. Recent scholarship allows us to more precisely date *The Deeds* between 1328 and 1337, about 100 years after Francis' death.

Ugolino was a Franciscan in the Spiritual Tradition. He always remained loyal to the institutional church, avoiding the extremes of other Spirituals.

His principal sources came through the oral tradition as opposed to a written tradition. Ugolino apparently heard stories from James of Massa (who knew Clare of Assisi, Leo, Masseo [d.1280], and Giles), John of Perugia (who knew Bernard of Quintavalle and Giles), John of Penna (who knew Philip) and John of La Verna (who also knew Masseo). It is obvious from this list that the oral tradition could go back to important sources for the life of Francis. However, because of the second- and third-hand nature of this information, its historical accuracy is highly suspect. Many of the stories show fanciful developments and additions from the other previously discussed sources. Those sources clearly included *The Major Legend* of Bonaventure, some of the writings of Francis' early companions (possibly including Leo of Assisi and the Three Companions), and the writings of the Spiritual Angelo Clareno.

The Deeds begins with stories about Francis. However, it gives considerable attention to the deeds of Francis' followers in Umbria and the Marches (the area northeast of Assisi). It supports some of the favored ideals of the Spirituals, especially poverty, which is the subject of stories in the last nine chapters. *The Deeds* speak in glowing terms about the friars in Umbria, helping scholars to determine its composition in that geographic area.

An unidentifiable Tuscan or Marches friar appears to have written the Italian translation of *The Deeds* that we call *The Little Flowers.* Many used to date *The Little Flowers* in the last decade of the 1300s because that is the date of the oldest known manuscript. However, modern scholarship believes that an earlier version, more in the form of an Italian translation of the *Deeds,* emerged shortly after *The Deeds,* i.e., after 1337. This is the version found in FA:ED. The version published in Habig follows the manuscript dated 1396, and consequently shows much of the editing that caused many scholars to originally believe *The Little Flowers* was more of a distinctive work influenced by *The Deeds* than a *translation* of *The Deeds*. One of the chief differences students will notice is that the later version found in Habig contains *The Considerations of the Sacred Stigmata,* which is not found in the earlier FA:ED version. In this workbook, I will use the traditional abbreviation *Fior* to refer to the version found in Habig and *LFl* to refer to the version in FA:ED III.

Both works contain numerous miracles, many unfound in other sources. They also highlight numerous animal stories, many of which contain miraculous aspects.

Evaluation

Frankly, I don't consider *The Deeds* or *The Little Flowers* sources for the life of Francis. They are much too late in the tradition not to be historically corrupted by hagiographic and political forces. Their reliance on the oral tradition further underscores this concern. Their very romantic approach and miraculous tendencies place the final nails in the coffin.

I caution my students to never use *The Deeds* or *The Little Flowers* as sources for the life of Francis. They could only be trusted if they corroborated an earlier source, in which case the earlier source should be cited. However, as in the case of Bonaventure's legend for its period, *The Deeds* and *The Little Flowers* tell something about Franciscan spirituality in the 14th century. We simply need to understand that this is not what we are studying at the present moment.

I also find it unfortunate to report that *The Little Flowers* is probably the most published life of Francis in English and perhaps in all languages. I suspect this is due to the fact that its spirituality was very appealing during the middle part of the 20th century. It also means there are a lot of inaccurate images of Francis in the popular mind today.

The Chronicle of Thomas of Eccleston

Date and authorship

The dating and authorship of major chronicles that are sources for the life of Francis are generally reliable. Thomas of Eccleston, who entered the English province of the order between 1229 and 1232, wrote the first chronicle. Thomas studied at Oxford and was proud of the scholarly reputation of the English movement within the order. Some feel he betrays an arrogant attitude that his province was superior to others in the order. Whether this is true or not, his chronicle is a reliable witness for the most part to the issues about the English Province. He is sometimes inaccurate with dates and details of events occurring outside England.

Organization

As a chronicle, the work presents the origins of the English Province. His work begins with 1224 (a date variant from the correct 1223) with the approval of Francis' *The Later Rule* and ends in 1257 or 1258. A few stories about Francis are included as they shed some light on the origins of the English Province. His work is somewhat disorganized and shows little appreciation for distinguishing between important and unimportant material.

Sources and evaluation

Thomas relies heavily on his own experience and accounts he heard from the early members of the province. When speaking from this experience and these sources, he appears quite accurate. When he talks about places and events in the far northern reaches of the province or on the continent, he is less reliable. In these cases, it is good to find verification from other reliable sources.

Suggested reading

- Sheehan, Maurice. "St. Francis in the Chronicle of Eccleston." *Francesco d'Assisi nella storia: secoli XIII–XV.* Ed. Servus Gieben. Rome: Istituto Storico dei Cappuccini, 1983. 201–218.

The Chronicle of Jordan of Giano

Date and authorship

Jordan wrote his chronicle in 1262. His personal history is sketchy. He was born around 1195 and may have been from Umbria, the Italian province containing Assisi. It appears he entered the order before 1219. Based on his chronicle, we know he was part of a delegation of friars who went to Germany in 1221. He easily could have met Francis at the general chapter that sent the delegation.

Sources and organization

Jordan's work appears highly reliable because of its dependence on Jordan's own experience. His work deals with three general areas. The first (paragraphs 1–16) deals with the early years of the order in general. This section talks about Francis and the early missionary journeys of the brothers. Part two (17–35) treats of the establishment of the order in Germany. The final part (36–78) discusses the development of the Saxony Province.

Evaluation

Jordan proves to be reliable as a historical source. He tries to be objective and manages to be entertaining at the same time. Jordan's chronicle makes three other important contributions. The first is that he shows Francis as an organizer and leader in the order. This is not so clearly portrayed in other sources. Secondly, Jordan testifies that Francis' biographers chose, selected and edited stories for their works. While we can take this for granted after having studied the rules of medieval hagiography, it is impressive when a contemporary author makes a similar assessment. Finally, Jordan's chronicle provides information about Thomas of Celano that helps us evaluate Thomas as a source for the life of Francis. See my earlier chapter "Thomas of Celano's *The Life of St. Francis*" for this information.

The Archives of Assisi and Arnaldo Fortini

Numerous students of Francis' life have read Arnaldo Fortini's *Francis of Assisi* and concluded they previously never had such a clear and animated picture of the man. "Fortini brings Francis to life," one of my students commented.

It's easy to imagine why. Medieval biographies tend to portray flat and uninteresting saints. They provide little depth to their characters and rely on tools described earlier in this book that prohibit modern readers from easily encountering the warm human beings beneath the thick saintly veneer of hagiography.

How does Fortini do it? He presents the social, political, economic, and religious environment in which Francis lived.

Fortini lived nearly his entire life in Assisi. He served as the city's mayor and, as such, oversaw the economic rejuvenation of the city in the middle part of the last century. He had a passion for history and enviable access to the archives of Assisi. This background situated Fortini to write many books that are as much a biography of Assisi as they are a biography of Francis. Fortini brings Francis alive because he situates Francis in a living city: 12th and 13th century Assisi.

So Fortini's works fill in many gaps left by the medieval biographies about Francis. They give us access to information only found in the archives of Assisi and, thus, largely unavailable to casual students of Francis. He summarizes and particularizes general information about medieval life as it applies to Assisi. Fortini's work offers added resources and requires subtle cautions to studying the life of Francis. Several of the study guides provided in this book include citations from Fortini's book. These citations are provided when Fortini alone gives valuable data in English.

However, the student of Francis must be careful when reading Fortini's book. We must distinguish between what Fortini is saying about Francis and what he is saying about Assisi or medieval Italy in general. Just because something was generally true in Assisi does not mean it was true about Francis. As long as students make that distinction, Fortini's book will be of extraordinary value.

When you have finished your study of Francis' life, I encourage you to read Fortini's book from cover to cover. After having completed this course about Francis, you will enjoy his book even more and be able to evaluate it in a critical manner.

Sources cited

- Fortini, Arnaldo. *Francis of Assisi.* A Translation of *Nova Vita di San Francesco* by Helen Moak. New York: Crossroad, 1980 and 1992 in paper.

Work

About Worksheets

The next section of this book provides you with the opportunity to study the life and writings of Francis. I wish to make a few introductory comments before beginning the worksheets.

First, as I mentioned earlier, it is my bias that people learn best by doing the work themselves. I have never found spoon-feeding to be an effective pedagogical approach. These worksheets will help you do the work by providing the primary sources for your study and a series of starter questions and/or suggestions. Read the *entire* worksheet at the beginning of your study. There may be important ideas toward the end of the worksheet to facilitate your study.

Occasionally, I have provided a commentary as part of a worksheet. Generally, I do this when there is information that affects your study and comes from other scholarly works.

I also provide lists of recommended reading on numerous worksheets. Sometimes, these lists are simply for those who wish to explore a topic in greater detail. On other occasions, I strongly recommend additional readings from secondary sources because they provide essential insights into the topic.

The more work you do on these worksheets, the more you will benefit.

Second, I wish to recall my earlier admission to being biased in favor of a historical approach to studying Francis. I believe a valuable Franciscan spirituality can only be constructed upon good historical knowledge about Francis. Each of the worksheets provides questions and recommendations for doing historical-critical work. However, I wish to enumerate a number of common techniques that are applicable to most worksheets.

- I have previously outlined numerous characteristics of hagiography. Review them often. When you read something in the primary sources that smacks of non-historical, hagiographic influences, let your suspicions guide you. Don't blindly accept assertions or interpretations you consider historically doubtful.
- One of my favorite techniques is to compare the same story in various sources. These comparisons allow you to see what has been added, subtracted, or changed from earlier versions of the story. Always ask why these changes are occurring. Review frequently what you know about each of the various medieval sources, especially the biases that are part of each source. Try to see whether a source's biases are guiding the changes in the tradition. You also will be able to see the powerful forces of hagiography adjusting stories over time. Always be suspicious of changes in a story.

- Medieval hagiography loves the miraculous. Without it, medievals doubted a subject's sanctity. Thus, you are wise to be suspicious of miracles without closing off the possibility that the miraculous account is true. Many world-class historians who believe in miracles acknowledge that hagiography is fraught with more miracles than are believable. My principle is first to search for a humanly understandable rendering of a story. While that may leave us with little information about a story, it probably will leave us with a version that is reliable.

Third, I wish to emphasize that my worksheets are places to begin. At the beginning of my courses, a few students make presentations in which they go through the list of questions I have asked in a worksheet and provide an answer to each. This is not how I intend the worksheets to function. My starter questions and suggestions are only intended to get you thinking and asking questions. If you are making a presentation to a group based on your study, I suggest that you organize your findings in a way that is satisfying to you and interesting to others in your group. In doing so, you may not answer a single question I list on your worksheet.

Fourth, I realize that not everyone using this book is in the same situation. If you are using it alone, please do what works best for you. If you are part of a study group, I have some suggestions.

- Don't have everyone in the group do every worksheet. They take a significant amount of time, and you may not have enough time to cover most of Francis' life if everyone works on every worksheet. I typically work with groups of four to eight members. I generally go around the horn, assigning the worksheets in succession to different individuals. I then ask each person to prepare a presentation to the entire group. However, I usually ask everyone in the group to work on a few important topics. They include: "Francis Meets the Leper," "The Religious Experience at San Damiano," "Francis and Penance", "Francis' Eucharistic Writings," and "The Development of the First Order Rule."
- Groups make for interesting and helpful dynamics in this process. After the individual's presentation, I invite other group members to respond to and evaluate the conclusions of the presenter. Often, members of the group will disagree about the conclusions and criticize each other's reasoning. I generally let this type of discussion go on for a while, especially early in the course. It teaches the participants to be critical and to think on their own. I even play the devil's advocate by asking questions of the presenter and the other participants. I use this technique to loosen up the crowd, which is often hesitant in the beginning to question another presenter. After a few sessions of presentations, I

find I occasionally have to stop a discussion just to move on. There is only so much time for each topic.

- I also find that our discussions often raise other questions about religious life, liturgy, the teachings of the church, spirituality, and values in general. I generally allow these discussions to occur when they seem manageable and I am competent to guide them. Part of the reason we study Francis' life and writings is to deepen our faith life. With that as a goal, it seems self-defeating not to allow discussion on other topics that our study raises up.
- Occasionally, a group leader may have an expertise that is helpful to this study process. I encourage you to share your expertise with your students. However, I would be careful to preserve a general atmosphere where the students feel like they are doing the majority of the work. I only present things they could not otherwise know on their own. For instance, I generally lead the session on a paradigm for conversion found in this book. However, I always invite the reactions and questions of others in the group.

Fifth, because of space limitations, I do not deal with all the prayers of Francis. A few are discussed in worksheets devoted specifically to them; others are discussed in worksheets on related subjects. If you are interested in a prayer I do not discuss, I refer you to FA:ED. It contains all the writings of Francis, introductions to each, and helpful footnotes which will direct you to additional bibliography.

Sixth, each worksheet has a *topic*. The primary sources cited in the worksheet generally talk about many things unrelated to that topic. Occasionally, students are prone to report to their groups every bit of information provided in the worksheet's sources, even when it is unrelated to the topic. This is deadening! I encourage students to focus only on the material related to the worksheet's topic. In order to facilitate this approach, this revised edition of *Studying the Life of Francis of Assisi* uses lower case letters to indicate specific paragraphs within a cited section of a source. The letter *a* refers to the first paragraph, *b* to the second, etc. For instance, the reference AP 3b–4 refers to *The Anonymous of Perugia* beginning with the *second* (b) paragraph of section 3 through the entire fourth section. Unless the citation specifically refers to Habig's edition, the letters refer to paragraphs as they occur in FA:ED.

Related to point six is my encouragement to read "around" your worksheet's citations, i.e., before and after the cited text, if that text by itself seems out of context. Often the larger context gives the text of a citation a fuller meaning. However, in light of point six, be careful only to report on material that is directly related to the topic of your worksheet.

That's pretty much all the advice I have for you at this point. The thing to do now is to begin. If you are part of a group, divide up the first few worksheets and break up for the time being. Your next gathering promises to be an enriching learning experience.

Pietro Bernardone: Francis' Father

Sources

1C 8–15a, 53
LJS 6–9
AP 7–9
L3C 2, 9, 16–20, 23
2C 3, 12
LMj I 2; II 1–4; VI 1
LMn I 1, 5–7

Starter questions and suggestions

Study Francis' father with two approaches. First, look at each of the individual stories that involves Francis' father, seeing how it changes throughout the biographical tradition. Second, look at each medieval source individually to see how it uniquely presents its image of Pietro.

1. Read through all the citations listed above. As you read, separate the citations according to individual stories. E.g., group together all the stories about the naming of Francis, the stories in which Pietro puts Francis in chains, the stories of Pietro cursing Francis on the street, etc. Within each story group, arrange the citations chronologically by composition. Note any additions to, subtractions from, or changes in the information. Try to determine why there are variations among the different sources. Determine what you believe is historically accurate about each story.
2. Reread all the sources, one biography at a time. Compare the composite image of Pietro in each biography to the images in the other biographies. What differences do you notice in the various portraits of Pietro? What goals, purposes, or biases of the authors are shaping the various images of Pietro? Which images or parts of images do you believe to be accurate?

It is helpful to know of two trends in medieval hagiography that affect the picture we receive of Pietro. One portrays the saint-to-be as sinful and worldly. This contrasts with the grace-filled and otherworldly post-conversion life. The stark differences draw attention to the change in the person, highlighting the hand of God in the saint's conversion.

A second common portrait shows the saint as always disposed to a gospel life, often in contrast to a materialistic social and family environment. In this presentation, the reader is brought to awe by the saint's achievements *despite* the unsupportive environment. Are either or both of these paradigms present in the traditions about Francis? Which biases of the authors influence their choice of a paradigm? How do these choices affect the portrait of Pietro?

While doing these tasks, gather as much personal information about Pietro as you can: place of birth, age, occupation, marriage, children, religious practices, loyalties to political organizations etc. When you finish gathering your data, draw up a personality profile of Pietro. Describe Pietro's temperament, personal goals, driving forces, biases, and yearnings. Explain the relationship between Pietro and Francis. Answer these questions: Did Pietro love Francis? Did he take good care of Francis? What were Pietro's hopes for Francis? Were those hopes unreasonable, cruel, or not understandable? Do you like Pietro? Who is responsible for the break in their relationship: Pietro, Francis or both of them?

My groups have often discussed whether Pietro's family was dysfunctional. It can be a difficult topic. One problem is determining whether we can apply a modern concept like dysfunction to a medieval family. It certainly would be unfair to *judge* the family as good or bad using standards from a different time and place. However, it is not unfair to try to name a reality using our terminology even though medievals would have no clue about what we are talking! The trick is to retrieve enough reliable data from medieval documents to make a reasonable determination. If it is helpful, try to address this issue for yourself.

Suggested reading

- Trexler, Richard C. *Naked before the Father: The Renunciation of Francis of Assisi*. Humana Civilitas 9. New York: Peter Lang Publishing, 1989. Trexler presents novel ideas about Francis' family constellation, suggesting that Pietro was Pica's second husband and that Francis and Angelo were half-brothers with different fathers. Chapter one studies Francis' family tree (pages 7–29).

Pica: Francis' Mother

Sources

1C 13
LJS 8
L3C 2, 9, 18–19
2C 3
LMj II 3
LMn I 1

Starter questions and suggestions

Study Francis' mother with two approaches. First, look at each of the individual stories that involve Francis' mother, seeing how it changes throughout the biographical tradition. Second, look at each medieval biography individually to see how it uniquely presents the image of "Pica."

1. Read through all of the citations listed above. As you read, separate the citations according to individual stories. E.g., group together all the stories about Francis' birth and naming, the stories about loosing Francis' chains, etc. Within each story group, arrange the citations chronologically by composition. Note any additions to, subtractions from, or changes in the information. Try to determine why there are variations among the different sources. Determine what you believe is historically accurate about each story.
2. Reread all the sources, one biography at a time. Compare the composite image of Pica in each biography to the images in the other biographies. What differences do you notice in the various portraits of Pica? What effect do the allusions to Elizabeth and Simeon in the birth stories have on the reader? What goals, purposes, or biases of the authors are shaping the various images of Pica? Which images or parts of images do you believe to be accurate?

While doing these tasks, gather as much personal information about Pica as you can: place of birth, age, occupation, marriage, children, religious practices, etc. When you are finished gathering your data, draw up a personality profile of Pica. Describe Pica's temperament, personal goals, driving forces, biases, and yearnings. Explain the relationships between Pica, Pietro and Francis.

Suggested reading

- Trexler, Richard C. *Naked before the Father: The Renunciation of Francis of Assisi*. Humana Civilitas 9. New York: Peter Lang Publishing, 1989. Trexler presents novel ideas about Francis' family constellation, suggesting that Pietro was Pica's second husband and that Francis and Angelo were half-brothers with different fathers. Chapter one studies Francis' family tree (pages 7–29).

Francis' Brother

Sources

L3C 9, 23
2C 12
Eccleston 6 (Chronicles 126)

Starter questions and suggestions

Do the three sources agree in content, tone, and image when discussing Francis' brother? If not, what are the differences?

What was Francis' relationship with his brother? Do we have a complete picture? Why is nothing said about Francis' brother until *The Legend of the Three Companions*? How do these stories suddenly get into the biographical tradition in 1246? Do you believe the characterization of his brother? Why or why not? What do you historically know about his brother? Give as many personal characteristics as possible: age, temperament, name, schooling, relationship with Francis before and after Francis' conversion, etc.

Obviously, it is impossible to answer many of the questions I list above. We don't have very much information about Francis' brother. In light of that, how accurately can we form any judgment of what his brother was like? Do you trust the narrow image that this very short story portrays?

Suggested reading

- Trexler, Richard C. *Naked before the Father: The Renunciation of Francis of Assisi.* Humana Civilitas 9. New York: Peter Lang Publishing, 1989. Trexler presents novel ideas about Francis' family constellation, suggesting that Pietro was Pica's second husband and that Francis and Angelo were half-brothers with different fathers. Chapter one studies Francis' family tree (pages 7–29).

Francis' Education and Literary Ability

Sources

Test 19
LtOrd 39
1C 22, 23, 89
AP 11a
L3C 10c, 21d
AC 10a, 109 (LP 83, 103)
2C 102, 141a, 145b
LMj I 1; XI 1; XV 5
LMn IV 3
Eccleston 6 (Chronicles 126)
Jordan 50 (Chronicles 57)

Commentary

Some sources are straightforward about Francis' education and literary ability. Others are more obscure in that clues about Francis' reading ability are indirect. Examples include those stories where Francis needed help reading the Gospels. However, other sources say he recited the Liturgy of the Hours, which might necessitate reading or might assume that he knew at least the psalms by memory.

Few medievals were educated. Few could read or write. Time and place certainly made a difference. I once read that fewer than 5% of medievals could read. I have no way of knowing for sure and am uncertain how anyone could know. I suspect historians are guessing when they make such estimates. But it is certain that an education was not taken for granted and that the literacy rate was low.

That being the case, Francis would seem better educated than most; he could read, write, and do basic arithmetic. He knew a little French and Latin. The fact that he left school to work early in life is an indication that his education was not extensive, but enough to conduct the business of his father's shop. His writings that do not seem touched up by others testify to the limits of his education: his sentences run on; he makes grammar mistakes; and he literally translates Italian idioms into Latin. Much of this is not visible to us who read the sources in English translation. However, recent studies are increasingly questioning this long-standing description of Francis' poor literacy. Articles by Fumagalli and Paolazzi listed in the suggested reading section below make strong arguments for a "better" educated or literate Francis.

Francis probably received a typical parish school education, which is not to say a parish school education was typical. This would mean Francis and his classmates learned to read and write by using the scriptures and liturgical books. Remember, books were both expensive and scarce. The scriptures and liturgical books would have been most available. The New Testament and Psalms were the most common biblical texts in liturgical books. So, Francis probably used them most while learning to read. He also may have used liturgical prayers including the creeds, gloria, introits, canons, etc.

Don't confuse this type of schooling with that of the great universities of his day. Francis, though more educated than most medievals, has typically been portrayed as crudely educated compared to some of the highly educated men who joined him later. It is not hard to understand how conflict could arise among them. Still, as historians study Francis' writings, many are amazed at his knowledge and mastery of scriptural, patristic, and monastic sources despite his lack of formal training. Robert Karris' study of *The Admonitions* is one superb example. Fumagalli and Paolazzi are amazed at Francis' mastery of cursus and other literary techniques of the day.

As a point of interest, the Church of San Giorgio, (where Francis attended school) is currently incorporated into the Basilica and Monastery of St. Clare in Assisi. The current buildings were constructed after Clare died. These "new" buildings allowed the Poor Clares to move within the "new" walls of Assisi and afforded them the physical protection that they lacked outside the walls when they lived at San Damiano. Clare of Assisi is buried in the basilica's crypt.

Starter suggestions

Read the sources listed above and prepare your own presentation to your study group about the nature of Francis' education.

Suggested reading and sources cited

- Fumagalli, Edoardo. "Saint Francis, the Canticle, the Our Father." Trans. Edward Hagman. *Greyfriars Review* 19.supplement (2005) 1–87.
- Karris, Robert J. *The Admonitions of St. Francis: Sources and Meanings*. St. Bonaventure NY: The Franciscan Institute, 1999. See especially his introduction on pages 1–16. However, Karris documents Francis' mastery of ancient sources throughout his study.
- Schmucki, Oktavian. T. "Francis's Level of Education." Trans. Paul Barrett. *Greyfriars Review* 10.2 (1996) 153–170.
- Paolazzi, Carlo. "Francis and His Use of Scribes: A Puzzle to be Solved." Trans. Edward Hagman. *Greyfriars Review* 18.3 (2004) 323–341.

Bishop Guido II

Sources

Francis renounces his father before Guido
1C 14–15
LJS 9
AP 8
L3C 19–20
2C 12
LMj II 4
LMn I 6–7

Guido questions the severity of Francis' life
AP 17b–e
L3C 35b–c

Guido has no church for the brothers
AC 56a–d (LP 8a–e)
2MP 55a–c

Guido helps the friars in Rome
1C 32
AP 32
L3C 47

Guido interrupts Francis in prayer
AC 54 (LP 6)
2C 100

Francis reconciles Guido and the Podestà (mayor) of Assisi
AC 84 (LP 44)
2MP 101

Francis appears to Guido
2C 220
LMj XIV 6
LMn VII 6

Guido instills clerical respect in Francis
AC 58f (LP 15b)
2MP 10g

A sick Francis stays in Guido's palace
AC 70a (LP 28)

Various stories about Bishop Guido of Assisi can be found in the sources about Clare of Assisi. The best English edition is:

- Armstrong, Regis, ed. and trans. *Clare of Assisi: Early Documents.* Second revised edition. New York: New City Press, 2005. The original edition of this work was published by Paulist Press in 1988. The first revised and expanded edition was published at St. Bonaventure NY by Franciscan Institute Publications in 1993. Page references here are from the New City Press edition.

Legend of Clare 7 (pp. 285–286)
Process of Canonization of Clare,
Witness 1, #8 (p. 146)
Witness 2, #12 (p. 152)
Witness 6, #14 (p. 170)

Arnaldo Fortini, the former mayor of Assisi, gathered substantial information about Guido of Assisi from the archives of Assisi. I recommend you look up Guido of Assisi in the index of his book *Francis of Assisi* translated by Helen Moak (Crossroads, 1980, 1992 in paper). Read the references to Guido (p. 710). I also suggest you reread the earlier section in this book about Fortini's writing.

Starter questions and suggestions

Our purpose here is to learn about Guido. Many of the stories that talk about Guido are also cited in other worksheets throughout this book. Do not focus so much on the stories themselves or what we learn about Francis. That will be the subject of subsequent worksheets. Rather, focus on what we learn about Bishop Guido.

Notice how many of the stories are either exclusively found in the Leonine tradition (AC–LP and 2MP) or not found anywhere in the Leonine tradition. Only the story of Guido interrupting Francis at prayer is found in a mix of a Leonine source (AC–LP) and another source (2C). Perhaps more than most topics, this one helps us see the different values of the various traditions. Clarify which values are important to which traditions (E.g., official, Egidian or Leonine traditions).

First, study each story separately. Note any changes in the story across the sources. Determine what you believe to be an accurate rendering of each individual story. Then take all the stories as a whole and develop a character sketch of Guido. Describe Guido's relationship with the order What role did he have in the foundation and development of the order? Describe his personal relationship with Francis and the other brothers. List Guido's personal characteristics. Was he a good bishop? Be prepared to defend your opinion!

Fortini's portrayal of Guido is different from that found in the Franciscan sources. This is probably due to the secular sources Fortini used. Describe the general picture of Bishop Guido coming from the Assisian archives at Fortini's disposal. How is that description of Guido different from the hagiographical sources? How can these different portrayals be reconciled?

Suggested Reading

- Fortini, Arnaldo. *Francis of Assisi.* Trans. Helen Moak. New York: Crossroad, 1980 and 1992 in paper.
- Robson, Michael. "Assisi, Guido II and Saint Francis." *Greyfriars Review* 12.3 (1998) 225–287.

Personal Information about Francis

Sources

1C 1–3 (do not confuse with prologue), 17, 83
LJS 1
AP 3b–4
L3C 2–3
AC 50j, 51a, (LP 2b–3b)
2C 3
LMj I 1

Starter questions and suggestions

There is no hidden agenda to this worksheet. All we want to do is gather personal information about Francis before his conversion. Note information about his birth date, name, character, physical characteristics, etc.

What was Francis like before his conversion? What were his natural qualities, fears, and concerns? What did he enjoy? What were his family and social life like?

Note differences in the way the various sources describe Francis before his conversion, his family life, and the social environment of Assisi.

War with and Imprisonment in Perugia

Sources

L3C 4
2C 4
Fortini chapter 4

Starter questions and suggestions

These Franciscan sources tell us very little about the war, Francis' motivations and preparations for the war, his family's attitudes about it, or the social stakes. With the help of Fortini, can you guess what some of these things might be? If you are reporting to a group about this topic, begin by summarizing Fortini's background information about this war.

Portends about one's future greatness are common in hagiography. Are Francis' prison predictions real or the addition of later hagiographers?

Note how little we really know about these powerful experiences in Francis' life. Why did the hagiographers deal with them so slightly?

Francis' Illness before His Conversion

Sources

1C 3–4, 89a
LJS 2
LMj I 2
LMn I 2

Starter questions and suggestions

Focus on the nature of Francis' illness and its cause(s). The medieval sources portray Francis' illness as "divine unction." This is an ambiguous term. What do you think the medieval authors were trying to say? Do they intend to say that God intervened in history and intentionally made Francis ill to change him? Could the medieval authors simply intend to describe the same grace through which God works in all our lives? Did Francis' "stubbornness" merit his illness? How do you explain the changes in Francis' response to his beautiful surroundings after he began to recover?

How do you understand God's role in Francis' illness?

As with the worksheet "War with and Imprisonment in Perugia," note how little we know about the causes and nature of this powerful experience in Francis' life. The medieval sources focus more on its effect than its nature or causes. Why did the hagiographers deal with the details so slightly?

The Expedition toward Apulia

Sources

1C 4–6
LJS 2–3
AP 5–7a
L3C 5–6
2C 5–6
LMj I 2–3

Starter questions and suggestions

List each source chronologically by composition on the top of a wide piece of paper. As you read each source, write data from the account down the column under the name of its source. Place similar information in different sources on the same horizontal plane. Place a check or some other mark next to information that represents an addition to, subtraction from or change of information from the previous sources. Determine whether the story is intensifying as it moves through the various biographies. If you are studying Francis' life with a group, it may be helpful to reproduce this schema for others in the group.

Determine why Francis left for Apulia. Look for more than one level of motivation. How do his motives relate to his previous experiences you already studied?

Decide whether you believe Francis' experiences in the stories to be dreams, visions, apparitions, revelations or growing self-awareness. Are all of the "dreams" historical? Evaluate the various authors' interpretation that God was intervening in Francis' life to lead him to his true vocation.

There are numerous allusions in these stories to biblical stories and sayings, and other saints' lives. Footnotes in the sources should help you identify them. What impact do these allusions have on the presented image of Francis? Trace the development of *interpretation* about Francis as the tradition chronologically develops.

Why did Francis decide not to continue on to Apulia? Again, explore various levels of motivation. Were his hagiographers covering up for a coward?

After completing this process, make a list of short, concise statements that portray what you believe reliably happened. Then make a list of short, concise statements portraying what you believe was going on inside Francis. Try not to confuse the two lists.

After looking at the historical Francis through this story, you may want to explore several theological concepts that affect us today. The first is our notion of the *will or desire of God.* The medieval presentations of this story imply that God has very specific plans for individuals, as if individuals cannot take other courses without displeasing God. Explore your own ideas about the *will or desire of God.* What exactly does God care about? What does God *want* us to do or be?

Related to the *will of God* is the notion of *vocation.* This word comes from a Latin word meaning *to call.* Does God will *specific* vocations for each individual? Do faithful Christians have *choices* to make in forging a vocation? What concerning our individual vocations does God care about?

Finally, this story focuses us on *grace* and causes us to ask how God acts in our lives. This story about Francis almost appears mechanistic in its approach to grace. Can we see grace in the story even if we conceptualize it differently than the medievals? More importantly, discussing grace in the life of Francis can cause us to examine it in our own lives. How do you experience grace operative in your life?

A Period of Prayer and Reflection including the Hunchback Fantasy

Sources

1C 6–7
LJS 4
L3C 8, 12
2C 8–9b (don't go beyond the second paragraph of section nine; don't report on the leper story)
LMj I 6b–e

Starter questions and suggestions regarding this reflection time in general

Focus on the internal process going on in Francis. Try to discern what all the anxiety was about in his life. Determine the role others played in his life at this time. Of what was Francis afraid?

What was the point of Francis hiding what was going on inside of himself from so many other people? Was Francis afraid of others or himself? Try to explain Francis' lack of confidence in himself as he goes through this process.

Using language that average people today would understand, describe what was going on in Francis.

Starter questions and suggestions regarding Francis' pilgrimage to Rome

Francis processes his conversion in two different ways. Sometimes he seeks secluded places to pray. At other times he looks for crowds among which he acts out his developing conversion. How is Francis' experience at the gates of St. Peter Basilica in Rome like and different from his solitary experiences around Assisi? How do they function in his ongoing conversion?

Starter questions and suggestions regarding Francis' hunchback lady fantasy

Only L3C and 2C relate this fantasy. What are the differences between the two sources? Why do you think there are differences in the accounts? Is this supposed to be a dream, paranoia, an imagining by Francis, or something else? Was the hunchback woman a historical person, a fearful image of Francis' future should he continue down this road, the image Francis was coming to understand himself to already be, or something else? Regardless of her historical or ahistorical existence, was the woman an outcast? If so, in what sense? What did the woman represent for Francis?

Is the devil cited in the sources a real being? Does the devil represent something within Francis? If so, what? A former student described the image of the hunchback as "an allegory of Francis' inner struggle." Do you agree?

How do you explain the "divine command" found in the 2C source? Does this message come from the real (audible) voice of God, Francis' understanding of God's call, Celano's interpretation of the event, or a different possibility?

The Lord of Revels Incident

Sources

1C 7
LJS 5
L3C 7
2C 7

Starter questions and suggestions

Compare the sources and see how the stories vary. Note how the sources' characterizations of Assisi's youth change as the story is related in later sources. Try to separate what actually happened from how the medieval biographies interpret the event. What does this event say about Francis *before* his conversion? How much were his friends part of the conversion process? Did they try to ward off Francis' conversion? At what point in the conversion process do you think this story occurs?

Is this story for real? What's for real?

Suggested resources

Arnold Fortini provides a description of the youth group that seems to be discussed in L3C and 2C on pages 129–137 of his book *Francis of Assisi*. Fortini provides much background that will bring this story alive. As much as I appreciate the contributions of Fortini, I always advise my students to be cautious when using him as a resource. Be sure to review my previous chapter, "The Archives of Assisi and Arnaldo Fortini."

Francis Meets the Leper and the Friars' Continuing Relationship with Lepers

Sources

Francis meets the leper during his conversion
1C 17
LJS 12a
L3C 11a–b
2C 9c–d
LMj I 5a

Francis' own testimony
Test 1–3

Francis and the friars live and work with lepers
ER VIII 10; IX
1C 17, 39, 103
LJS 12
L3C 11–12, 55
AC 9, 64–65d (LP 102, 22–23b)
2C 66, 98
LMj I 6; II 6; XIV 1
LMn I 8; VII 1
Jordan 33+39 (Chronicles 46+48)
2MP 44

Francis eats out of a leper's bowl
AC 64 (LP 22)
2MP 58

Francis heals a leper in body and soul
DBF XXVIII
LFl and Fior 25

Starter questions and suggestions

When I teach this course to a group, I ask all the members to work on the story of Francis meeting the leper during his conversion. Not only is it an important story, but studying the story also helps students see how hagiographic forces work on a story over time. If you are working with a group, I recommend that you too ask all the members of your group to do the same. That involves working with the first six sources cited at the top of this worksheet. The citation from

Francis' *Testament* is very important, as it is his own reflection on his experience with lepers.

I further recommend that all students in the group put a clean sheet of paper on its side. An oversized sheet is quite helpful. Divide the paper into five vertical columns. List the top of each column with one of the medieval biographies *in chronological order* (i.e., 1C 17, LJS 12, L3C 11, 2C 9, and LMj I 5). Briefly outline the story from 1C in the first column using black ink. Spread it out over the entire column so there is some space between entries. Do the same in the second column with the story from LJS also using black ink. Write the elements of the story next to the same elements found in 1C to the left. However, whenever LJS includes new material or changes some detail as compared to 1C, use red ink so the change stands out visually.

Next, write the elements of the story as found in L3C in the third column across from the same elements in the first two columns. Write elements that are identical in detail to the account in 1C in black ink. Elements that accept the additions or changes in LJS should be written in blue ink. Use red ink for elements that are added or changed for the first time in L3C.

Continue by putting the elements of the story found in 2C and LMj in the fourth and fifth columns respectively. Again, elements that repeat information from 1C go in black ink. Any additions or changes found in previous versions that are incorporated by 2C or LMj should be written in blue ink. Write all new changes or additions that are unique to 2C or LMj in red ink.

After completing the chart, use it to help you analyze how hagiographic forces shaped the story through its development. Note where most of the red ink is and ask why. Pay special attention to changes or additions that contribute to making the story more miraculous. I am often amazed at how once a source adds or changes something in a hagiographic tradition, that change is usually carried on in all subsequent versions. Is that true here? Check out the blue ink!

Which version of the story do you believe is the most historically reliable? Tell your group what you think really happened. I suggest you be as simple and cautious as possible.

After you have focused on the history of the story, I suggest you turn to its meaning. What was going on in Francis before he met the leper? What did the meeting do to Francis? What does the kissing of the leper indicate?

Some of the biographies present Francis' meeting with the leper in connection with his conversion. Do they present this event as the *cause, result* or *proof* of conversion in Francis? What is historically true in this regard? Is the leper theme overplayed in importance in Francis' conversion (both in the medieval and modern legends)?

Try to break the leper story down into three levels of interpretation: the historical event; the intention of Francis; the meaning of the event. What does your analysis shed on the medieval understanding of Francis? Does it or should it influence the way we understand Francis?

Fear is the best word to describe the medieval attitude toward leprosy. Given this, might Francis' embrace of the leper be an embrace of his *fear*? If so, fear of what?

If you are doing your study in a group and usually assign each worksheet to a different person, but had everyone study the story of Francis meeting the leper, I suggest you have only one person do the rest of this worksheet. The following questions and suggestions are aimed at the remaining sources.

Trace the development of leper stories in the medieval sources. Note the changes that occur through the tradition in each story. What historical judgments can be made? What were the authors trying to do with their changes? What is objective history in each story? Is one source more reliable in regard to each individual story? If so, which source, and why do you value it more than other sources?

What role did presence with lepers play in the formation of new men joining Francis' movement? Why do lepers seem to enjoy such special attention and affection from Francis? Is there a parallel between the early friars' formation among lepers and your formation as a Franciscan?

Which virtues or religious attitudes of Francis are connected to the leper stories? Do you think the stories really portray the virtues the medieval sources cite? Today, would we attribute similar virtue to equivalent actions? Give examples.

Suggested reading

- Fortini, Arnaldo. *Francis of Assisi.* Trans. Helen Moak. New York: Crossroad, 1980, 1992 in paper. 208–210. Fortini reconstructs a ritual "investiture" of a leper. Anyone familiar with the rituals of marriage, religious profession, or ordination will be struck by the similarities of structure. His reconstruction demonstrates how society formalized its relationship with a leper like it formalized its relationships with a priest through ordination or a religious through investiture and profession.

An Example of Using the Method: The Leper Stories

The story of Francis meeting a leper is among the best for showing how to use historical-critical methods to study hagiography. Because of that, I provide here my own study, which you can compare to your study with the previous worksheet. The example should also help use the method with other worksheets.

I strongly recommend that you *do not* read this example until you have completed your work on the previous worksheet. You can learn a great deal by having to struggle with the material before you are biased by my attempt. Once you have finished your study of Francis meeting the leper, I hope you learn even more from what follows.

This article was originally published in *The New Round Table* 38 (1985) 107–130 and is reprinted here with permission. However, I have abridged sections of the original article that have been repeated earlier in this workbook, especially in the section on hagiography.

Introduction

The meeting took only a moment. At least one of the participants, perhaps both, was caught off guard by the encounter. There was no time for preparation or avoidance. The moment was thrust upon these two actors in life, actors whose parts have been played and replayed for every generation that cared to watch. The scene is classic: high emotion; poignant silences of uncertainty; compelling, unpredictable action; catharsis; self-revelation; ultimate life-questions. The scene of the transforming Francis accidentally meeting a leper has long caught the Franciscan imagination. It is a scene fraught with innuendo, full of magic, and inexhaustible in its symbolism. The episode was a necessity for medievals, a watershed for moderns.

This pivotal episode and its consequences are the object of my study. I start by examining the reliable historical facts that are Francis' life. I will attempt this critical approach first with the specific accounts of Francis meeting the leper and second with Francis' and his early brothers' general practices and relationship with lepers. I will conclude by attempting to build on this historical foundation a reconstruction of Francis' personal psychology relative to his behavior and relationship with lepers.

Francis meets the leper: A historical analysis

When Franciscans gather to tell the stories of Francis, there generally is a presumption that the stories are known by all in relatively the same form.

However, the modern Franciscan may be amazed to pick up a given medieval version of Francis' life and not find some aspect of the story he or she had always assumed was there! The story of Francis meeting the leper is a pointed example. A comparison of the various medieval accounts of the story sheds light on our understanding of that event and offers a unique view into the world of hagiography.

This comparison will involve five medieval biographies: both major works about Francis written by Thomas of Celano, *The Life of St. Francis* written by Julian of Speyer, *The Legend of the Three Companions*, and Bonaventure of Bagnoregio's *The Major Legend of St. Francis*. I will examine the five works in chronological order, highlighting the additions and changes in the story over their thirty-five-year span.

The earliest account of Francis unexpectedly meeting a leper occurs in Celano's *The Life of St. Francis* (17). Celano wrote between 1228 and 1229 with the purpose of popularizing Francis as a saint after his canonization by Gregory IX in 1228. While Celano's legend is predictably fraught with miracles, it is especially important to note that, in this first account of Francis meeting a leper, Celano refrains from any use of marvelous or miraculous material. His portrayal of the meeting is brief, simple, humanly understandable, and almost incidental to Celano's larger concern to portray Francis as increasingly coming into control of some undesirable reality inside him.

Celano relates the entire incident in two simple sentences. Francis meets a leper, overcomes something inside himself, and kisses the leper. That is the end of the account. It is preceded by testimony regarding Francis' typically medieval abhorrence of lepers. It is followed by the observation that, henceforward, Francis increasingly gained control over that imperfect internal dynamic until he effectively conquered it, whatever it might have been. This *conversion* manifested itself in respect, charity, and compassion for other poor people.

Historically speaking it is important that this event is related in the earliest of all biographies about Francis. The story has an early origin. At the same time, it is striking that the story is told without any miraculous accoutrements. Certainly, if any miraculous aspects existed in the early oral versions of the story, Celano would have made use of them given his propensity to use such devices to establish the sanctity of Francis.

Julian of Speyer provides a second account of the incident in his *The Life of St. Francis* (LJS 12). Julian wrote on the heels of Celano: sometime between 1234 and 1235. His hagiographic goals are the same as Celano's. Again, Julian relates the incident with striking brevity and simplicity, avoiding any hint of the miraculous. Given goals similar to Celano's, if miraculous aspects of this story were circulating at the time of composition, Julian certainly would have included them. He did not.

The Legend of the Three Companions marks the beginning of additions to the basic story first presented by Celano. In general, the additions serve to *fill-in* the story. These details show the condition of Francis when he encounters the leper: riding a horse. Besides kissing the leper, Francis also gives him a coin, a common enough charitable act. Finally, the leper is portrayed as giving Francis a kiss of peace. This final addition, in which Francis risks contagious infection, could be edging into marvelous material. While no miraculous phenomenon is explicitly mentioned, the inclusion of this detail heightens the sense that something significant is happening. The encounter stirs the notion of a prediction in the making, a portent foreshadowing who Francis was to become: a friend of lepers and the poor.

The Legend of the Three Companions was written in 1246. It is difficult to know from where the author received this additional information. Possibly someone with first-hand knowledge of the event came forward. Perhaps it reflects the natural organic process by which stories about saints accumulate more details. Finally, the additions could be the personal work of the author attempting to provide a more interesting narrative for a powerful incident. In the latter two cases, the additions would have to be discounted from a historical point of view.

Whatever the case, great concern is not warranted. The additions barely change the tone or content of the original Celanese account. Only the image of the leper giving the kiss of peace to Francis raises the spectrum of hagiographic forces molding the developing story. Still, this is done within the acceptable limits of normal human interaction.

The Remembrance of the Desire of a Soul, completed by Celano in 1247, presents a significant departure from earlier works regarding the emphasis of the leper story (2C 9). Celano declares that his second major work, written for the friars, will provide *new* material about Francis' conversion, material not known to Celano earlier (2C 2). In the case of the leper story, Celano is certainly accurate. He incorporates all of the additions of *The Legend of the Three Companions*, with the exception of the kiss of peace by the leper.

Still, Celano builds on the notion of a portent contained in the leper's kiss of peace. At the conclusion of Celano's second account, Francis remounts his horse and, in an area without hiding places, loses sight of the leper. The effect of the disappearing leper would not be lost on medieval readers, especially the friars. Celano clearly intended to introduce miraculous material into the narrative.

Popular medieval images of saints encountering Christ in a poor or sick person abounded at the time. An image such as St. Christopher carrying Jesus across a river—a medieval addition to the more ancient legend—was widespread in Europe (*Acta Sanctorum* Julii VI: 125–149). Likewise prominent was the legend of Martin of Tours, who gave half his cloak to a cold poor man. In

Martin's subsequent dream, the poor man was revealed to be Jesus (Sulpicius Severus 106–108). More locally, areas had traditions as that of Julian the hospitaller, who after caring for a supposed leper—who in reality was a messenger from God—was assured by the messenger that his sins were forgiven (*Acta Sanctorum* Januarii III: 590).

Images of such miraculous encounters were lodged prominently in the minds of the people. Given this tradition, Celano altered the portrait of the leper as a suffering human being to that of the disguised Christ at best, an emissary-angel at least.

The possible sources of the new material are similar to those outlined in regard to *The Legend of the Three Companions*. The significant difference is that Celano's addition tests the limits of normal human activity. Given the late introduction of this miraculous detail and our exhaustive knowledge of the medieval hagiographic requirement to include such miraculous material in the lives of the saints, we can only conclude that Celano or his sources changed the scope of the story. With Celano's *The Remembrance*, this story in the legends about Francis of Assisi made a common jump, desired and believed by medievals, but challenging to moderns.

The final version to be studied is from *The Major Legend of St. Francis* by Bonaventure of Bagnoregio (LMj I 5). Bonaventure completed this work by 1262 upon the request of the General Chapter of Narbonne held in 1260. While Bonaventure incorporated all the major points of Celano's second major narrative, including the additions, he refrained from making any new additions of his own. Bonaventure needed no additional details. Celano had passed on to him a rendition that suited Bonaventure's purposes perfectly.

Bonaventure modified the standard notion of medieval hagiography by using the life of Francis to write a work of spiritual theology. This spiritual model could then be imitated, especially by the friars. Like other works of hagiography, Bonaventure's is not concerned with objective history, but it goes further in highly systematizing the inner spiritual life of Francis. In so doing, Bonaventure portrays Francis walking in the path of salvation history with the great figures of the scriptures, leading up to the poor, crucified Christ. The effect of the disappearing leper could not be lost by the reader of this spiritual treatise, which concludes this powerful identification with the scene of the stigmata on La Verna (see Armstrong, *Spiritual* esp. 44–55).

What are reliable historical conclusions that can be drawn from this study of the story of Francis meeting the leper? A glance at the summary of the five accounts in the chart at the end of this chapter—even without bothering to read the words written there—makes evident the significant amount of additions to the original account of Celano. While this expansion in *The Legend of the Three Companions* only fills in insignificant detail without infringing upon the original story, Celano, in his *The Remembrance*, and Bonaventure add the detail of the disappearing leper. This addition alters the emphasis of the story from the personal, internal dynamic in the converting Francis, to the *election* of Francis by the crucified Christ. Undoubtedly included in this election are the roles of founder and stigmatic (see Iriarte 453). The addition is unbelievably spectacular. Furthermore, it is introduced into the tradition twenty-one years after the death of Francis and after the completion of three previous, well-circulated legends. The disappearing leper simply cannot be accepted as solid historical material. The earlier additions of *The Legend of the Three Companions*, while not necessarily *historical*, are credible.

The most dependable version of the story is to be found in Celano's original life and secondarily in that of Julian of Speyer. Their accounts are short, sparse, eminently believable, and without any trace of the influence of miraculous tampering. As spiritual documents, they are concerned with the internal spiritual development of Francis. However, in this particular case, the authors do not detract from the historicity of the story by enlisting miraculous events to make their point. What dependably happened is summed up in Celano's original two sentences: " . . . he met a leper one day. Made stronger than himself, he came up and kissed him" (1C 17).

One of our goals is to discover what impact this meeting had on Francis. Given the starkness of this concluding statement, the event may appear robbed of *any* significance. This is not so. Before exploring the possible impact on Francis, we first had to strip off of the story those layers of additions which —written for contemporarily good reasons—distract us moderns from the answers to *our* questions, with the language and images of *medieval* answers.

Lepers and Francis' early continuing formation: A historical analysis

All too often, the episode of Francis meeting the leper has been the primary focus of studying Francis' relationship with lepers. While it is a watershed-like experience, it is only the beginning of a lifetime of relationships from which much more can be learned. At the beginning of his final testament, Francis himself, by recounting the role lepers played in his conversion, testifies to the enduring effect lepers had in his life:

> The Lord gave me, Brother Francis, thus to begin doing penance in this way: for when I was in sin, it seemed too bitter for me to see lepers. And the Lord Himself led me among them and *I showed mercy* to them. And when I left them, what had seemed bitter to me was turned into sweetness of soul and body. And afterwards I delayed a little and left the world. (Test 1–3; FA:ED I 124)

In his testament, Francis begins with thirteen autobiographical verses. He recapitulates the primary experiences and principles of his early life. Francis begins by recounting his early experiences with lepers, using language that confirms the basic realities underlining the account of Francis' unexpected meeting with the leper. Before the completion of his conversion, Francis was horrified at the very sight of lepers. He felt that a force outside of himself directed him into their midst. Francis identified this movement with God. In the midst of the experience, Francis was able to go beyond his admitted fear and *relate* with lepers.

Armstrong renders the Latin phrase in *The Testament* "et feci misericordiam cum illis" (Esser 307) as "and I showed mercy to them." The phrase is clearly idiomatic and requires a free translation to adequately convey the intended meaning. The use of the preposition *cum* (with) implies a greater sense of mutuality between Francis and the lepers than I believe is expressed in this translation. I prefer to translate verse two as "And I experienced compassion with them." Regardless of the translation, the nuances of the line indicate that Francis had a significant experience in the presence of lepers. After touching them—and being touched by them—Francis was changed. He indicates that he could no longer live in his accustomed ways ("... I delayed a little ..."). Ultimately, Francis links this experience to his choice of a new lifestyle ("... and [I] left the world.").

Strikingly, Francis begins his testament with an explanation of how he began to live his new and different life ("... to begin doing penance ...") by focusing explicitly on his experience with lepers. He does not talk of other episodes narrated in the medieval biographies as part of his conversion: sickness, military experiences, imprisonment, dreams (especially at Spoleto), pilgrimage to Rome, religious experience at San Damiano, or renunciation before the bishop. Without satisfying our desire to know more of the *personal* impact of his leper experience, Francis clearly tells us that it was paramount to his personal conversion. To understand more deeply, we must explore other stories of Francis' early relationship with lepers.

The medieval biographies about Francis provide references to Francis and lepers both while he was living alone and after he began to attract followers. As in the case of the story of the meeting with the particular leper, these more general stories develop and augment as the hagiographic tradition advances. Celano's early life of Francis presents the meeting with the leper as a flashback in a larger section that recounts Francis' general dealings with lepers after his renunciation before Bishop Guido. Celano tells us that during this period, Francis lived with and served lepers "for God's sake." This included washing their sores. Celano links these experiences with lepers as part of Francis' growing "victory over himself" (1C 17). Julian of Speyer recapitulates Celano's presentation (LJS 12).

The Legend of the Three Companions talks of Francis' interaction with lepers before the scene in the bishop's piazza. The setting for the account is a divine answer to Francis' prayers for direction:

> Francis, everything you loved carnally and desired to have, you must despise and hate, if you wish to know my will. Because once you begin doing this, what before seemed delightful and sweet will be unbearable and bitter; and what before made you shudder will offer you great sweetness and enormous delight. (L3C 11a; FA:ED II 74)

After the narrative of the meeting with the leper, the legend tells us that, some days later, Francis took a large sum of money to a leper hospital and distributed it, kissing each leper on the hands. The narrative concludes by telling us that Francis became a friend of the lepers (L3C 11–12).

In *The Remembrance*, Celano characteristically takes up the additions provided by *The Legend of the Three Companions*, citing the divine response to his prayers. Celano further heightens the *personal* dimension of Francis' struggle by connecting two narratives: that of Francis' relationships with lepers and that of the devil's temptation in which, if Francis continued down his path of conversion, he would become like a monstrously hunchbacked woman in Assisi. With the stakes raised by Celano to include both spiritual and physical consequences, Francis' encounter with the leper appears even more spectacular and victorious. Celano concludes with the same narrative of Francis taking money to a leprosarium, but with the intensifying variation that Francis also kissed the lepers' *mouths*, not only their *hands* (2C 9)!

Bonaventure passes on Celano's elaborations. He tells us that Francis visited lepers' houses frequently, giving them alms and kissing their hands and mouths. Bonaventure also makes his own addition by telling us that Francis was so desirous of giving his whole self that he often gave away the very clothes he was wearing. Thus, Francis came to despise himself and serve God (LMj I 6). Bonaventure also relates Francis' life with lepers after his renunciation before Guido. He tells that Francis both lived with and served the lepers. His description is detailed: washing their feet, bandaging ulcers, drawing pus, and kissing their wounds (LMj II 6). Bonaventure ties these activities to Francis' desire to be humble (LMj II 6) and his respect for Christ, who was despised like a leper (LMj I 6).

Finally, just as Francis seems to have begun his life of penance in the presence of lepers, so the medieval biographies suggest that he longed to end it there. Again, the early account of Celano and those of Julian and Bonaventure affirm that, at his death, Francis longed to go back to serving lepers (1C 103; LJS 67; LMj XIV 1). This reported nostalgic glance back to Francis' early days appears confirmed by his obvious alertness in *The Testament* to the role lepers played in his conversion.

Reviewing these other stories from the medieval biographies about Francis, we can clearly see the growth in the tradition. Still, they steer clear of introducing marvelous or miraculous material like *The Remembrance* and Bonaventure's *Major Legend* did in the story of Francis meeting a particular leper. The accounts remain consistent among themselves and receive the personal confirmation of Francis via *The Testament*.

Given this reliability of the sources, we are able to make the following basic conclusions. Francis' unexpected meeting with the leper was not an isolated event; rather, it was a fountainhead for continued interaction with lepers. In the beginning, Francis visited the lepers, giving them alms and fraternizing with them. In time, after his renunciation before Guido, Francis lived among lepers, caring for their wounds. The importance of these activities for Francis was not only in being a benefactor to the poor. He was somehow changed through the relationship. Francis testifies to this and describes the change as related to his spiritual life. The relationship is tied to his decision to lead a life of penance and to leave the world. He talks of having been led to this spiritual experience by God himself. It was an experience that changed the way he looked at life (Test 1–3). In the end, Francis experienced something *with* the lepers. He and they became friends, even sisters and brothers. The intensity of their experience leads Iriarte to characterize Francis' time with lepers as his novitiate (Iriarte 463). Our natural curiosity longs to hear Francis explain this inner dynamic for himself. However, too many lacunae in our understanding of what happened to Francis remain.

Francis, the early community, and lepers: A historical analysis

Francis mentions lepers only three times in his own writings. One, in his testament, we have already considered. This scarcity of personal testimony is a disappointing fact. The writings of Francis are clearly the best sources for trying to understand the mind of the man. Certainly the medieval biographies can provide this in part, but their overarching hagiographic goals are too dominant to resist *shaping* an image of even the mind of Francis. A supposed quotation of Francis in a medieval biography must at least be questioned as the actual words of Francis. If Francis himself had written more about his experiences, attitudes, and feelings about lepers, our curiosity would be greatly satisfied. As things stand, we are left to consider bare actions of Francis and the early community, without any clear understanding of their motivations and goals.

The remaining two references to lepers in Francis' writing are found in *The Earlier Rule*. Here, Francis mentions lepers in regard to the relationships of the friars. At the end of chapter eight, which deals with prohibitions against handling or seeking money, Francis extends this prohibition to include collecting money for places where the friars may work, even though the money may not be for the brothers themselves. This included their work in almshouses: houses for the poor, indigent, or lepers (see Flood 26–29). In verse ten, however, Francis clarifies that the collection of general alms (i.e., not in the form of money) could be done by the friars in the case of evident necessity of lepers (ER VIII 10; compare translation differences in AB 117, FA:ED I 70, and Flood 77). What this line affirms is that at least some of the early friars worked in leprosariums and sought alms for lepers. Celano confirms this agency of the friars with the sad story of a friar who disobediently picked up a coin to give to a leper (2C 66).

The second reference to lepers in *The Earlier Rule* follows immediately in chapter nine. This chapter concerns the pride with which the friars should live among the poor. It is a further clarification of chapter seven which most likely existed earlier in the historical development of the rule. Chapter seven affirms the friars in supporting themselves with their own work as long as they are not compensated with money. It further stipulates that, should the fruit of their labors not be sufficient, the friars may have recourse to begging for alms as the poor do (ER VII 1–9). In light of this, in chapter nine, Francis exhorts all the brothers to imitate the humility and poverty of Christ (ER IX 1). Like Christ, "They must rejoice when they live among people considered of little value and looked down upon, among the poor and the powerless, the sick and *the lepers*, and the beggars by the wayside" (ER IX 2; FA:ED I 70; emphasis added). Again, chapter nine affirms that the early friars lived among lepers. Furthermore, it links this practice of the friars with that of Jesus, whom Francis describes as poor, transient, and dependent on alms (ER IX 5). For Francis, "Alms are a legacy and a justice due to the poor that our Lord Jesus Christ acquired for us" (ER IX 8; FA:ED I 71). Francis saw living with and sharing the life of lepers, among other powerless people, as imitating the life of Jesus, Mary, and the apostles.

The accounts from the medieval biographies offer a variety of confirmatory witnesses to the early friar-community's relationship with lepers. In general, this material avoids sensationalizing the data, often providing information in passing comments. This peripheral nature of many references lends greater credibility to their accuracy as they are less the object of hagiographic manipulation to make editorial comments.

The earliest legend makes the simple statement that some of the early friars did live with lepers (1C 39; also see AC 64 or LP 22). *The Legend of the Three Companions* would seem to reinforce the idea of some mutual relationship by its suggestion that lepers later used the huts of the early friars at Rivo Torto (55).

Further familiarity with lepers is suggested by the narration of two stops Francis made at leper houses while traveling with a companion. The first was near Borgo San Sepolcro (2C 98; also see LMj X 2); the other near Trevi (AC 65 or LP 23; 2MP 59). The chronicle of Jordan of Giano, written in 1262, likewise affirms such casual relationship when it recounts a chapter of the friars held at a leprosarium in 1223. This occurred in Germany at Speyer (Jordan 33; *Chronicles* 46). Later, Jordan testifies that, upon the friars' arrival in Erfurt, they lived with the lepers' chaplain until better arrangements could be provided (Jordan 39; *Chronicles* 48). Cardinal Odo of Châteauroux, papal legate of Urban IV (1261–64) in Paris, confirms this view of the early community in his *Sermon on St. Francis* of 1262. Odo states that, besides ministering to the sick and begging for them, Francis and his friars lived in leper houses and cared for them (Doyle 148–149).

The Leonine tradition (*The Assisi Compilation* and *The Mirror of Perfection*) adds some force to the tradition by relating that, in the beginning of the fraternity, Francis *wanted* the friars to live in leprosariums, warning prospective members that they would have to serve lepers. Francis' goal in this practice was to establish the neophytes in humility and poverty (AC 9 or LP 102; 2MP 44). While it is compatible with the other sources that living with lepers was part of early friar-formation, the depiction of force and necessity conveyed in the Leonine sources is a unique nuance.

While the above listed accounts refrain from sensationalizing Francis' and the early community's relationship with lepers, there is one story that does. Again, it comes from the Leonine tradition with all its attendant critical questions (AC 64 or LP 22; 2MP 58). According to the narrative, Francis recommended lepers to Brother James, who was like a doctor to the sickest lepers. On a specific occasion, Francis reproached James for bringing a leper to the Portiuncula. Regretting his admonition as despising and saddening the leper, Francis confessed his sin to Peter Catanii and asked that his penance be to eat from the same dish with the leper. Peter granted the penance. It is difficult to know if the purpose of the story is to convey Francis' attitude toward lepers or to portray Francis as a strict ascetic, an image that conforms to other sections of *The Assisi Compilation*. Again, while the story confirms previously established facts—that the friars lived and worked with lepers and that Francis experienced empathy with lepers—the precise historicity of this event may legitimately be questioned in light of its relationship to one of the legend's hagiographic goals: to portray Francis as a model of strict observance.

General historical conclusions

This analysis leaves us with the following basic elements to the relationship among lepers, Francis, and the early community. Like all medievals, Francis feared contact with lepers. Perhaps his fear was more acute than normal. In spite of this fear, interacting with lepers became the test for Francis' growing desire to imitate Christ in humility and poverty. The unexpected meeting with a particular leper presented Francis with the opportunity to finally overcome the distance created by his fear. In a cathartic gesture, Francis kissed the leper.

After the incident, Francis continued to visit lepers, often giving them alms. As he solidified his new way of life, Francis actually lived among lepers, caring for their wounds. This early formative period was very important in Francis' spiritual life. While we cannot fully understand the inner dynamic of Francis at this time, he clearly links these experiences with lepers to his growing conversion and new lifestyle.

As Francis began to attract followers, contact with lepers and at times living with them continued to be an important part of Franciscan life. Some of the friars appear to have been more involved with lepers. This relationship with lepers included: living with lepers, physically caring for them, and seeking non-monetary alms for lepers' benefit. Francis and his companions apparently felt enough mutuality with lepers that they would stop to rest at leprosariums while traveling. Francis felt strongly enough about this that, at one point in the development of the rule, he explicitly held up living with lepers—among other powerless people—as an honorable way to imitate the poor and humble Christ. Finally, we know that this relationship remained valued by Francis up to his death when, longing once again to serve lepers, he fondly looked back on their role in his early conversion and seemed to have regretted a diminishment in interaction with them.

The meaning of Francis meeting the leper: An attempt to remythologize

If one has come to the point where the standard critical tools of historical research are accepted for use on hagiographic material, the demythologization of Francis' and the early community's relationship with lepers is relatively easy and immediate. The most difficult step for those brought up in the traditional cult of saints is the acceptance of what appears to be new techniques. The techniques are actually nearing three centuries of existence (see Schoeck iii–v)! Still, the historian remains at a faith disadvantage, for the lives of the saints are indeed intended by the church to inspire modern faith and good works. Because of our modern cultural setting which values objective history, demythologizing is a requirement. We want our faith to be based on and nourished by historical truth. Once that is done, however, we are no different from the medievals in our need to attach meaning to these lives and events through a rejuvenating process of remythologization.

This is not an easy task; nor should we expect it to happen immediately. As snug as the assigned medieval meaning may appear to us, we must remember that those works incurred significant resistance in their own day and appear in part to be authored as responses to and corrections of one another. Celano's original life was clearly needed to further popularize the cult of Francis, newly canonized. Bonaventure's *The Major Legend of St. Francis* was in part directed toward critics of Franciscanism at the University of Paris, diocesan clergy, and suspicious bishops. The Leonine tradition represents the thought of a series of redactors who appear concerned to portray Francis as more occupied with the strict observance of the rule than is portrayed in other biographies. The simple fact is that the original mythologization of Francis was not accomplished overnight; rather, it took close to a century for the various traditions to fully establish themselves, and then never in complete agreement.

Once we arrive at what we reasonably conclude is objective history about Francis, we cannot expect an adequate remythologization to occur immediately. In fact, it may be best that the historian not attempt both tasks: demythologization and remythologization. In reality, the two tasks require different processes, although the one must build on the work of the other. Furthermore, we must willingly acknowledge a variety of attempts to give meaning to the life-events of Francis.

Keeping in mind these cautions, I wish to conclude this study with my own attempt to remythologize the story of Francis unexpectedly meeting the leper. This is a psychological approach. It is an attempt to view the meeting of the leper and Francis in a way that can give new meaning to modern readers. While my imaginations are based on the indications I find in historical research, ultimately, such projections can never be historically verified. With this reconstruction, I am moving beyond the realm of history, hoping to better understand the world in which we live and the responses that best express our faith. Here is my projection of what happened the day Francis met the leper.

> Joltingly, the sight of a leper on the road before him shook Francis. His natural instinct of horror—understandably held by most of his setting but particularly acute in Francis—stiffened his posture. He feared the contagion that stood before him. This terror found root in medical fact and fiction, theological speculation, and social policies of isolation and rejection. Such an instinctive reaction was the result of a powerful, cultural symbol: the person of the leper. Still, fear was co-experienced with self-dissatisfaction: the feeling in Francis that he was not what he wanted to be or thought he should be. He was impacted by the available legends of saints who somehow overcame their fear. Through them came a call Francis interpreted to come from God. In the language of the day, this call was to see God everywhere, even where mortals normally could not see God. Previously, Francis had not seen God in the lepers. He could not. His fear, natural as it was, blinded him. But the saints disturbed that lack of vision.

With time, Francis' changing vision of life outside himself began to change his vision of life inside himself. Francis began to ask the question so normal to human life: "Why me?" Still, Francis asked this normal question from a most unusual perspective. Generally, this question asks why pain and suffering happen to me, as if somehow I am unjustly sentenced to singular or disproportionate struggle. Francis' question, on the contrary, asked why he was *not* suffering in light of all the suffering around him. Regardless of whether luck is good or bad, Francis seems to have recognized it to be what it is: luck! There was no reason for these events in life. Francis wanted to look deeper for the differences among people that called for the sharp divisions of his era and place. He could find none. With that conclusion, Francis realized the sameness between himself and others so shunned by his society. A recovering alcoholic friend I have often quotes me the old adage: "There go I but for the grace of God." Francis seems to have accepted the adage—probably not known in his day—without any qualifier. His deep realization that resulted from improved vision was simply: "There go I!"

This tension propelled Francis forward. His old and steady companion, fear, reeled back at the sight of the leper. Still, new and growing thoughts and convictions finally became strong enough to demand equal behavioral attention from Francis. In this moment, if Francis gratified his fear, his growing spiritual insights would visit him with guilt. On the other hand, if Francis acknowledged his insight by touching the leper, his fear of leprosy may have actualized with unbearable social consequence. Francis, at least this time, chose the new direction. It took sheer energy to accomplish this feat. Francis' fear was strong and not about to bow in deference to spiritual insight. For the moment, Francis had to refuse to feel in order to overcome that fear. Like the horrified child determined for the first time to hold his or her breath under water, Francis abandoned all reason in self-resignation, struggling to abide by the proclamation of a different type of reason. Like the child feeling the rush of adrenaline that assists the plunge, Francis kissed the leper.

With that, Francis hurdled the first and largest of a series of walls that for too long had held him hostage. In that emotional, cathartic, and symbolic moment, Francis embraced himself. "There go I," Francis acknowledged to himself. Francis could once again feel his fear, not running from it, but embracing it! Francis could now accept who he really was. He recognized the luck that gave him stature in society and insulated him from the ultimate tragedies and suffering that are part of everyone's life. Francis was a leper.

Francis left the meeting at peace experiencing the emotional release that comes with embracing the reality of who one truly is. Fear no longer dominated his life. Francis' personal spiritual insight, passed on to him by centuries of traditions, was now able to direct his life. The rest was simple denouement, though nonetheless dramatic. The die was cast in Francis' personal, internal life. He had finally approached the crucial choice in his life and decided to leap in faith. Once Francis experienced the peace and satisfaction that only a few others of his day would understand, he would less and less be able to live with the divisions that separated him from himself. Francis could not live without personal integrity. He could no longer bear the thought that his very life would be the most significant lie he could tell. He had to live in truth: Francis and the leper were the same.

Sources cited or consulted

- *Acta Sanctorum.* Eds. Joannes Bollandus et al. 1643–1786. New edition. Eds. Joannes Carnandet et al. 63 vols. Paris: Victor Palmé, 1863–1887. 6 vols. Brussels: Socios Bollandianos, 1894–1940.
- Armstrong, Regis J. *The Spiritual Theology of the* Legenda Major *of Saint Bonaventure.* Diss. Fordham University, 1978. Ann Arbor: University Microfilms International, 1978. 7814881.
- Doyle, Eric, trans. and ed. *The Disciple and the Master: St. Bonaventure's Sermons on St. Francis of Assisi.* Chicago: Franciscan Herald Press, 1983.
- Flood, David, and Thadée Matura. *The Birth of a Movement: A Study of the First Rule of St. Francis.* Trans. Paul Schwartz and Paul Lachance. Chicago: Franciscan Herald Press, 1975.
- [Iriarte], Lázaro de Aspurz. "'El Señor me llevó entre los leprosos': La Vía de la Conversión en San Francisco de Asís." *Laurentianum* 8 (1967) 452–468.
- Schoeck, Richard J. Preface. *The Legends of the Saints: An Introduction to Hagiography.* By Hippolyte Delehaye. Trans. V.M. Crawford. Notre Dame, IN: University of Notre Dame Press, 1961.
- Sulpicius Severus. *Life of St. Martin, Bishop and Confessor.* Trans. Bernard M. Peebles. Eds. Roy Joseph Deferrari, et al. The Fathers of the Church 7. New York: Fathers of the Church Inc., 1949. 101–140.

Francis Meets the Leper
A Textual Comparison

1C 17 - LJS 12	L3C 11	2C 9	LMj I 5
Francis was generally repulsed by sight of lepers.	Francis always felt an overpowering horror of lepers.	Francis naturally abhorred lepers.	Francis felt sick at the sight of lepers.
	F was riding near Assisi.	*F was riding near Assisi.*	*F was riding on plain below Assisi.*
F met leper.	F met leper.	F met leper.	F met leper**, an unforeseen encounter.**
F was made stronger than himself.	F made great effort and conquered his aversion.	F prepared himself to kiss leper **not wanting to break his word.**	*F remembered his resolve to be perfect and a knight of Christ*
	F dismounted.	*F dismounted.*	*F dismounted.*
F kissed leper.		**F prepared to kiss leper.**	*F prepared to kiss leper.*
		Leper held out hand for alms.	*Leper held out hand for alms.*
	F gave coin to leper and kissed leper's **hand.**	*F gave leper money* and kissed leper's *hand.*	*F put money in leper's hand* and kissed leper's *hand.*
	Leper gave F kiss of peace.		
	F remounted and rode away.	*F remounted.*	*F remounted.*
		Leper vanished from F's sight in an open area with no obstructed view.	*Leper vanished from F's sight in an open area with no obstructed view.*
F later considered self less and less until he reached perfect victory over self.	F increasingly considered self less and less until with God he won complete victory.	**F was filled with joy.**	F was full of wonder *and joy.*
			F resolved to do more in future.
F continued contact with lepers (see beginning of text).	F continued contact with lepers.	F continued contact with lepers.	

Francis — indicates the 1C version carried throughout.
Francis — indicates a new change or addition.
Francis — indicates a change or addition carried throughout.

Francis' Religious Experience at San Damiano

Sources

L3C 13–15
2C 10–11
LMj II 1
PrCr

Starter questions and suggestions

If you are working in a group, I suggest that all group members prepare this worksheet. The story is very important in Francis' life. However, assign one group member to make a presentation to the group. Focus your study on the story involving San Damiano, not the unrelated material. Nevertheless, read a little before and after the San Damiano story to understand its context. You may want to share general observations about the context of the story with your group. However, again, do not share a detailed analysis of how those contextual passages change and develop. This worksheet is about Francis' experience at San Damiano.

Place a clean piece of paper on its side (oversized is helpful). Divide the page into three vertical columns and label the top of each column with one of the first three sources in chronological order (i.e., L3C 13–15, 2C 10–11, LMj II 1). Briefly outline the story about San Damiano from L3C in the first column using black ink. Spread it out over the entire column so there is some space between entries. Do the same in the second column with the story from 2C. Write the elements of the story next to the same elements found in L3C to the left. Continue to use black ink, except when 2C includes new material or changes some detail as compared to L3C. In those cases, use red ink so the changes stand out visually.

Next, write the elements of the story as found in LMj in the third column across from the same elements in the first two columns. Write elements that are identical in detail to the account in L3C in black ink. Elements that accept the additions or changes in 2C should be written in blue ink. Use red ink for elements that are added or changed for the first time in LMj.

Look at the red ink on your paper and note what was added, subtracted or changed. Analyze your chart and determine what you believe historically happened. What was the historical reality of the "voice" in this story? What is the importance of what happened?

What theological ideas are visible in the various authors? What is the role of the hagiographic tradition in the development of the accounts? Does that hagiographic tradition cloud the historical reality? Why is Francis' preoccupation with the passion tied to this experience? How is the idea of repairing the church and the passion of Christ tied together?

This story first appears in L3C, which is dated 1246. 1C, LJS, and AP ignore the story, and all three sources were interested in the conversion period of Francis' life. What meaning could this fact have for your historical evaluation of the story? Can you think of any reason why the story is missing from those sources?

Read Francis' *The Prayer Before the Crucifix*. Many believe that this prayer was once written on cloth hanging in front of San Damiano's altar. The editors of FA:ED date it 1205/06, making it the earliest of Francis' extant writings. Does the prayer reflect the spiritual theology of the biographical accounts listed above or another reality? What relationship can you see between the prayer and this story? Explore the feelings and aspirations of the prayer.

Suggested Readings

- Bigaroni, Mariano. "San Damiano—Assisi: The First Church of St. Francis." *Franciscan Studies* 47 (1987) 45–97.
- Lehmann, Leonard. "Prayer before the Crucifix." Trans. Paul Barrett. *Greyfriars Review* 11.1 (1997) 1–12.
- Picard, Mark. *The Icon of the Christ of San Damiano*. Assisi: Casa Editrice Francescana. 1989.

Francis' Trial before Bishop Guido

Sources

1C 14–15
LJS 8d–9
AP 8a–b
L3C 19–20
2C 12
LMj II 3–4
Fortini pp. 222–230

Starter questions and suggestions

There are many variations in this story across the different versions. Put a clean sheet of paper on its side. More than one sheet and oversized paper are quite helpful. Divide the paper into six vertical columns. Mark the top of each column with one of the medieval biographies in chronological order (i.e., 1C, LJS, AP, L3C, 2C, LMj). Briefly outline the story from 1C in the first column using black ink. Spread your outline over the entire column so there is some space between entries. Do the same in the second column with the story from LJS also using black ink. Write the elements of the story next to the same elements found in 1C to the left. However, whenever LJS includes new material or changes some detail as compared to 1C, us red ink so the change stands out visually.

Next, write the elements of the story as found in AP in the third column across from the same elements in the first two columns. Write elements that are identical in detail to the account in 1C in black ink. Elements that accept the additions or changes in LJS should be written in blue ink. Use red ink for elements that are added or changed for the first time in AP. Continue this procedure in columns four, five, and six.

After completing the chart, use it to help you analyze how hagiographic forces shaped the story through its development. Note where most of the red ink is and ask why. Pay special attention to changes or additions that contribute to making the story more stupendous. I am often amazed at how once a source adds or changes something in a hagiographic tradition, that change is usually carried on in all subsequent versions. Is that true here? Check out the blue ink!

Which version of the story do you believe is the most historically reliable? Note that only some of the sources relate that Pietro first petitioned the civil authorities to deal with Francis. Also note that the earliest and the latest sources (1C and LMj) relate that Pietro retrieved his money *before* summoning Francis to court. The other sources portray the retrieval of money occurring during the trial before Bishop Guido. Tell your group what you think really happened. I suggest you be as simple and cautious as possible.

What was the meaning of this event for Francis?

Commentary

I recommend Fortini's book here with some reservations. More than usual, he seems to fill in details he imagines happened. That is a concern. Remember, Fortini's value is his knowledge of the laws and customs of Assisi during Francis' lifetime. When he imagines what an event might have been like, you want to evaluate whether he appropriately or inappropriately uses the other medieval primary sources.

I recommend you consult Fortini in this case to understand what legal basis Pietro might have had to accuse Francis and the reason Francis successfully may have bid to be tried before the bishop rather than civil authorities.

Pietro's charge against Francis appears to be more than simple theft. If the charge were only theft, Pietro's case would have been severely damaged once his money was returned. Furthermore, Francis earlier squandered lots of Pietro's money without precipitating legal action by Pietro.

Rather, it appears Pietro was initiating a process through which he was disinheriting Francis. This appears to have required a legal proceeding. The accusation needed to be based on the child's rebellion against the parents' authority. Fortini describes the legal and social situation and consequences of this scenario.

Secondly, during this period of medieval Italy, there often existed a two-tiered legal system. The civil legal system affected most people. However, people in the service of the church could claim exemption from civil proceedings and demand that the competent church official hear their cases. While Francis was a lay and secular person at this time and the exemption generally applied to clerics and religious, he managed to secure a church hearing. Again, Fortini describes the legal and social processes involved in these situations. So consult Fortini, but be careful.

A more recent study by Richard Trexler sheds enormous light on the question of this being a disinheritance trial. Trexler uses his knowledge of medieval families, financial arrangements, and marriage to forward a more complex theory. The citation is below.

Suggested reading

- Trexler, Richard C. *Naked before the Father: The Renunciation of Francis of Assisi*. Humana Civilitas 9. New York: Peter Lang Publishing, 1989. Trexler presents novel ideas about Francis' family constellation, suggesting that Pietro was *Pica's* second husband and that Francis and Angelo were half-brothers with different fathers. This would have put Francis and Pietro in competition for *Pica's* money, perhaps her dowry. Thus, Trexler strongly suspects that the "trial" before the bishop was a legal event in which Francis renounced his right to inherit or use his *mother's* fortune. Chapter one studies Francis' family tree (pages 7–29). Chapter two explores the written documents for clues as to the real *issue* of the "trial" before the bishop (pages 30–69).

A Paradigm for Understanding Francis' Conversion

I like to think of doing history as a three-part process:

1. collecting data in a critical way;
2. organizing that data in meaningful ways; and
3. interpreting the data.

These three activities need not be done in order; usually, all three are going on simultaneously in a historian's mind.

At this point in our study of Francis, I like to pause with my study group to organize the data we have collected about Francis thus far. In so doing, I hope we will be able to interpret the data in ways that give deeper insight into Francis' experience. I also believe this process helps students to gain a deeper understanding of themselves. This usually happens when my students are part of a formation program for religious life.

The medieval hagiography that discusses Francis' early life does so in the context of conversion. Each legend or florilegium has its unique slant on the nature of Francis' inner transformation. I usually find that postulants and novices are attuned to the theme of conversion even if they cannot articulate much about it in their own lives. They know changes are happening in their lives. Adjustments in their lifestyle may be difficult and stressful. Their values are being challenged and questioned by both their formators and the people with and to whom they minister. Talking about conversion in Francis is often an outlet for them to talk about their own current experience of change.

However, surprising as it may seem, my students seldom begin to organize the data they are learning about Francis in a way that helps them to understand his conversion. The method presented in this book is new to many students, and they concentrate on preparing good reports to present to the entire study group. So, I usually suspend our use of the study sheets about this time and invite them to reflect on conversion in Francis' life.

I begin by offering a paradigm or model of his conversion that I have come to experience as both accurate and helpful. In very simple terms, the paradigm has four parts:

1. the former status quo;
2. jarring experiences;
3. withdrawal;
4. gradual reinsertion.

The first step in this paradigm of conversion is the person's status quo before the conversion process actually begins. Of particular interest to me is an understanding of the person's worldview, her or his understanding of how the world is or ought to be. Our worldviews allow us to function socially. They give us a framework out of which we make sense of the world. It is impossible for people to function positively when their worldview makes no sense, because they are unable to decipher a workable framework for meaningful action. So, this first point in my conversion paradigm is the point just before the conversion begins, that point when one's worldview still makes sense.

The second moment in the paradigm is jarring experiences that bring that worldview into question. Worldviews are like theories. We continue to regard them as possibly true as long as the data we know are consistent with the theory. On the other hand, once we encounter data that are inconsistent with a theory, we know adjustments need to be made in the theory, if the theory is to be kept at all. Worldviews can be challenged by data in a variety of forms. Some of those forms can be as safe as a university classroom. However, I believe the deepest conversions, and especially deep *religious* conversions, are precipitated by jarring experiences.

These jarring experiences are of numerous types, but all have the ability to shake us at our cores. Special circumstances sometimes account for these jarring experiences. Many veterans have described their Vietnam or Iraq War experience in this way. Some medical personnel involved in abortions have later described their experiences to me in this way. Working with poor people or those with AIDS could be a jarring experience that challenges one's worldview.

These jarring experiences can also be experiences most people have in life. The death of a parent, friend, or relative can put this spin on people. Losing a job or an important relationship can also do the trick. Coming to terms with one's limits, as in a mid-life crisis, might call into question everything the person previously thought true about him or herself, and his or her place in the world.

I understand this phenomenon as a question of adequacy: Is someone's worldview adequately able to explain these new jarring experiences? If not, if the way a person has previously thought about life is shaken to the core, the person will be tremendously troubled. Such people often feel insecure. They no longer are comfortable in previously familiar situations. Sometimes, people lose their effectiveness; they can no longer function like they used to. When these issues are viewed or experienced as religious, the person is at the beginning of a religious conversion.

The third moment in the paradigm of conversion is withdrawal. It is an understandable reaction to the confusion and dysfunction the person is experiencing. Once one's worldview is no longer adequate to interpret the important experiences that are part of our lives, we begin a process of constructing a new worldview that is able to interpret these new experiences. While withdrawal provides relief from those situations that cause dissonance and distress to people going through conversion, it also gives them the space and time to build something new that will serve them better.

This is not done overnight. It takes time, sometimes years. However long it takes, it will continue until the process is complete. To not complete the process is to condemn oneself to a life of inner dissonance and confusion.

People withdraw in a variety of ways. The obvious way is to physically remove oneself from familiar surroundings and activities. So, one might move, take an extended vacation or leave from work, go on a sabbatical, or secretly desert friends, family, and loved ones. A person in withdrawal could also physically stay right where she or he has been, but withdraw from activities and associations that previously were enjoyable or rewarding. So, one might quit all the social clubs she belonged to, stop going to church, not join the gang for a drink after work, or not attend the annual family reunion.

Withdrawal could also be doing things we generally haven't done or going to places we seldom visit. A person in the midst of conversion might visit a soup kitchen, volunteer in a local social service program, make a retreat, make a pilgrimage (not necessarily a typical religious pilgrimage), seek out an old trusted friend to talk, or start seeing a spiritual director.

A less healthy form of withdrawal would be a psychological withdrawal in which a person continues to do the things he has always done but without the psychological presence of the past. Others may think such a person is withdrawing inside. He may stop communicating with those who love him the most. This person might become crabby and irritable. Pretty soon, others don't want to be around him.

People in religious conversion begin to reinsert themselves into society after they fairly well have constructed a new worldview that adequately interprets all the new and old experiences they have had. This begins the fourth moment of the paradigm. Actually, I believe this moment begins by *testing* new behaviors that might express the new worldview. They actually are testing two things: the adequacy of their new worldview, and the adequacy of their new behaviors to express that new worldview. If the new worldview fails to satisfy, the person will have to make adjustments. If certain new behaviors don't cut the mustard, the person will have to seek out different behaviors that might do the job.

As people progress in this moment of the paradigm, they increase their inner peacefulness and sense of well being. They regain energy and feel comfortable in social situations that reflect their new worldview. People at this stage are able to be productive, though they may be productive about different things.

So, just as someone in withdrawal may have volunteered at a soup kitchen to withdraw into a new space to think, another person might decide to volunteer one day a week at a soup kitchen to express her newly formulated worldview. Some will change jobs or begin entirely new careers to express their newfound vision.

It is important to understand that while the intensity of a conversion may encompass a short period of time, we can seldom declare the conclusion of a conversion at a specific moment. People generally deepen in their conversion over periods of time that continue long after the intensity of the experience abates.

It is also important to realize that all conversions are not positive. Religious people in particular tend to think of conversion in exclusively positive terms. However, people can convert to evil as easily as to good. Conversion is a neutral term describing basic types of changes in our lives, both positive and negative.

I generally begin this presentation on conversion by listing each of the four moments in my conversion paradigm horizontally across a blackboard. I explain each of the moments and invite my students to ask questions.

However, the process becomes clearer to the students when I ask them to identify elements of each moment in Francis' life. I begin this by asking them to describe Francis as they believe he was *before* his conversion process began. I list the characteristics under *status quo* in the first column. They usually include many of the following characteristics: generous, happy-go-lucky, a spendthrift, a party-person, narcissistic, an upper-class merchant, and playboy. (This last characteristic generally precipitates a lengthy discussion regarding whether or not the primary sources support an assertion that Francis was sexually promiscuous before his conversion.)

Next, I ask the students to list experiences in Francis' life that may have jarred him to the point of questioning the adequacy of his worldview. I list these experiences in the second column under *jarring experiences*. They generally include defeat in war with Perugia, imprisonment in Perugia, illness during and/or after his imprisonment, Francis' fantasy about the hunchback woman, and his growing awareness of lepers. Some mention his failed trip to war in Apulia, but generally this suggestion begins a discussion as to whether or not the sources support an interpretation that this was a jarring and confronting experience for Francis.

As the group moves to the third moment in the paradigm, they experience more difficulty in agreeing about whether some actions in Francis' life portray his withdrawal or represent new behaviors to express his new worldview. The group usually includes the following, which I write in the third column under *withdrawal*: a time of greater prayer and reflection, seeking out solitary places with a trusted friend, Francis' trip to Rome, and Francis' religious experience at San Damiano. Some view Francis' imprisonment and illness as both a jarring experience and an imposed withdrawal. Certainly they were times when he thought about his worldview and, perhaps, began to make changes in it. It is important to think of withdrawal as not necessarily temporally long or getting away from people, but events that helped Francis construct a new worldview. That is why my students almost always include Francis' religious experience in San Damiano, though it lasted only a short time.

Finally, I write down the group's list of Francis' new attempted behaviors in the fourth column: embracing the leper, continued presence and work among lepers and other outcasts, returning his clothes to his father before Bishop Guido, the embrace of poverty, and the rebuilding of three churches. Obviously, Francis' conversion lasted a lifetime. I try to list here those events that were part of the intense moments of that conversion. I return to this paradigm frequently in class, adding more events as the class makes more presentations.

This exercise helps students understand the paradigm. More importantly, it helps them to organize the data they have been collecting through their work with the worksheets. This organization helps many of them to interpret the data in ways they previously did not. It's an enriching experience for me to see students achieve such insight.

When I have taught this course to postulants or novices, I also have found this paradigm and application to Francis' life to be of personal benefit for the students. Postulants in my province spend half of their day with poor people. That experience and other parts of the postulancy program are designed to help postulants enter into a conversion process. In the beginning they are overwhelmed and often don't know what to make of their experiences. Frequently, they experience frustration and confusion.

Examination of this conversion paradigm usually helps them make sense out of their own jarring experiences with the poor. Many begin to understand what is happening to them in different ways. Often, this discussion on conversion leads to greater peacefulness and a willingness to "go with the flow" of postulancy. Resistance to aspects of their postulancy program diminishes. Many begin to appreciate their postulancy experiences and value the opportunity this year offers them.

Suggested reading

- McMichaels, Susan W. *Journey out of the Garden: St. Francis of Assisi and the Process of Individuation.* New York: Paulist, 1997. McMichaels applies concepts of Jungian developmental psychology to Francis' conversion, resulting in a fresh look at Francis. Her treatment is short and easy to read for those unfamiliar with Jung's theories.

- Brunette, Pierre. *Francis of Assisi and His Conversions.* Trans. Paul Lachance and Kathryn Krug. Quincy IL: Franciscan Press, 1997. A short text about Francis' "conversions" written at a popular level.

Francis' "Exile"

Sources

1C 16
LJS 10–11
LMj II 5–6a

Starter questions and suggestions

These stories portray Francis as he left Assisi and his trial before Bishop Guido. The accounts are straightforward and simple. Perhaps the important thing to notice is that Francis did not have a clear idea of what he wanted to do. However, he was imbued with strong feelings of joy and happiness.

If you are studying with a group, relate the simple stories. Explain his euphoria. Describe the nature of his conversion at this time. You may want to reflect on the monks whom Francis visited. What do you think of them? Were they "unchristian"? There are no hidden secrets in the stories.

Francis Rebuilds Three Churches

Sources

1C 18, 21
LJS 13–14
AP 7c + 8c
L3C 21–24
2C 11, 13–14
LMj II 7–8

Starter questions and suggestions

Some of the sources cited are lengthy and involve information about other matters. Focus on the material concerning the rebuilding of the three churches and the meaning this activity had in Francis' life.

Which three churches are we talking about? What is the relationship between Francis' earlier religious experience at San Damiano and his rebuilding projects? What was Francis seeking to overcome inside himself as he rebuilt the churches? What steps in Francis' conversion occurred during this period? How do the hagiographers use the rebuilding stories to interpret Francis' life and purposes? What is the significance of Francis changing clothes while rebuilding San Damiano?

What other importance is tied to the various locations besides the fact that Francis rebuilt the buildings?

Critically evaluate the hagiographers' connection of Francis rebuilding three churches and the three Franciscan orders.

Suggested reading

- Bigaroni, Mariano. "San Damiano—Assisi: The First Church of St. Francis." *Franciscan Studies* 47 (1987) 45–97.

The Apostolic Life Movement

The Franciscan movement did not develop in a vacuum. In fact, many students of Francis hold that what makes Francis' vision unique is the way he put elements from various traditions together, not the elements themselves. Whether or not that is true, it is true that the apostolic life movement, which predates Francis by well over a century, had a major impact on the lifestyle he pioneered.

This movement receives its name from the Latin phrase *vita apostolica*. People in the eleventh through thirteenth centuries used it to refer to what they thought was the lifestyle of Jesus and his apostles. It marks a period in history when Christians sought to return to the evangelical (gospel) and historical sources of Christian life as a guarantee of authenticity (Chenu 204). There was a sense that Christianity was drifting away from authentic Christian life. The opulent and hedonistic lifestyle of many church people spawned numerous attempts to reform the church and its ministers. Church officials masterminded some reforms as in the Gregorian Reform (1073–1085) and the four Lateran Councils (1123, 1139, 1181, and 1215). Others were grassroots movements begun by reform-minded clergy, religious or lay people.

The phrase gained popularity in the eleventh century when monks used the term to describe their monastic lifestyle. Abbot Rupert of Deutz (d. 1130) wrote that the apostles were the first monks. He argued that contemporary monastic life modeled the internal life of early Christian communities. The core element of this similarity was the "abandonment of all private goods in favor of the common life" (Chenu 206). Monastic institutions merely formalized the pattern of the early Christians.

Those applying the term to monastic life often cited Acts 4:32–37 as a point of comparison. This passage describes how the early believers were of one heart and mind, holding everything in common. Everyone was given what she or he needed. Other similar summarizing and idealized descriptions were found in Acts 2:42–47 and 5:12–16. The citation of these supporting scriptures begins the collection of what I call the apostolic texts. More passages were added to the list as the notion of early Christian life developed.

It is interesting to note that those using this notion to bolster monastic life generally ignored the work and ministry of the early apostles and Christian community. Rather, they focused on the early community's lifestyle, which they compared favorably to contemporary monastic life. Thus, they equated the apostolic life with community life. Using this model, they focused on simplicity of food, clothing and shelter, modest manners, fraternal corrections, and the penitential nature of manual labor (Chenu 207).

Yet, the comparison limped in many people's estimation. While individual monks were technically poor, their grand monasteries were the center of medieval economic power and wealth. As the social role of the monastery expanded, it increasingly swallowed the very world it eschewed. It was difficult to live in the shadow of medieval Europe's great monasteries and imagine them to reflect the simplicity of the early Christian community (Chenu 207–208).

Furthermore, the monks were increasingly moving away from the manual labor previously encouraged in Benedict's rule. Others were brought into the monastery to perform menial and manual jobs so that the monks could devote more time to prayer (Chenu 208–210). The use of texts that described the early Christian community at Jerusalem invited criticism of monasticism while hoping to bolster its image at the same time.

The medieval idea of the apostolic life developed with the growth of the canons regular. Unlike monks, canons often lived in cities and ministered actively among the people. Their ministries included celebration of the sacraments with the people, preaching, teaching, and social outreach. For example, the Canons of San Rufino taught Francis at the church of San Giorgio just outside the walls of Assisi. Canons continued to live in community and, thus, seemed to embody the principles of apostolic life emphasized by the monks. However, canons wedded apostolic action to the image of that life (Chenu 214). In retrospect, it is amazing that monks felt they could invoke images of the apostles to sanctify their monastic lifestyle without also incurring the criticism that, unlike the apostles, monks did not actively engage in evangelization of the people through ministry. After having accepted the teachings of Jesus, what was more impressive about the apostles than the way they spread that teaching!

While the canons developed the notion of the apostolic life within the confines of a clerical and celibate lifestyle, the lay apostolic movement adapted the notion to lay people open to marriage, though many forwent marriage. These lay people sought expressions for their religious fervor as the canons and monks before them did. Unimpeded by commitments and responsibilities to monasteries or cathedrals, many lay apostles tied itinerant (traveling) preaching with their simple lifestyle, something no monk or canon could easily do. Those who remained in one place often banded together for corporal works of mercy: caring for the sick and dying; burying the dead; feeding the hungry; providing shelter to travelers and pilgrims; etc.

These lay apostles (whether stationary or itinerant) gravitated toward cities where new classes of people gathered: merchants, artisans, manual workers, and clerks. In fact, many members of lay apostolic groups came from these new classes. They sought to provide spirituality, ministry, and religious outlets to these people too often ignored by traditional religious institutions that proved unable to adapt to the new situation.

Both the canons and lay apostles took on values that the monks derived from their reading of the early *vita apostolica*: simplicity of food, clothing and shelter; modest manners; fraternal correction; and penitential manual labor. However, they added the dimension of active ministry, which included preaching, and tending to people's social and economic needs. These new groups hungered to hear the gospel in particular and all the scriptures in general. They shared reflections on the scriptures and worked to produce vernacular editions of the scriptures. They were the antithesis of the monks by dwelling in the heart of the very "world" the monks sought to flee.

It is amazing that all three groups could appeal to the same notion of the apostolic life and live it in such strikingly different ways.

This movement, which began as a monastic renewal in the 11th century and developed in its canonical and lay forms through the 12th, reached its pinnacle in the 13th century with the birth of the mendicant orders, including the Franciscans and Dominicans. The mendicant orders further blended the freedom from stability of lay groups with the common life of the canons and other religious. Obviously, this development is what we want to study. However, it is important to understand this broader and significant development that preceded Francis.

As groups began to broaden their idea of the apostolic life beyond monastic stability (people committing to live in a particular monastery for life), they also began to expand the scriptures to which they appealed to justify and support their lifestyles. I encourage you to take some time to read these scripture passages. After a while, their emphases become very clear. Once you develop an eye for these passages I call apostolic texts, you will easily identify them in the stories of Francis' life.

Acts 2:42–47 Acts 4:32:37 Acts 5:12–16	These passages describe the ideal early Christian community at Jerusalem. They are the foundation of the monastic renewal based on the apostolic life. The monks used the texts because they described the internal life of the early Christians in terms they could apply to monastic life. The passages emphasize common life, not ministry.
Acts 6:1–7	When people began to challenge the adequacy of monastic life exemplifying the apostolic life because it lacked a thrust toward ministry, the monks began to appeal to this passage to show that the apostles appointed others (deacons) to assist with the daily needs of the faithful, freeing the apostles up for prayer and service to the word.

Matt. 10:1–42 Matt 28:16–20 Mark 6:7–13 Mark 16:14–18 Luke 9:1–6 Luke 6:12–16 Luke 10:1–12 Luke 24:44–49 John 20:19–23	The call and commissioning of the apostles are favorite themes of the apostolic passages. The commissioning passages deal with events both before and after Jesus' resurrection. The canons and especially lay apostles latched on to these passages that portray the apostles, and in one case the seventy-two disciples, as preachers of the word.

The lay dimension of this movement surmised that every Christian was called to be a preacher of God's word. Using these texts, they acquired the notion that the early apostles were poor praying pilgrims, who preached penance and peace, and resultantly experienced persecution. They expected the same to be true of themselves more than a millennium later.

Arnold of Brescia, Peter Waldo, who founded the Waldensians, and Stephen of Muret (d. 1124), who founded the Pauperes Christi in Grandmont, were three important figures in this movement before the time of Francis. Their movements often suffered misunderstanding and persecution from the church. However, Pope Innocent III forged a new policy toward these groups and attempted to achieve reconciliation. His ultimate hope was to harness their religious fervor for the service of the church. Thus, Innocent either forged a reconciliation with or chartered the following groups: the Humiliati in Milan who were mostly cloth weavers, the Poor Catholics led by Durand of Huesca, a group led by Bernard Prim, and our own Francis of Assisi. Certainly, Innocent's new and innovative policy created the environment that allowed groups that would become the mendicant orders to firmly establish and later flourish.

In the end, I believe the notion of apostolic life changed because monasticism became inexorably connected to feudalism. As feudalism fell apart, monasticism was bound to lose its appeal (see Chenu 230–231). All the things on which feudalism stood were giving way: the preeminence of land in the economy, stability of places and people, personal relationships forged by oaths between nobles and their lessers, the granting of benefices, and serfdom. The new Europe was centered in cities and towns with their markets and merchants. Money and people were in increasing circulation. Liberty from serfdom was increasingly achieved. Guilds and leagues of workers, artisans and merchants replaced feudal oaths of fealty. Medieval people were beginning to understand themselves as autonomous individuals and part of the natural world at the same time.

The monastic world was losing touch with the pulse of the changing medieval world.

I encourage you to return to this chapter often during your study of Francis. The influence of this movement is tremendously important to understanding Francis and the Franciscan movement.

Suggested reading and sources cited

- Bolton, Brenda. *The Medieval Reformation.* Foundations of Medieval History. London: Edward Arnold Publishers, 1983.
- Chenu, M.-D. *Nature, Man, and Society in the Twelfth Century: Essays on New Theological Perspectives in the Latin West.* Trans. Jerome Taylor and Lester K. Little. Chicago: University of Chicago Press, 1968. Pay special attention to chapter six, "Monks, Canons, and Laymen in Search of the Apostolic Life," pages 202–238, and chapter seven, "The Evangelical Awakening," pages 270–309. Chenu is a highly respected authority on this period of European history. This collection of essays in translation includes many articles considered classics in the field. You can't go wrong reading Chenu.
- Chinnici, Joseph. "Evangelical and Apostolic Tensions." *Our Franciscan Charism Today.* New Jersey: Fame, 1987.
- Constable, Giles. *The Reformation of the Twelfth Century.* Cambridge: The University Press, 1996. While only short passages deal with the Apostolic Life Movement specifically, Constable offers a broad description of the need for reform and resulting movements slightly before the time of Francis of Assisi. Constable is a world-class medieval historian.
- Davison, Ellen Scott. *Forerunners of Saint Francis and Other Studies.* Ed. Gertrude R. B. Richards. Boston: Houghton Mifflin Co., 1927. Part One (3–284) provides a more extensive discussion of pre-Franciscan reform movements influenced by the apostolic-life idea.
- Lambert, Malcolm. *Medieval Heresy: Popular Movements from the Gregorian Reform to the Reformation.* Rev. ed. London: Blackwell, 1992. This work focuses on heretical groups but discusses underlying currents that also influence orthodox lay movements.
- Lapsanski, Duane V. *Evangelical Perfection: An Historical Examination of the Concept in the Early Franciscan Sources.* Theology Series No. 7. St. Bonaventure, New York: Franciscan Institute Publications, 1977. Lapsanski's work follows the idea of evangelical perfection through the first century of the Franciscan movement. Thus, the entire volume may be of interest to you. However, Part One (6–50) discusses pre-Franciscan apostolic movements.

- Lawrence, C.H. *Medieval Monasticism: Forms of Religious Life in Western Europe in the Middle Ages*. Second Edition. New York and London: Longman, 1989. Focused on the development of monasticism, this work explains the changes of Cistercian life that prepared ground for the novel mendicant movement, including the Franciscans.
- ____. *The Friars: The Impact of the Early Mendicant Movement on Western Society*. London and New York: Longman, 1994. This book is a small treasure chest of information about the social and church environment spawning the Franciscans. However, the first two chapters are particularly relevant about causes of the Apostolic Movement and its expression in the Franciscans.
- McDonnell, Ernest W. "The *Vita Apostolica*: Diversity or Dissent." *Church History* 24 (1955) 15–31.
- Rivi, Prospero. "Francis of Assisi and the Laity of His Time." *Greyfriars Review* 15. Supplement (2001) v–vii, 1–108. Chapter one succinctly describes the laity's reawakening from the 11th century until the time of Francis of Assisi.
- Southern, R. W. *Western Society and the Church in the Middle Ages.* New York: Penguin, 1970. The chapters on religious orders provide background to the apostolic movement.
- Vauchez, André. *The Spirituality of the Medieval West: The Eighth to the Twelfth Century*. Trans. Colette Friedlander. Kalamazoo MI: Cistercian Publications, 1993. Succinctly describes the changing spirituality of the masses that helped create and then embrace the Franciscans.
- Vicaire, M. H. *The Apostolic Life*. Chicago: The Priory Press, 1966. Focuses on the Dominicans, but much of this book is applicable to the Franciscan movement.

The Call to the Apostolic Life and Francis' Response

Sources

1C 21–23
LJS 15–17
L3C 25–27
AC 101e–g (LP 67c–d)
LMj III 1–3
Matt. 10:7–14 (parallels are in Mark 6:8–11 and Luke 9:1–5) [missionary discourse to the twelve]
Luke 10:1–12 [missionary discourse to seventy-two disciples]

Starter questions and suggestions

Parts of this worksheet also are covered later in the worksheet on the development of the First Order Rule: "Francis Hears a Gospel in Honor of the Apostles, 1208." You or your group could choose to study the story in only one of the two places. However, I have found it beneficial to study this worksheet in detail at this time to continue to understand Francis' ongoing conversion. Later, I recommend you at least review the topic when studying the development of the rule. Commentary relevant to studying the rule's development will be provided then. For now, the following questions and suggestions should prove helpful.

How did Francis conceive his mission? What gave shape to his vision? Review the apostolic texts from the previous section. How might those texts and the groups that frequently referred to them have affected Francis?

What does Francis' change of clothing signify? Francis changed his self-conception from what to what? Try to find words or phrases that describe what Francis thought he was (i.e., categories of his day which gave him an identity). How was Francis' conversion furthered in this story?

What attitudes about and approaches to scripture did Francis reveal in this story?

Now focus on Francis' preaching after having his experience during eucharist. What was the nature and content of Francis' preaching? How did people receive him? Why did they receive him in this fashion? Do you like what he preached? How was Francis different from other preachers? What did Francis mean by *peace, penance* and *perfection*?

Suggested reading

There is quite a bit of debate about precisely which scripture is the one Francis heard in this story. Scholars are not even in agreement that this story took place on the Feast of St. Matthias. The answers to these questions are not necessary to profitably do this worksheet. However, if you are interested in these questions, I recommend you read the following article:

- Schmucki, Octavian. "The 'Way of Life According to the Gospel' as It Was Discovered by St. Francis of Assisi." Trans. Patrick Colbourne. *Greyfriars Review* 2.3 (1988) 1–56. The most pertinent pages are 4–10.

The Preaching of the Early Friars

Sources

Test 23
1C 23, 29–30, 89
LJS 16, 19–20, 23
AP 15–16, 18–24
L3C 33–34, 36–41b, 60 (If you are using Habig, note that page 921 is a misplaced reproduction of page 923. Skip page 921, moving directly from 920 to 922.)
LMj IV 6

Starter questions and suggestions

Over the years, the sources listed for this worksheet have expanded and contracted. That's because the material about preaching is often intertwined with other topics. The current list of sources takes a moderate approach. Still, while these texts may refer to many things, focus your attention on *the preaching* of the early friars: their message and style, the reaction of the people, etc. If you have trouble situating a story, read a few paragraphs before your text. They may help you better understand the text that concerns you.

Distinguish between the various preaching trips that are described in these sources. Where did the friars go? How did they go? How did they identify themselves? What about the early friars raised suspicion or admiration in the people? What did they preach? Into what problems did they run?

Why do AP and L3C devote so much space to these trips, while the other sources do not?

What is the relationship between the friars' preaching and their example? Was the effectiveness of their preaching due to their preaching, example, both, or neither?

What were the characteristics of the early friars while preaching?

Francis' earlier idea of his life style seems to have involved living poorly and begging. Suddenly, preaching appears to be a constitutive part of his mission. Is his mission changing, developing, or staying the same?

Suggested Reading

- Anderson, C. Colt. "Clerics, Laity and Preaching the Gospel among the Early Franciscans." *Franciscan Evangelization: Striving to Preach the*

Gospel. Ed. Elise Saggau. Washington Theological Union Symposium Papers 2007. St. Bonaventure NY: The Franciscan Institute, 2008. Pp.55–77.

- Chinnici, Joseph. "The Impact of Clericalization on Franciscan Evangelization." *Franciscan Evangelization: Striving to Preach the Gospel*. Ed. Elise Saggau. Washington Theological Union Symposium Papers 2007. St. Bonaventure NY: The Franciscan Institute, 2008. Pp.79–122.

Approbation of *The Primitive Rule* (1209/10)

Sources

Test 14–15
1C 32–33
LJS 21
Roger of Wendover's Chronicle 5–6 in FA:ED I 598–599
AP 31–36
L3C 46–53
2C 16–17
LMj III 8–10
LMn II 3–5

Starter questions and suggestions

We will look at these sources later when we study the development of the First Order's rule. At that time we will be most concerned with the nature of the rule's text. Right now, we are concerned with the story about the presentation and approval of the rule.

Place an oversized piece of paper on its side and create seven vertical columns, one for each biography. (*The Testament* and Wendover can be read after the stories in the hagiography have been compared.) Outline the accounts so that similar information is horizontally adjacent in the various accounts. Note additions, subtractions, and changes.

Pay attention to the chronological order of the events in the various accounts. How do you account for the variations in chronology? Which order seems to make the most sense to you?

Evaluate the historicity of each of the component parts of the total story. Are there aspects of the story you do not believe are historical?

The text of this form of the rule, called by many *The Primitive Rule*, has been lost. Use your sources to come up with a description of *The Primitive Rule*.

Why did Francis write a rule at this time? Why did Francis seek *papal* approval of the rule? Why could he not be satisfied with local diocesan approval, which he probably would have received? Who went to Rome? What was the manner of relating among the brothers on the way to Rome? Are the authors unduly comparing the early brothers to Christ and the apostles? What is the point of such a comparison? What exactly does Innocent approve? What is the nature of his approval? What does Innocent tell the brothers to do? Does Innocent consider this the final version of the rule?

Why are the friars given a tonsure (circle of shaved hair over top-back part of head)? What does the tonsure signify in the accounts? Does this event in the life of the order say anything about Francis' relationship with church authority? Does this have anything to do with obedience? If it does, to whom or what? If it has something to say about obedience, is that obedience blind, or does Francis fight for what *he* wants?

Can you discern political, social or church realities that might make this approval by the Bishop of Rome more important than it would first seem?

Suggested Reading

- Powell, James M. *Innocent III: Vicar of Christ or Lord of the World?* 2nd expanded edition. Washington DC: Catholic University of America Press, 1994.

Living at Rivo Torto

Sources

1C 42–44
LJS 25b–26
L3C 55
AC 92 (LP 55)
LMj IV 3–5
2MP 36

Starter questions and suggestions

There are numerous stories comprising the tradition about Rivo Torto: the early lifestyle of the friars, the admonition to Emperor Otto of Brunswick, the intrusion of a man with a donkey, and the entrance of Giles into the community. Separate the stories and note how each one changes as the tradition develops. Try to determine what concerns of the various authors might be shaping the story with additions and changes. Note which stories stop appearing in the tradition. Pay attention to the different tones found in the various sources. Decide and report what you believe truly happened at Rivo Torto.

These stories talk about ownership, poverty, bodily mortification, prayer, and quiet. Many of the additions to the stories listed above speak about the early life of the friars. By studying the changes, try to determine which values go back to the early friars and which later writers may have read back into their situation. Critique their spiritual values. Many of the values were commonly held in the church of their day. Are the values of our modern church different? Which of these values do you believe engender holiness? Note any values you do not share and explain why.

Commentary

The name *Rivo Torto* means twisted or crooked river. The stream that runs near this place is no more than a creek today. Nothing at the site today goes back to Francis' life. The stone huts constructed inside a moderately sized church on the site today were built long after Francis died.

Rivo Torto is a pleasant 30-minute walk into the valley below Assisi. A beautiful southern panoramic view of Assisi is visible from Rivo Torto.

Stories from the Leonine tradition (AC and MP) seem to be about an earlier period than those in the other sources. This seems so because 1C places the stories just after Francis and a group of eleven friars returned from Rome with approval for their *Primitive Rule*. The Leonine sources clearly place the number of followers at three with Giles, dating the story before the trip to Rome.

The Starving Friar

Sources:

2C 22
LMj V 7
AC 50a–h (LP 1)
2MP 27a–h
ER IX 10–12
Compare the values of the starving friar story with those found in AC 53 (LP 5) about eating grapes with a sick friar.

Starter questions and suggestions

This is a good story to see the effect different goals can have on shaping a particular story within various hagiographic traditions. Pay particular attention to this shaping dynamic as you prepare your presentation.

Read the four versions carefully. Note that after Francis gives his admonition about charity and understanding, the Leonine sources (AC and MP) add that Francis will never break his fast like this again because it would be neither religious nor upright.

If you are working with a group, tell the core story that all four sources present. Next, tell what the Leonine sources have added. The Leonine addition seems to negate the original intention of the story (i.e., to portray Francis' understanding and compassion, and his lesson about discernment). Explain which goals of the Leonine tradition may be motivating this change in the story. Do you believe the addition is historical?

Explore reasons for this story not being in the Egidian sources (AP and L3C). What significance is there in the fact that it is not in 1C? How does the citation from the *Earlier Rule* cause you to understand this story? How does that same text influence your evaluation of the addition to the story by AC and MP?

Now turn your attention to Francis' notion of penance. Tell the group what we can learn about his vision of penance from this story. Do you think Francis had a balanced approach? Do you think Francis' vision is being misrepresented in any of the sources? Do the various versions tell us more about Francis' vision of penance or that of the author?

Do you like the vision of penance presented in the story? Do you live this way yourself? Why or why not?

Now turn your attention to the hungry friar. What psychological forces do you see operating in him (e.g., attitudes that determine expectations, behavior, and feelings)? Tell us if you think the friar reflected a healthy attitude. Tell us what you believe to be the view of life underlying the practices talked about in this story.

The Conversion of Friars and Robbers

Sources

ER VII 13–14
AC 115 (LP 90)
2MP 66
DBF XXIX
LFl 26

Starter questions and suggestions

Note that this story only occurs in the Leonine tradition, possibly because its site is a hermitage, a favorite theme of the tradition. Do you find it odd that it's not mentioned anywhere else in the medieval sources? The versions in AC and 2MP are nearly identical. However, there are quite a few differences between them and the version found in *The Deeds* and *The Little Flowers*. Do you think these are the same stories? What differences do *The Deeds* and *The Little Flowers* emphasize? How is Francis portrayed differently in the two versions? Which do you like better? What is your assessment of the historicity of the story in its two versions?

Is the emphasis in the story on how the friars affected the robbers or on how the robbers affected the friars? Compare your conclusions with how the friars interacted with lepers. What importance does the fact that the robbers were outcasts have in the story?

Which virtues and religious values are tied to this story? Are the actions of the friars *ministry* or simply living authentically their Franciscan way of life?

How do the stories differ in their portrayal of authority in the order and the role of Francis as founder? How do the early friars look to Francis? Reflect on your own approach to Francis. What do you hope to receive from Francis?

Finally, could the citation from the *Earlier Rule* listed above have prompted late hagiographers to create a story, in the absence of any earlier story, to illustrate a certain and early Franciscan value?

Beggars and Francis

Sources

The poorly treated beggar before conversion
1C 17c
LJS 12b
AP 4
L3C 3
LMj I 1

Francis' resolution to help the poor
1C 17c
LJS 12b–c
AP 4
L3C 3
2C 5
LMj I 1

Francis' generosity toward a poor knight
L3C 6
2C 5
LMj I 2

Francis' attitude toward the poor and beggars
1C 76
LJS 45
AC 114 (LP 89)
2C 78, 83, 85
LMj VIII 5

Francis responds to various requests
L3C 28
AC 31–34 (not in LP)
2C 86–89
LMj VIII 5
2MP 29–32

Francis gives away a New Testament
AC 93 (LP 56)
2C 91
2MP 38

Someone poses as a beggar to trick Francis
2C 78–79

Other stories during Francis' conversion
L3C 8–10

Francis' philosophy of receiving alms
AC 15 (LP 111)

Starter questions and suggestions

Many of these stories have already been encountered in previous worksheets. The goal here is to summarize the relationship of Francis to beggars in a general way. I recommend that you take each of the areas mentioned above and study them critically like you would any worksheet. However, if you are presenting to a group, I do not recommend that you report the specifics of each story to the group. That would take a great deal of time.

Rather, I suggest that you do the detail work and then generalize about Francis' relationship with beggars. This latter material should be shared with the group. Use examples only to illustrate the points of your summary.

Try to discover what beggars represented to Francis. Why was Francis so resolved to respond to them. What did the economic situation of beggars elicit out of Francis? What did Francis see as his spiritual and economic relationship with beggars?

The Fourth Lateran Council (1215)

Pope Innocent III held the Fourth Lateran Council at his Roman cathedral, St. John in the Lateran, in 1215. Some have called it the "Great Council" because Innocent mounted a massive movement to address major Catholic Church concerns of the day, including various heresies, growing disrespect for the church and its leaders and ministers, the reform of the church's episcopacy and priests, the reform of eucharistic practice, and the initiation of a new crusade to the Near East.

The council is particularly important for students of the Franciscan movement because many of these themes appear in Francis' writings, clearly showing the influence of the council. Knowledge of several canons from the council proves invaluable to better understand Francis' writings, especially the development of his rule, and his eucharistic and penitential writings.

I provide here a summary of important canons. English editions of the entire document from the council can be found in:

- Tanner, Norman P., ed. *Decrees of the Ecumenical Councils*. 2 vols. Washington D.C.: Georgetown University Press; London: Sheed & Ward, 1990. 1:227–271.

Canons 1–3: These canons are directed against heresy in general, but especially Joachimism.

Canon 10: Bishops are to be preachers. Ignorance among them is condemned. If a bishop cannot preach for any reason, he should provide clerics who can. Bishops should provide for the needs of preachers.

Canon 11: Every cathedral church and others of means shall appoint a master to teach clerics and poor students at no cost. Metropolitans shall provide a theologian to teach the clergy about the *cura animarum* or the care of souls.

Canon 12: All orders are to hold chapters every three years. Two Cistercians shall guide the chapters. Those in authority shall conduct visitations of their religious houses. Superiors shall work for reform and regular observance.

Canon 13: There shall be no new rules for religious orders. New monasteries must accept a rule that the church has already approved.

Canon 17: This canon laments priests who are lax in the Christian life and their priestly duties. It specifically cites priests who celebrate eucharist as infrequently as four times a year, do not even attend eucharist, or are not attentive during eucharist. This canon calls for a diligent and devout celebration of the Liturgy of Hours and eucharist.

Canon 19: Non-sacramental items (e.g., household goods) should not be stored in churches. It calls for greater care for the cleanliness of church buildings and the general care of sacred vessels and vestments.

Canon 20: Chrism and consecrated eucharistic breads should be reserved in locked places that protect them from rash people. The penalty for not doing this is suspension for three months.

Canon 21: The faithful should confess once a year to a parish priest and receive communion at least once during Easter under the penalty of excommunication. Priests who reveal confessed sins should be stripped of their priestly office and relegated to a monastery of strict observance for the rest of their lives.

Canon 27: Incompetent persons must not be promoted to the priesthood or given the direction of souls. It is better to have fewer good ministers than many poor ministers.

Canon 71: This canon is actually composed of numerous decrees that deal with preparations for a new crusade. It is four pages long!

Finally, let me provide you with some information about various papal bulls that were issued after the Fourth Lateran Council. A papal bull is a common genre of medieval papal literature. They are called bulls because popes signed them with lead seals bearing their insignia called bulls. The bull is a form through which the pope made announcements and pronouncements to the church. They often were responses to requests or problems. Papal copyists often made hundreds of copies that were delivered across Christendom. Local church officials often had their copyists make copies of the copies to distribute among their people. I provide these summaries of the bulls, but the full texts for some bulls can be found in FA:ED. Pope Honorius III wrote all of these bulls except *Quo elongati*, which was written by Gregory IX, the former Cardinal Hugolino, cardinal protector of the Franciscans.

Cum dilecti filii (11 June 1219)

- addressed to church officials;
- instructs the reader to receive the Friars Minor as *Catholics* and believers;
- clarifies that the Friars Minor have been sent to preach in the world.

The full text is found at FA:ED I 558.

Sane cum olim, also known as *Expectavimus hactenus* (22 November 1219)

- calls for serious consideration of canon 17 of the Fourth Lateran Council concerning eucharistic abuses and the devout praying of Liturgy of Hours;
- calls for serious consideration of canon 19 of the council urging that churches be kept clean and the sacred vessels and vestments be cared for properly;
- calls for serious consideration of canon 20 regarding the reservation of eucharistic bread, the scriptures and the oils in a safe and locked place.

Note that this bull does not refer to canon 21, which mandates yearly confession and communion during Easter. An English translation is found in FA:ED I 55, note a.

Pro dilectis filiis (29 May 1220)

- addressed to church officials in France;
- notes the hostility that has been shown the Friars Minor;
- instructs the reader to regard the Friars Minor as *Catholics* and devout;
- instructs bishops to admit Friars Minor into their diocese as true believers.

The full text is found at FA:ED I 559–560.

Cum secundum consilium (22 September 1220)

- addressed to the priors (sic) and custodians of the Friars Minor (This is an odd form of address since the Franciscans abhorred the title *prior* used by other religious men. The title implied privilege and rank to the Franciscans who sought to be minors. Custodians were the ministers of custodies, which were divisions of the provinces. It appears Honorius was addressing this bull to all the various ministers of the Franciscans.);
- forbids religious profession without a year of probation (i.e., novitiate);
- forbids anyone to leave the order after profession;
- forbids other orders or dioceses from receiving someone who has left the order;
- forbids anyone in the order to wander outside obedience or to debase poverty;
- threatens ecclesiastical censure by superiors of the order for those who do any of these forbidden things.

The full text is found at FA:ED I 560–561.

Fratrum minorum (18 December 1223)

- addressed to church officials;
- summarizes the points of *Cum secundum consilium*;
- tells the readers to observe the excommunication of friars by the superiors of the Friars Minor.

This bull highlights the fact that the Friar Minors were having difficulties that required excommunications and that church officials were not accepting the authority of Franciscan leaders. I presume these conditions existed earlier for such a bull to be warranted.

Quo elongati (28 September 1230)

Our primary interest in *Quo elongati* is in regard to comments on *The Testament* and the Franciscan rule. However, it does comment on a number of other things that I included in this summary.

- declares that *The Testament* is not a legally binding document;
- the friars must observe *only* those precepts *explicitly* found in the rule, not those found in the gospels in general;
- provides for agents to care for the material needs of the friars;
- announces the friars shall have no individual or communal property;
- only public mortal sins need to be confessed to the provincial;
- trained preachers may preach; others need the approval of the general minister;
- the custodians (leaders of custodies, a sub-division of provinces) elect one representative to go with the provincials to the general chapters;
- friars may enter only the public areas of cloistered nuns.

The full text is found at FA:ED I 570–575.

Francis and Penance: *The Letter to the Faithful* *(Admonition and Exhortation to the Brothers and Sisters of Penance)*

Preliminary comments

My students regularly have difficulty identifying the proper texts for this worksheet. Thus, indulge this brief explanation of their various names. The Paulist Press edition of the writings (AB in 1982) called these documents the first and second versions of *The Letter to the Faithful*. The table of contents of FA:ED I calls the first document *Earlier Exhortation* and the second document *Later Admonition and Exhortation*. The headings on the pages of the documents (FA:ED I 41 + 45) complete these titles with the phrase "...to the Brothers and Sisters of Penance." Then FA:ED also lists the older name from AB. Finally, the abbreviations used by FA:ED reflect the older names (1LtF and 2LtF), and its footnotes use the older names. I believe that the older names will continue in popular English usage and, thus, continue to use them here.

The Letter to the Faithful was written by Francis to encourage and teach a life of penance. Though broad in appeal, the letter seems addressed particularly to lay people.

The Letter to the Faithful comes to us in two versions, an earlier and a later, also called the first and second versions. The first version is sometimes called by the Latin name *recensio prior*. For a long time, it has been called the *Volterra Letter* because the French historian Paul Sabatier first discovered a manuscript containing it in the Guarnacci Library in Volterra, Italy. Sabatier published the work in 1900. Most scholars largely ignored it until Kajetan Esser included it in his 1976 critical edition of Francis' writings as an authentic and important writing expressing Francis' ideas on penance. Some argue that Francis offered the earlier version as a guide for groups of lay penitents who asked Francis for guidance.

Raffaele Pazzelli's study of these letters has caused scholars to be more tenuous about suggesting that these two documents are different versions of a single document. (Compare the different introductions in AB 62 + 66 and FA:ED I 41 + 45, including note a on page 41.) Still, the literary similarities throughout the letters suggest to me a value in considering the two documents in a dynamic relationship, if not in continuity.

The difference between the two versions is mostly style. The second version corrected the grammar and scriptural quotations of the first. The tenses of verbs were changed. A different psalter (version of the psalms) was used. The second version opted for the genre of a formal letter. Other changes reflect the use of more concrete examples of penance. Those examples reflect the growing concern Francis had for certain issues as he and his order grew older: orthodoxy, respect for clergy, eucharist, confession, and the implementation of the Fourth Lateran Council (1215).

The editors of FA:ED date the first version between 1209 and 1215. They date the second version about 1220.

The *Letter to the Faithful* itself

Sources

1LtF (FA:ED I 41–44)
2LtF (FA:ED I 45–51)

Starter questions and suggestions

I often find the discipline of outlining helpful to understand the message of a document. I strongly recommend that you outline both versions of this letter. Start with the first version. Go for the broad strokes; don't become overly concerned with detail. Your outline for the first version should be about one page in length.

Considering your outline, try to summarize Francis' approach to penance. Pay attention to the images and how they interact with Francis' ideas. Is Francis' description general or specific? Is it positive or negative? Does Francis' idea of penance in this letter match or differ from our modern ideas about penance?

Next, outline the second version. The outline should not exceed a page and a half. How is the second version different from the first? Note what was added. How do the additions affect the organization of the original version? Why does the second version become lengthier? Why more specific? Does the second version maintain the same tone as the first? Can you see the influence of the Fourth Lateran Council in the second version? Where? Be specific!

If you are working with a group, discuss how you might be surprised by Francis' approach to penance in the letter. Talk about your own ideas of penance. Discuss how Francis' ideas might cause you to think differently about penance. Remember, Francis envisioned the totality of his life with his brothers in the First Order as a life of penance. This is an idea that most of my students have difficulty understanding at first. Because of our training, we tend to think of penance as penitential practices. While Francis certainly engaged in penitential practices, his idea of a penitential life style (as found in this letter) is much more positive. How can you envision your life to be a penitential lifestyle?

The relationship between the *Letter to the Faithful* and a rule for lay penitents

Sources

1C 36–37
LJS 23
AP 41
L3C 54, 60
AC 74j–o (LP 34)
LMj II 8; IV 6; XII 8

Starter questions and suggestions

Several of the sources cited above portray Francis as promising a rule of life or guidelines for lay people to live a penitential lifestyle. Many writers believe the *Letter to the Faithful* is that promised way of life.

How do you evaluate the relationship between Francis and lay penitents? Some point to these passages as proof that Francis founded the Third Order. Do you find evidence to support this claim? If you do, in what sense might Francis be considered the *founder* of the Third Order: organizer, leader, inspirer, charismatic figure, lawgiver, or another way? Did Francis leave some guide for life to lay penitents? If he did, could the *Letter to the Faithful* be this guide?

What was Francis' appeal to lay people?

Commentary

Before reading this commentary, I recommend that you finish your personal attempt to outline the *Letter to the Faithful*. I wish to provide here my own outline of the two versions, which you can use as a point of comparison. I believe you stand to learn the most if you try to construct your own outline before even peeking at mine.

First version

I. To those who do penance (emphasis on *life*)

A. Addressed to those who (a predisposition):
1. love the Lord with their whole heart
2. love their neighbors as themselves
3. hate their bodies with their vices and sins
4. receive the body and blood of the Lord
5. produce worthy fruits of penance

B. The Spirit of the Lord dwells in those who do these things.

C. They are in relationship to Christ as:
1. *spouses*: the Holy Spirit joins their souls to Christ
2. *sisters/brothers*: they do the will of the same Father
3. *mothers*: they carry Christ in their hearts and bodies through love and give birth in their holy manner of working, which is an example

D. A proclamation of praise for this wonderful relationship with the Father as spouse, brother, and son.

The high priestly prayer of Jesus found in John 17 is part of this proclamation. That text talks of Jesus' care for his followers, which is like the Father's care for Jesus.

II. To those who do not do penance (emphasis on *death*)

A. Addressed to those who (a predisposition):
1. are not in penance
2. do not receive the body and blood of Christ
3. practice vice and sin
4. don't observe their promises to the Lord
5. bodily serve the world by the desires of the flesh and cares for the world

B. These are held fast by the devil.

C. They are in relationship to the devil and knowingly lose their soul to the devil; they:
1. are children of the devil whose deeds they do
2. are blind for not seeing the light of Christ
3. don't possess spiritual wisdom for they don't possess Christ

D. Proclamation of damnation:
1. they are blind, deceived by their enemies: the flesh, the world and the devil
2. they have nothing in this or the next world (deceived in thinking they do)
3. they will die a bitter death if given the chance to do penance and ignore it
4. all things will be taken from them
5. their relatives will curse them for not leaving them more inheritance
6. they will be tormented in hell without end

III. Concluding injunction

A. Read this with acceptance.
B. If you are illiterate, have it read to you.
C. Preserve these words of Jesus Christ; they are spirit and life.
D. Those who do not do so will be accountable at judgment.

Second version

Introduction

A. Addressed to Christian religious, clergy and lay, men and women, all in the world.

B. Since Francis is sick and unable to visit, he sends this letter.

I. Proclamation of the Christ event

A. Historicity of the nativity and the humanity of Christ.
B. Though rich, Christ and Mary chose poverty.
C. Recount of the Last Supper eucharist.
D. Recount of the agony in the garden showing Christ's obedience.
E. God's will was Jesus' sacrifice on the cross for our sins.
F. All of which leaves us an example.
G. Concluding with the proclamation that the Father desires us to be saved and to receive him.

II. The response of those who do penance

A. A description of true worshipers (in spirit and truth)—they:
   1. ✓love the Lord and do God's commandments
   2. pray always
   3. confess to a priest
   4. ✓receive the body and blood worthily
   5. ✓produce the fruits of penance
   6. ✓love their neighbors as themselves
   7. if judges, are merciful
   8. have charity and humility
   9. give alms for their sins (the rewards of charity are taken to heaven)
   10. fast and abstain from their vices and sins, explicitly from excesses of food and drink

11. are Catholic
12. visit churches frequently
13. venerate clergy for the reason of their office and admin istration of eucharist
14. ✓hate their bodies with their vices and sins
15. love their enemies
16. observe the commandments
17. are obedient as they promised
18. if in authority, are lesser, have mercy, and are patient
19. are simple and humble
20. hold themselves in contempt and scorn
21. never desire authority

B. The Spirit of the Lord dwells in those who do so.

C. They are in relationship to Christ as:
1. *spouses*: the spirit joins them to Christ
2. *sisters/brothers*: they do the will of the same Father
3. *mothers*: they carry Christ in their hearts by love, giving birth by their holy works and example

D. A proclamation of praise for this wonderful relationship with Christ:
1. who prayed the High Priestly Prayer found in John 17
2. Francis ends with a Christological hymn celebrating that Christ is all we have and need for salvation

III. The response of those not in penance

A. A description of who they are:
1. not in penance
2. do not receive the body and blood
3. practice vice and sin
4. don't observe what they have promised
5. bodily serve the world, the desires of the flesh, and the cares of the world

B. They are deceived by the devil.

C. They are in relationship with the devil because they are not with Christ:
1. they are blind because they don't see Christ, the true light
2. they have no spiritual wisdom because the don't have Christ within
3. they know and do evil, and so lose their souls

D. A proclamation of their damnation:
   1. they are deceived by the devil, world, and flesh because
      a. sin is sweet to the body
      b. all proceeds from their hearts
   2. they have nothing in this or the next world
   3. they die bitter deaths for placing trust in their relatives and friends, and not doing penance and restitution
   4. all will be taken from them
   5. their relatives will curse them for not leaving them more inheritance
   6. they will be tormented in hell without end

IV. Conclusion

A. Receive these words and observe them.
B. Pass them to others.
C. May God bless those who observe them.

NB: ✓ = these elements were also included in the first version of the letter. This section (II A) has been expanded in the second version.

Suggested reading

- Cusato, Michael F. "To Do Penance/*Facere poenitentiam*." *The Cord* 57.1 (2007) 3–24. Cusato successfully explains Francis' upbeat understanding of penance as many others do. However, he provides concrete examples from the 13th century that clarify the idea by illustrating it with concrete examples. This makes his treatment unique.
- Esser, Kajetan. "A Forerunner of the 'Epistula ad Fideles' of St. Francis of Assisi." *Analecta Tertii Ordinis Regularis Sancti Francisci* 129 (1978) 11–47.
- Lehmann, Leonard. "Exultation and Exhortation to Penance: A Study of the Form and Content of the First Version of the Letter to the Faithful." Trans. Timothy Gottschalk. *Greyfriars Review* 4.2 (1990) 1–33.
- Pazzelli, Raffaele. "The Title of the 'Recensio Prior of the Letter to the Faithful': Clarifications regarding Codex 225 of Volterra (cod. Vo)." Trans. Nancy Celaschi. *Greyfriars Review* 4.3 (1990) 1–6.
- Manselli, Raoul. "Francis of Assisi and Lay People Living in the World: Beginning of the Third Order." Trans. Edward Hagman. *Greyfriars Review* 11.1 (1997) 41–48.

- Menestò, Enrico. "A Re-reading of Francis of Assisi's Letter to the Faithful." Trans. Edward Hagman. *Greyfriars Review* 14.2 (2000) 97–110.
- Rivi, Prospero. "Francis of Assisi and the Laity of His Time." *Greyfriars Review* 15. Supplement (2001) v–vii, 1–108. Chapter one succinctly describes the laity's reawakening from the 11th century until the time of Francis of Assisi. Chapter two shows how Francis electrified this movement by tapping into its most basic desires. It also reviews the evidence for Francis' relationship with the lay apostolic movement.
- Schmucki, Octavian. "The Third Order in the Biographies of St. Francis." Trans. Nancy Celaschi. *Greyfriars Review* 6.1 (1992) 81–107.
- Stewart, Robert M. *"De illis qui faciunt penitentiam" The Rule of the Secular Franciscan Order: Origins, Development, Interpretation.* Rome: Istituto Storico dei Cappuccini, 1991. Distributed in the USA by the Franciscan Institute at St. Bonaventure University. Pages 91–133 discuss the historical context leading up to the 13th century penitential movement. Pages 135–179 provide a detailed analysis of 1LtF and 2LtF as well as a good summary of recent scholarly writing about them. I recommend this readable resource.

Francis' Tension between Leading an Eremitical or Ministerial Life

Sources

1C 35b, 91
LJS 23a
LMj IV 2; XII 1–2
DBF XVI 1–13
LFl 16a–c

Starter questions and suggestions

There were at least two periods in which Francis struggled with the form of life for himself and his group in regard to prayer and apostolic activity. When did they occur? What was the nature of the tension? What were his pre-conceptions that created the tension in him? What were Francis' motives? How did he resolve the tension?

Do you believe Francis made the "right" choice? Elaborate.

Suggested reading

- Brady, Ignatius. "The History of Mental Prayer in the Order of Friars Minor." *Greyfriars Review* 19.3 (2005) 207–236.
- Cirino, André and Josef Raischl. *Franciscan Solitude.* St. Bonaventure NY: Franciscan Institute Publications, 1995.
- Schmucki, Octavian. "Mentis Silentium: Contemplation in the Early Franciscan Order." Trans. Ignatius McCormick. *Greyfriars Review* 4.2 (1990) 35–71.

Franciscan Eremitical Life

Sources

The Rule for Hermitages
AC 56i–n (LP 9b–10)
2C 18–19, 178

Starter questions and suggestions

Read *The Rule for Hermitages*. List the component parts of Franciscan eremitical life as found in this rule. Is this a simple or complicated rule? What is the relationship between solitude and sister-brotherhood? While Francis wrote a rule for hermitages, it is important to realize that he included no requirements about the eremitical life in the legislative documents of the order (ER and LR). Why do you think Francis didn't legislate about this matter?

The Portiuncula was an important early Franciscan hermitage. That's why some of the citations are included. Describe life in hermitages as portrayed in the medieval biographies. Liturgy of the Hours and personal prayer are emphasized in these documents. Neither eucharist nor *lectio divina* (using spiritual writings—especially scripture—as the starting point of personal prayer) are mentioned at all. Why do you think this is so? How does this shape a modern program of prayer for Franciscans?

What place did hermitages play in the life of the friars in general?

Suggested reading

- Cirino, André and Josef Raischl. *Franciscan Solitude.* St. Bonaventure NY: Franciscan Institute Publications, 1995.
- Schmucki, Octavian. "Mentis Silentium: Contemplation in the Early Franciscan Order." Trans. Ignatius McCormick. *Greyfriars Review* 4.2 (1990) 35–71.

The Office of the Passion

Sources

The Office of the Passion
The Prayer Inspired by the Our Father
The Praises To Be Said at All the Hours
LegCl 30 (found in a separate collection of sources for Clare of Assisi's life. See the page of abbreviations for details.)

Commentary

Every now and then, a new publication changes individuals and the general public's appreciation and view of its subject. The recent *The Geste of the Great King: Office of the Passion of Francis of Assisi*, published after the first edition of this workbook, is having that effect regarding *The Office of the Passion*. It is the first book-length treatment in English of this writing by Francis. Its introductions and commentaries open the depth of meaning and feeling contained in the prayer by placing it within its historical context and unlocking the code for its interpretation. Since many of the aids from this outstanding source are not included in FA:ED I, I will continue to provide explanatory notes here as I did in the first edition. However, I strongly encourage users of this workbook to read *The Geste of the Great King*.

Before discussing the office itself, it is helpful to briefly describe Francis' Christology, which undergirds the prayer. This further places the office in a context. Francis' theology of Christ (Christology) is intimately tied to his beliefs about the pattern he sees within the triune God (Trinitarian theology), the human condition (anthropology), and the way God saves us (soteriology). Though all of creation comes from God, it finds itself seemingly hopelessly separated from God. Typically, Christians understand *sin*, *original sin*, or *human finiteness/limitedness* as ways to explain this. However, in Francis' view, this separation is not part of God's plan for humanity or the rest of creation. We are intended to be united with God, and God works to repair the breach. How God does this is the object of Francis' continuous meditation.

What we see of God's method is most clearly visible in Jesus. However, it is important to understand that, as a disclosure of the invisible God, the saving pattern we can see in Jesus is truly a reflection of the saving pattern within the triune God. For Francis, the roles of the persons of the Trinity explain the process. The *Father* signifies the Godhead's desire or will that all of creation, which came from God, return to God. The *Word/Son* signifies the disclosure of God's desire in incredible self-emptying. The *Word* is the person who implements the *Father's* desire and, thus, is often portrayed as the *doer* within God. The *Spirit* signifies the recognition of the Father and the Word's relationship, often described as *love*.

Jesus becomes the focus of Francis' meditation on this saving pattern in God. As the Word made Flesh, Jesus discloses the otherwise less visible saving pattern in God. As divine, Jesus has the "rights" of divinity, i.e., the nature of divinity with its powers and abilities. However, in the historical Jesus, the Word forgoes or gives up these prerogatives of his divinity in order to join himself to creation through our humanity. This is the great mystery of the Incarnation in which the Word *emptied* itself, not of divine nature, but of divine prerogative. In theological language, we call this pattern of self-emptying in Jesus *kenosis*; Francis liked to call it Jesus' poverty and humility. I find it most beautifully expressed in the Christological hymn found in Paul's *Letter to the Philippians*.

> Let the same mind be in you that was in Christ Jesus, who, though he was in the form of God, did not regard equality with God as something to be exploited, but emptied himself, taking the form of a slave, being born in human likeness. And being found in human form, he humbled himself and became obedient to the point of death — even death on a cross. Therefore God also highly exalted him and gave him the name that is above every name, so that at the name of Jesus every knee should bend, in heaven and on earth and under the earth, and every tongue should confess that Jesus Christ is Lord, to the glory of God the Father. (Phil 2:5–11; I quote at length because this hymn succinctly describes many dimensions of Francis' spiritual intuition to be discussed.)

Francis envisions the *entire* Jesus-event as part of the Father's saving plan and thus disclosing of the invisible saving pattern within God. The Incarnation does not simply or even primarily refer to Jesus' birth. It refers to the *entire* time a divine and a human nature are united in the person of Jesus. It refers to the entire earthly life of the historical Jesus beginning at his conception (Annunciation) and continuing into the present. Since this self-emptying is part of every moment of Jesus' life, his entire life has that saving quality. However, for Francis, Jesus' self-emptying quality is particularly *evident* in his birth as a vulnerable infant, and his passion and death because of their radical witness.

If we are saved through our incorporation into a three-fold pattern of salvation—in the triune God, in Jesus, in us—it is eminently logical that Francis' spirituality would focus on following in the footprints of Jesus. This imitation begins with a keen observation of the pattern, which occurs for Francis through his meditation on the Incarnate Word in general and Jesus' passion and death in particular.

Within the sources about Francis' meditation, he gives little evidence of holding that Jesus' death was an appeasement of a highly offended God. Far from wanting reparation in the form of compensation or remuneration, God desires our conversion, our turning away from sin and toward God. In fact, our salvation occurs in that very conversion through the self-emptying example or pattern found in Jesus. This leads Francis to a profound attitude toward Jesus' passion and crucifixion, which is an extraordinary example of the divine self-emptying that is part of every moment of Jesus' earthly existence.

Using the image of photographs, I would say that Francis does not capture the saving quality of Jesus as a *series* of photographs that display a chronological succession of events leading to a conclusion. Rather, Jesus' entire life is a single snapshot that captures all moments in every moment. Thus, Jesus' early life is not unimportant as if nothing vital happened until the passion began. Jesus' salvific activity is occurring during his private and his public life before his passion. Equally important to Francis is the understanding that Jesus' resurrection is not a later-granted reward for his sacrifice on the cross. Instead, the new life of the resurrection is grounded in the self-emptying divine life so visible on the cross.

I believe that many medieval artistic depictions poignantly grasp the *simultaneous* nature of Jesus' saving work and consequent resurrection. The San Damiano Crucifix, familiar to most Franciscans, is a wonderful example. In this depiction, Jesus is crucified but painlessly *alive*. Furthermore, more than one "event" is depicted at the same time. While Jesus *is presented* on the cross, he is also depicted as victoriously ascending to the Father. Further, as Jesus is on the cross and ascending, he is simultaneously sanctifying the people who are part of the passion narrative, later local and universal saints, and people living at the time of the crucifix' painting. All of this goes on *at the same time* within the depiction of the San Damiano Crucifix. It is a depiction of the crucifixion from *The Gospel according to John*, which understands Jesus' life, death, and resurrection in a similar way.

This *simultaneity* addresses more than whether there is chronology or a lack of chronology in Jesus' saving activity. It more importantly focuses us on the pattern that genuinely saves us. Though some talk of Jesus paying the debt of our sin, Francis' view seems to place most notions of debt aside. Instead, in his perception, Jesus simply gratuitously invites us into what can really save us: a self-sacrificing obedience to the will of God. That in itself saves us or gives us life.

Though the San Damiano Crucifix predates Francis' birth, it beautifully depicts this mystery. Jesus is alive and victorious *while* he is on the cross. The clearest expression of Jesus' perpetually obedient *kenosis* (his passion and death) achieves salvation/life/resurrection in its very expression, as does Jesus' entire life. Thus, the cross both expresses the cost or extent to which God is willing to go to bring us to himself and also illustrates the triumph and victory contained in the very means.

This is the framework out of which to understanding Francis' *The Office of the Passion*. He could focus on Easter Sunday when the victory is fully visible. However, Francis focuses instead on Holy Thursday and Good Friday, the days of the passion and crucifixion when the victory is graphically tied to the means. In Francis' view, Jesus' self-sacrificing obedience is both the means to and experience of true life.

So, Francis celebrates new life in Jesus by meditating on the self-sacrificing obedience most visible in his passion. To do this, Francis developed this devotional office, capitalizing on the medieval association of five moments in Jesus' passion and death with five specific hours on Holy Thursday and Good Friday. Francis' *The Office of the Passion* juxtaposes those times with five specific hours from the official *Liturgy of the Hours*. Thus, the agony in the garden on Holy Thursday night is associated with Compline (night prayer). The trial before the Jewish Sanhedrin coincides with Matins in the middle of the night. The trial before the Roman tribunal of Pilate on Good Friday is connected to Terce around 9:00 am. The crucifixion coincides with Sext at noon. Jesus' death was thought to have happened around 3:00 pm, the time for None. Two other hours are inserted into this schema. Prime is celebrated at sunrise and continues to celebrate the *light* and *new life* of Jesus' victory celebrated at that time in the *Liturgy of the Hours* (as does modern Lauds or Morning Prayer). Finally, Vespers is celebrated at sunset and, within *The Office of the Passion*, is intended to summarize and celebrate the entire cycle of the day. Thus the daily pattern of this office looks like this:

Compline	at bedtime—meditating on Jesus' arrest on the Mount of Olives
Matins	at midnight—meditating on Jesus' trial before the Jewish Sanhedrin
Prime	at the first hour, i.e., sunrise—an interlude celebrating Christ as the light of a new day
Terce	at the third hour, i.e., 9:00 am—meditating on Jesus before the Roman tribunal of Pilate
Sext	at the sixth hour, i.e., noon—meditating on Jesus' crucifixion
None	at the ninth hour, i.e., 3:00 pm—meditating on Jesus' death
Vespers	at sunset—recalling and celebrating the entire daily cycle

When I outline this schema in my classes, many students protest that Francis really focuses on the "price that Jesus paid" and not on the victory of the resurrection. For them, his look at Jesus' passion seems so filled with vengeance. It is hard for many to conceptualize how the passion itself is an expression of the victory. A helpful analogous image might be childbirth. I am repeatedly amazed at the accounts mothers give of the pain of childbirth. Still, all those whom I have talked to unequivocally testify to the preciousness of the experience. Giving birth involves pain. It is achieved through pain. It coexists with pain. Birth does not occur *after* the pain. It is in the midst of pain. Francis' meditation on Jesus' passion is a bit like someone hoping to understanding a mother's love, not by focusing on the image of a newly delivered infant lying on a smiling mother's lap, but on the grimaces of a mother in painful labor. There is where the measure of love is found. It is a labor of love. Jesus' labor of love also gives new life, and that labor amounts to self-sacrificing obedience to the desire of the Father.

This victory in the midst of self-sacrificing passion is also visible in the order of prayer in *The Office of the Passion*. There are six elements to the celebration of each hour. All hours follow this same structure (unlike the *Liturgy of the Hours*). Only the psalm *selection* is different for each hour. This is the structure you would follow if you wanted to celebrate this devotional office.

Our Father (Gallant and Cirino prescribe only the simple *Our Father* with a doxology. However, the manuscripts cite this prayer as "O Our Father Most Holy," which are the opening words of *A Prayer Inspired by the Our Father*.)	FA:ED I 158–160
The Praises To Be Said at All the Hours with its concluding prayer	FA:ED I 161–162
antiphon honoring Mary	FA:ED I 141
psalm (Directions found in the manuscripts indicate that Francis prayed three psalms here: one honoring Mary of Nazareth; one of Francis' choosing; and one on the passion. We have no way of knowing which were the first two. However, the manuscripts provide the psalms on the passion. Most attempts to recreate this office simply provide for the single psalm on the passion at each hour.)	see chart below
antiphon honoring Mary	FA:ED I 141
dismissal prayer	FA:ED I 141

Within this format, each of the seven hours begins with the *Our Father*, a prayer that gives unreserved allegiance to God's will: "Thy will be done on earth as it is in heaven." The format then celebrates the victory of Jesus in *The Praises To Be Said at All the Hours,* which begins with three strong verses from *The Book of Revelation* that depict the four living beings, the twenty-four elders, and the heavenly hosts as singing the praises of the slain but victorious lamb (see Rev 4:2—5:12). *The Praises* conclude by inviting all of creation to join in this acclamation of praise. The antiphon used before and after the psalm in each hour highlights the obedient cooperation of Mary with the plan of God for Jesus. As such, she is seen as part of the mystery playing out in this office. Finally, the dismissal prayer again focuses on the *living* or victorious Jesus and again calls on all to praise him. Thus, the format of each hour moves from a proclamation and celebration of Jesus' victory, to a psalm that recounts some aspect of his passion/death, and returns to proclamation and celebration in its conclusion. In other words, this format surrounds Francis' meditation on Jesus' passion and death with the affirmation of Jesus' victory and, thus, further connects the two simultaneously in a single celebration of prayer.

A few more comments on the technicalities of this prayer will help the student with only FA:ED as a resource. There are five parts of the office, which correspond to five liturgical seasons or feasts. Knowing the parts assists the user to select the proper psalm. The parts are:

Part I: for the triduum and weekdays during the year
Part II: for the Easter season
Part III: for Sundays and principal feasts
Part IV: for Advent
Part V: for the Christmas season

	Part I	Part II	Part III	Part IV	Part V
Compline	1	8	8	13	15
Matins	2	9	9	14	15
Prime	3	3	3	3	15
Terce	4	9	10	10	15
Sext	5	9	11	11	15
None	6	9	12	12	15
Vespers	7	7	7	7	15

I have been using the word *psalms* without distinguishing Francis' psalms from the 150 psalms found in the Hebrew Scriptures. The psalms that compose this office do not correspond to any psalm in the Hebrew Scriptures. Rather, they are collages that take bits and pieces from various psalms, canticles, other biblical passages, and liturgical prayers to make a new composition. Walter Viviani calls the result a "biblical concentration." He defines a biblical concentration as the total result of the diverse scriptural recollections with which Francis wanted to express a specific idea. These concentrations need to be seen as a *whole* to express an idea. As with a collage, the composite image is of importance. Each individual piece is important only as it contributes to the composite image (Viviani 109).

This dynamic is very visible when studying these "psalms" that Francis composed for *The Office of the Passion*. Each verse is strategically chosen to help the user penetrate the event of the passion associated with its particular hour in the office. This utilizes the common Christian medieval idea that the Hebrew psalms prefigure Christ to the degree of sometimes being considered primarily about him. Thus, the parts of the story that make up Jesus' passion can be found within the various lines of the Hebrew psalms. Francis weaves verses often from diverse psalms into a single unit in order to better enter into the story of that particular hour.

Other examples of this method can be found in other writings by Francis: *The Exhortation to the Praise of God, The Earlier Rule* V 9–12 (on minority), *The Earlier Rule* XVI: 10–21 (on persecution), the first version of the *Letter to the Faithful* I 14–19 and the second version of the same letter 56–60 (concerning God's care for those who do penance).

Finally, I wish to emphasize that Francis did not intend this devotional office to replace the official Liturgy of the Hours. Francis prayed it in addition to the official office. We have no idea how often Francis or anyone else celebrated this office. Dominique Gagnan mentions twice in his article that Francis prayed this office daily (1 and 52). He gives no source for this statement. While Francis was devoted to the passion of Jesus, I am aware of no evidence to indicate he prayed this office on a daily or even frequent basis.

Starter questions and suggestions

Begin by reading the introduction to *The Office of the Passion* (FA:ED I 139). Skim through the office itself, paying attention to the antiphon and prayer, and reading the footnotes, which explain some of the structure of the office. Next read the introductions and texts of *The Prayer Inspired by the Our Father* (FA:ED I 158–160) and *The Praises To Be Said at All the Hours* (FA:ED I 161–162). In all cases, pay attention to the biblical and liturgical sources for the various parts of these writings. Finally, if you can locate a copy of Gallant and Cirino's *The Geste of the Great King*, read as much of it as you can to understand the spirituality and mechanics of *The Office of the Passion*.

I next suggest that you explore the biblical concentrations of some of the psalms that Francis composed. Psalms 1, 2, 4, 5, and 6 are good examples with which to begin since they correspond to the five-part story rhythm of this office each day. Taking as many pages of clean paper as necessary, fold them into two side-by-side columns. At the top of the page, list the number of the psalm and the part of the passion story it narrates, i.e., psalm one—arrest on the Mt. of Olives, psalm two—trial before the Sanhedrin, psalm four—trial before Pilate, psalm five—crucifixion, or psalm six—Jesus' death. In the left column, write out Francis' psalm leaving space between each verse. In the right column, write every image, analogy, and implication that each psalm verse suggests about the related moment in Jesus' passion and death. Pay particular attention to the movement in Francis' psalms from a symbolic description of the historical moment and the human feelings associated with it to an expression of hope and trust that victory is sure for the one who does the desire of the Father. Finally, pull back from the individual verses of the psalm and describe their overall accumulative effect. Repeat this exercise for as many psalms as possible.

If you are making a presentation about *The Office of the Passion* to a group of fellow students, provide them with a summary of the spirituality and theology that undergirds the office. Then work through one of the psalms with the entire group as I suggest in the previous paragraph.

Finally, I suggest that you pray a few of the hours to experience them as intended by Francis. Gallant and Cirino's book will make this easy. Like them, I suggest that you use the simple *Our Father* and not *The Prayer Inspired by the Our Father*. I find that praying all seven hours for about a week allows me to experience the focused effect of the devotion in a way that only cursory use does not. Also, prolonged use of this devotional office allows Francis' spiritual intuitions about Christ to better penetrate one's spirituality.

Suggested reading and sources cited

- Constable, Giles. "The Ideal of the Imitation of Christ." *Three Studies in Medieval Religious and Social Thought*. Cambridge: The University Press, 1995.
- Delio, Ilia. *Franciscan Prayer*. Cincinnati OH: St. Anthony Messenger Press, 2004. While not specifically aimed at *The Office of the Passion*, Delio's book offers a general overview of Franciscan prayer that has many connections to *The Office*.
- Dolan, Gerald M. "Words of Hope in Troubled Times: Francis of Assisi in the Presence of the Mystery of the Trinity." *In Solitude and Dialogue: Contemporary Franciscans Theologize*. Ed. Anthony M. Carrozzo. St. Bonaventure NY: The Franciscan Institute, 2000. 9–45.
- Doyle, Eric, and Damian McElrath. "St. Francis of Assisi and the Christocentric Character of Franciscan Life and Doctrine." *Franciscan Christology*. Ed. Damian McElrath. St. Bonaventure NY: Franciscan Institute Publications, 1980. 1–13.

- Gagnan, Dominique. "*The Office of the Passion*: The Daily Prayer of St. Francis of Assisi." Trans. Sergius Wroblewski. *Greyfriars Review* 7.supplement (1993) 1–89. An excellent work on the spirituality of *The Office of the Passion.*
- Gallant, Laurent and André Cirino. *The Geste of the Great King: Office of the Passion of Francis of Assisi*. St. Bonaventure NY: The Franciscan Institute, 2001.
- Matura, Thaddée. *Francis of Assisi: The Message in His Writings*. Trans. Paul Barrett. St. Bonaventure NY: Franciscan Institute Publications, 1997. A shorter more popular treatment of Francis' Christology than Nguyên-Van-Khanh's.
- Nguyên-Van-Khanh, Norbert. *The Teacher of His Heart: Jesus Christ in the Thought and Writings of St. Francis*. Trans. Ed Hagman. Eds. Louise Hembrecht and Bernard Creighton. St. Bonaventure NY: The Franciscan Institute, 1994. The best book-length study of Francis' Christology in English.
- Nguyên Van Si, Ambroise. "The Theology of the Imitation of Christ According to St. Bonaventure." *Greyfriars Review* 11.supplement (1997) I–181.
- Schmucki, Octavian. "The Passion of Christ in the Life of St. Francis of Assisi: A Comparative Study of the Sources in the Light of Devotion to the Passion Practiced in His Time." *Greyfriars Review* 4.supplement (1990) 1–101.
- Seubert, Xavier John. "The Cross and Death of Jesus: A Franciscan Interpretation." *In Solitude and Dialogue: Contemporary Franciscans Theologize*. Ed. Anthony M. Carrozzo. St. Bonaventure NY: The Franciscan Institute, 2000. 155–169.
- Viviani, Walter. *L'ermeneutica di Francesco d'Assisi: Indagine alla luce de Gv 13–17 nei suoi scritti.* Roma: Editrice Antonianum, 1983.
- Any commentary on the passion narrative as found in *The Gospel according to John*.

Francis' Eucharistic Writings

Sources

1LtCus
2LtCus
2LtCl
LtR
LtOrd
ER XX
Adm I, XXVI
1LtF
2LtF
Test 13
1C 46b–c
LJS 27b–28
AP 37e, 40b
AC 60 (LP 18)
2C 201
OfP Antiphon (FA:ED I 141) [compare to 1LtF and 2LtF regarding Mary's relationship]
Fourth Lateran Council, canons 17, 19–21 (see worksheet on the council)
Sane cum olim (See worksheet on the Fourth Lateran Council. An English translation is found at FA:ED I 55, note a).

Starter questions and suggestions (Please follow in order)

1. Read 1LtCus, 2LtCus, and 2LtCl. Write down their major ideas about eucharist. Read the summaries of canons 17, 19–21, and *Sane cum olim* in the worksheet on the Fourth Lateran Council. Note on your list of ideas those that are directly related to the four relevant canons of the council. Remember that the Fourth Lateran Council occurred in 1215. These three letters and *Sane cum olim* were written in 1219. Note themes that recur in Francis' three letters.

2. Now look at LtR (also 1219). Outline its major ideas, even those not related to eucharist. Which ideas are being linked in this letter? Try to divide the content of the letter into *pre-dispositions* that lead up to a conclusion (therefore…) in the letter. How and why is eucharist included in this letter? What is the central idea of the letter? Does this central idea of the letter surprise you?

3. Next, look at LtOrd (1225–1226). Note that it was written much later. Begin by listing in order the major ideas of the letter. Again, after you have listed the ideas, go back and note on your list those ideas that are directly related to the Fourth Lateran Council and *Sane cum olim*.

4. Read the remaining sources. List the ideas about eucharist like you did for the previous sources.

5. This point should be the main focus of your study of Francis' eucharistic writings. Reviewing all your notes, try to organize the thought of Francis about eucharist into a comprehensive schema rather than individual writings. First, identify and list principles of Francis' eucharistic approach. These principles can usually be expressed as basic beliefs Francis held about eucharist. Next, list practices that flow from Francis' eucharistic principles and that he encourages. Any conclusion that encourages *action* is a *practice*. Conclusions that indicate a *belief* without action are *principles*. (I find five principles and eight practices. But you may organize things differently.) Elaborate on each of the principles and practices after composing your lists.

6. After you have completed your schema, ask yourself how Francis reflected the eucharistic theology and practices of his day, especially as expressed in the Fourth Lateran Council and *Sane cum olim*. How does the eucharistic context of Francis' day compare to the context in our day? How does this affect the way we might approach modern Franciscan spirituality regarding eucharist? What in Francis' approach is lasting; what is time bound? Are there other lessons to be learned from Francis here? I like to think of Francis as a *conciliar man*, one who embraced the movement of the Spirit in the major ecumenical council of his day. What might this mean? What might it mean as we develop our modern eucharistic spirituality?

7. To continue the line of inquiry suggested in point six, I recommend that you read basic texts about eucharist in the post-Vatican II era. Better yet, attend classes or lectures on the topic. If Francis was a person of his council (Fourth Lateran Council), shouldn't we who follow him be people of our council (Second Vatican Council)? The basic liturgical documents of Vatican II and the documents of implementation that followed the council can be found in the bibliography below.

Commentary

I strongly recommend that you attempt to come up with your own list of principles and practices before looking too closely at my lists. In an article published in *The New Round Table*, I wrote down my own analysis of Francis' eucharistic writings. In that article, I identified five principles and eight practices in this way:

Principles

1. Eucharist is the only way we see Christ.
2. Without priesthood there is no eucharist.
3. Eucharist is essential to a life of penance and salvation.
4. Authentic eucharistic participation requires a proper disposition.
5. Eucharist is an encounter with the humility of Christ.

Practices

1. Proper reservation of eucharistic bread and the word.
2. Proper care of vessels and buildings used for eucharist.
3. Kneel at the consecration and during eucharistic processions.
4. Give priests unwavering respect.
5. Priests should live in ways consistent with their ministry.
6. The confession of sins.
7. Always admonish people to a life of penance.
8. Only one Mass celebrated daily in the houses of the brothers.

Francis' principles and practices very much reflect the eucharistic theology and devotion of his day. In many ways, he was a man of his council, the Fourth Lateran Council, which said so much about eucharist. We live in another time and need to be people of our council, the Second Vatican Council. It too has said much about eucharist and the church that celebrates eucharist. It is helpful to try to compare and contrast these two moments in the life of our church and discern how best to bring into our own time and place the spiritual insights of Francis coming out of his time and place. Many works cited in the following bibliography can help us do that.

Suggested reading

- Bynum, Caroline Walker. *Holy Feast and Holy Fast: The Religious Significance of Food to Medieval Women.* Berkeley and Los Angeles: University of California Press, 1987. See especially chapter two.
- Beltrame, Pedro. "La Eucharistia en la Vida de los Hermanos Menores: Carta a Toda la Orden." *Quadernos Franciscanos* 20 (1987) 69–80.
- Delio, Ilia. "Francis and the Body of Christ." *The Cord* 53.1 (2003) 26–35.

- Doyle, Eric, and Damian McElrath. "St. Francis of Assisi and the Christocentric Character of Franciscan Life and Doctrine." *Franciscan Christology*. Ed. Damian McElrath. St. Bonaventure NY: Franciscan Institute Publications, 1980, 1–13.
- Duffy, Regis A. " 'Hold Back Nothing of Yourselves': Contexts for a Franciscan Theology of the Eucharist." *In Solitude and Dialogue: Contemporary Franciscans Theologize*. Ed. Anthony M. Carrozzo. St. Bonaventure NY: The Franciscan Institute, 2000. 101–123.
- *Eucharisticum mysterium* [Instruction on the Worship of the Eucharistic Mystery]. Congregation of Rites. 25 May 1967. *Documents of Vatican II*. Rev. ed. Ed. Austin Flannery. Grand Rapids: Eerdmans, 1984. 100–136.
- Foley, Edward. "Franciscan Liturgical Prayer." *Franciscans at Prayer*. Ed. Timothy Johnson. The Medieval Franciscans 4. Gen. Ed. Steven McMichael. Leiden: Brill, 2007. While Foley's article addresses many aspects of Franciscan prayer, it begins with a large section on eucharist in the life of the early friars.
- Gerken, Alexander. "Historical Background of the New Direction in Eucharistic Doctrine." *Theology Digest* 21 (1973) 46–53. A translation and digest of "Dogmengeschichtliche Reflexion über die heutige Wende in der Eucharistielehre." *Zeitschrift für Katholische Theologie* 94 (1972) 199–226.
- Hoeberichts, Jan. "Francis' Letter to All the Brothers (Letter to the Entire Order): Title, Theme, Structure and Language." *Collectanea Franciscana* 78.1–2 (2008)5–85. Noting that many authors consider the central theme of this letter to be the eucharist, Hoeberichts explores alternative central themes.
- Hugo, William. "The Eucharistic Writings of Francis of Assisi." *The New Round Table* 41 (1988) 62–80.
- Jungmann, Josef. *The Mass of the Roman Rite: Its Origins and Development*. Trans. Francis Brunner. 2 vols. New York: Benzinger, 1951, 1954.
- *Liturgiae instaurationes* [Third Instruction on the Correct Implementation of the Constitution on the Sacred Liturgy]. Congregation for Divine Worship. 5 September 1970. *Documents of Vatican II*. Rev. ed. Ed. Austin Flannery. Grand Rapids: Eerdmans, 1984. 209–221.
- *Lumen gentium* [Dogmatic Constitution on the Church]. 21 November 1964. *Documents of Vatican II*. Rev. ed. Ed. Austin Flannery. Grand Rapids: Eerdmans, 1984. 350–423.

- Macy, Gary. *Treasures from the Storeroom: Medieval Religion and the Eucharist*. Collegeville: The Liturgical Press, 1999. Brilliant.
- Moloney, Raymond. "Eucharist." *The New Dictionary of Theology*. Eds. Joseph Komonchak et al. Wilmington DE: Glazier, 1987. 342–355.
- Rubin, Miri. *Corpus Christi: The Eucharist in Late Medieval Culture*. Cambridge: Cambridge University Press, 1991.
- *Sacrosanctum concilium* [The Constitution on the Sacred Liturgy]. 4 December 1963. *Documents of Vatican II*. Rev. ed. Ed. Austin Flannery. Grand Rapids: Eerdmans, 1984. 1–40.
- Schmucki, Ottaviano. "St. Francis's Letter to the Entire Order." Trans. Ignatius McCormick. *Greyfriars Review* 3.1 (1989) 1–33.
- Schroeder, H.J., ed. *Disciplinary Decrees of the General Councils*. St. Louis: Herder and Herder, 1937.
- Smits, Kenneth. "Franciscan Living: An Ecology of Prayer, Community, and Ministry." *The New Round Table* 37 (1984) 73–108.
- Tanner, Norman P., ed. *Decrees of the Ecumenical Councils*. Washington D.C.: Georgetown University Press; London: Sheed & Ward, 1990. 2 vols.
- Van Dijk, Stephan. "The Liturgical Legislation of the Franciscan Rules." *Franciscan Studies* 12 (1952) 176–195, 241–262.
- Van Dijk, S.J.P. and J. Hazelden Walker. *The Origins of the Modern Roman Liturgy: The Liturgy of the Papal Court and the Franciscan Order in the Thirteenth Century*. Westminster, MD: Newman, 1960.

The Development of the First Order Rule

Studying the development of the First Order Rule is one of the most exciting and enlightening ventures of Franciscan studies. It causes us to reassess our preconceived notions of how clear Francis and the early friars really were about their new form of life. At the conclusion of this study, we can see the organic nature of developing Franciscan life. Finally, we come to realize that Francis was a partner with his brothers, not an autocrat, as they wrote *their* rule.

Let me begin by clarifying whose rule this section is about. The First Order of Franciscans was and is composed of men who follow Francis through a celibate and community life style. Today, the First Order has three branches: the Friars Minor (OFM), the Conventuals (OFM Conv.), and the Capuchins (OFM Cap.). The Second Order of Franciscans is made of women who follow Clare of Assisi in her celibate and cloistered Franciscan way of life. The Poor Clares, Colletines, and Capuchinesses are some of the modern groups in the Second Order.

The Third Order of Franciscans was originally composed of lay and secular people, many of whom married, but some of whom were celibates. Eventually, some priests also joined this order. The attractiveness of this lifestyle was its union of Franciscan values to the everyday experiences of ordinary believers. With time, this order took two forms. The Third Order Seculars or Secular Franciscans remained predominantly lay and secular as the original members, while the Third Order Regulars took on many of the "religious" characteristics of the first two orders like celibacy and community living. The TORs are an example of a men's Third Order Regular group. Almost 200 American religious orders of Franciscan women that are outwardly ministering as health care workers, teachers, parish ministers, or social ministers are also Third Order Regular groups. Most Franciscan sisters in North America are members of a Third Order Regular group.

This is a study of the First Order's rule. It was never intended to apply to the Second or Third Orders.

This study of the rule spans the years from 1208 through 1226. It does not approach the subject as if there were multiple rules. My assumption is that there is a single First Order rule that organically developed for fifteen years. We are able to discern *glimpses* of that rule at various points of its development. The following is a timeline that highlights important events in this process.

The Development of the Rule of the Friars Minor

1208	1209/1210	1215	1217	1221	1223	1226
Francis hears a Gospel honoring the apostles ——— Bernard of Quintavalle joins Francis	*The Primitive Rule* is approved by Innocent III	Fourth Lateran Council	Chapters begin at the Portiuncula	*The Earlier Rule*	The lost rule of 1223 & *The Later Rule* is approved by Honorius III	*The Testament*

The First Glimpse: Francis Hears a Gospel Honoring the Apostles (1208)

Sources

1C 22
LJS 15
L3C 25
LMj III 1
Matt. 10:7–14 (Parallels are found in Mark 6:8–11 and Luke 9:1–5; missionary discourse to the twelve).
Luke 10:1–16 (missionary discourse to seventy-two disciples)

Starter questions and suggestions

We looked at these sources earlier when we examined Francis' reception of his call to the apostolic life. Our concerns here are different. The purpose of reexamining these texts is to discover a *pattern* of ritual actions that clarifies the meaning of the text from the Gospel. Can you find that pattern? If you find a pattern, does it suggest anything about the role of Matt. 10:7–12 in Francis' new life?

Commentary

I find a four-point pattern:

1. Francis heard a text (Matt. 10:7–12 or one of its parallels).
2. He assented to that text ("This is what I wish, this is what I seek, this is what I long to do with all my heart.").
3. He changed clothing as a sign of his commitment.
4. He lived out what he promised.

This pattern was identical to that of a person making profession in a religious order:

1. reading, hearing, and studying a text (i.e., the rule and/or constitutions of the particular order);
2. assenting to that text with a vow formula;
3. putting on a religious habit of profession;
4. living according to the rule and constitutions.

This pattern continues today with the exception that, in religious communities in which members no longer wear habits, a different object (e.g., cross, tau, pin) often becomes the symbol of profession.

This ritual pattern is important because it indicates that this single text from the Gospel expressed the way of life Francis intended to live. As such, it represents the beginning of his rule. Some may be amazed by my conclusion. After all, rules for religious orders were longer and more comprehensive. The Franciscan rule eventually became more so. However, it had clear moments of development and is distinguished by its organic growth. As a frequently changing document, this moment represents its uncomplicated and insufficient beginning. It is only a beginning, but it *is* the beginning.

Of equal importance is that this text is one of the apostolic texts favored by the traveling lay preachers of Francis' day. See my previous chapter, "The Apostolic Life Movement," to review why the Apostolic Life Movement and these texts are so important to understanding Francis and his rule.

By assenting to this biblical text as his rule, Francis placed himself in a new tradition of medieval ministry and at the beginning of a new form of religious life called the mendicant orders.

The Second Glimpse: Bernard of Quintavalle Joins Francis (1208)

Sources

1C 24
AP 10–12
L3C 27–29
2C 15, 109
LMj III 3
DBF I 10–46
LFl 2
Mark 10:17–22 (Parallels are found in Matt. 19:16–22 and Luke 18:18–23.)
Luke 9:1–6
Matt. 16:24-28 (Parallels are found in Mark 8:34–38 and Luke 9:23–27.)

Starter questions and suggestions

Our concern once again is to discern any ritual that may be present and similar to that in the story about Francis. I suggest you place the accounts side by side in chronological order to compare them. Note the differences in details and determine what you believe to be the true account.

Commentary

Many of my students believe I accept too much in this event as historical fact. They often conclude that the ritual pattern discerned in Francis' experience on the feast of an apostle is not historical in Bernard's experience because it is first clearly outlined in *The Anonymous of Perugia* (1240/41). 1C, which clearly portrays the pattern when telling of Francis' experience on the feast honoring an apostle, is less explicit in describing the pattern in Bernard's case. Could the tradition be amplifying Bernard's experience to create clearer parallels between the two men for hagiographic purposes (i.e., to embellish the story making it more marvelous)?

They have a point. However, even if the story of Bernard is not completely reliable as historical fact, the earliest testimony (1C) ties Bernard's commitment to an additional scripture text and notes that he was tied to Francis "by his life and by his habit." All that is missing is the verbal assent to the texts. This *ritual* deficiency is supplied in the tradition by *The Anonymous of Perugia*, which portrays Bernard using the same words as Francis.

Thus the same four point ritual commitment occurs in Bernard's case:

1. a text being presented (one to three gospel texts);
2. verbal assent to the text beginning in AP;
3. changing clothes to signify the change;
4. living according to the text.

Given this pattern, we see the rule expanding from a single text in Francis' experience to an additional three in Bernard's. Furthermore, all three texts added through the Bernard episode are also *apostolic texts*, further tying the early Franciscan movement to other lay apostolic movements of the day.

The Third Glimpse: Approval of The Primitive Rule by Innocent III (1209/10)

Sources

Test 14–15
1C 32–33
LJS 21
AP 31–36
L3C 46–53
2C 16–17
LMj III 8
LMn II 4–5
Jordan 15

Starter questions and suggestions

Again, we have looked at these sources before. Our concern this time is to create a description of *The Primitive Rule*. We have only a description of this version of the rule because the text itself is lost. Perhaps someone someday will find a copy on a dusty shelf of an old European library. It would be the Franciscan find of the century! Until that day, we must be satisfied with the description of *The Primitive Rule* found in the various medieval biographies.

Using data from these sources, compose your description of *The Primitive Rule*.

Commentary

The sources give the following description of *The Primitive Rule*:

1. short;
2. simple;
3. composed mostly of gospel texts;
4. containing a few other things for a holy life, including:
   a. the promise of Francis and his successors to be obedient to Innocent III and his successors;
   b. the promise of the brothers to be obedient to Francis and his successors;
   c. permission from the pope for the brothers to preach.

Although the texts do not mention it, it seems reasonable to assume that *The Primitive Rule* also contained some directives regarding entrance into the new group. Every group needs some norms or procedures for entrance.

Because this version of the rule occurs very early in the order's history, most Franciscan scholars assume the text would be very positive in tone. It probably was very idealistic and promoted the core values of Francis and the group's original inspiration. This would seem further substantiated by the fact that numerous church officials, including Innocent III, wondered if the rule was too severe.

Development between the Third and Fourth Glimpses (1209 to 1221)

Sources

The Admonitions (regarding *The Admonitions*, read: 1C 82, AP 37, and L3C 57–59)
A Letter to the Entire Order
A Letter to a Minister (especially 13–22)

Certain canons of the Fourth Lateran Council (1215) (See my previous chapter by the same name.)
Jacques de Vitry, *Letter I,* FA:ED I 580
Jacques de Vitry, *Historia Occidentalis* 9, (FA:ED I 583)
Cum dilecti filii (1219) (FA:ED I 558)
Pro dilectis filiis (1220) (FA:ED I 559–560)
Cum secundum consilium (1220) (FA:ED I 560–561)
Fratrum minorum (1223) (summary in my chapter "The Fourth Lateran Council")
1C 38, 84
AP 18, 37–40a, 43
L3C 35c–d, 57–60
2C 66,128,143,176
Jordan of Giano 10–15

Starter questions, suggestions, and additional information

The purpose of this section is to learn of the dynamic growth of the rule that occurred between 1209 and 1221. Each of these sources in some way testifies to this growth.

Begin by looking at *The Admonitions.* First, read the references about *The Admonitions* listed above. These references describe how Francis often addressed the brothers, especially during chapters.

Second, read the introduction to *The Admonitions* found in *Francis and Clare: The Complete Works* on page 25, or FA:ED I 128. They give some valuable information about the composition of *The Admonitions.*

It is helpful to keep in mind that *The Admonitions* are undated. They seem to be sayings of Francis that were collected by an unknown person or group of people at various points in Francis' life. Many Franciscan scholars suppose many of them originated during chapters, which began in 1217. They reflect and confirm Francis' general spirituality and enjoy a solid presence in the manuscript tradition. While some noted authors and scholars offer models of organization for *The Admonitions,* I personally am hard pressed to see a viable organizing principle among them. I simply conclude that they are various sayings of Francis, randomly gathered and assembled for the most part. Robert Karris' study, listed in the chapter "The Admonitions," makes the most convincing argument for some form of order.

Before moving on, read *The Admonitions* themselves. You will find many of their ideas and even expressions present in *The Earlier Rule,* which we will study later.

Next, read the other sources listed above. They provide descriptions of various general chapters (meetings of the international order), which began in 1217, and give us an idea of how they proceeded. The purpose of reading them is to gain appreciation for the banter and confusion that were part of chapters as well as the processes by which decisions were made. Since changes to the rule were discussed at chapters, this overall picture of chapters gives us insight into the development of the rule.

Often, students are uncertain why I am giving these particular citations. Because of this, I wish to note some of the more important pieces of information we learn from the sources.

A Letter to a Minister is particularly revealing about how experience and problems in the order helped shape the rule. This letter reveals a minister distraught over dealing with a friar who has fallen into sin. Francis proposed a solution and stated that he intended to bring the policy to the next chapter for inclusion in the rule. The letter testifies to the fact that Francis did not change the rule at will, but sought the approval of friars gathered in chapter.

The canons of the Fourth Lateran Council and the various listed papal bulls help our study in two ways. First, they raise numerous issues concerning the universal church to which the friars had to respond. After all, they were part of the church and had to adjust to what was going on in the church.

Secondly, the papal bulls testify to intense hostility toward the friars from some bishops and other church officials. Part of the resistance was related to the perception that the Franciscans were not good Catholics, or possibly even heretics.

It is important to realize that medievals considered many more people than those who denied church dogma as heretics. Those who challenged the authority of church officials or ignored church law could also be branded heretics. Some of the wandering lay preachers of the day were considered heretics for doctrinal reasons; others, because they criticized church leadership or practices. The Franciscans often *looked* like these "heretics" since they too wandered across the countryside, lived poorly, preached to whomever would listen, and *appeared* to have no legitimate church superior. Bishops and priests, much less the uneducated laity, often could not distinguish between the "heretics" and this new religious order of Friars Minor. This was a public relations problem for the Franciscans. The fact that the pope often needed to defend the friars in writing indicates that the friars had huge credibility problems. See the previous chapter entitled "The Fourth Lateran Council (1215) and Subsequent Papal Bulls" for an outline of each document. Some can be found in translation in FA:ED I.

1C 38 indicates that the name for the Franciscans found in late versions of the rule goes back to the time shortly after Francis and the eleven returned from Rome. Paragraph 84 confirms Francis' intention to follow the Gospel, which became the core and opening lines of *The Earlier Rule* and *The Later Rule*.

The Anonymous of Perugia 18 confirms that the friars worried about not having educated members. The concern would seem to be in response to canons 10, 11, and 27 of the Fourth Lateran Council, which sought to improve preaching in the church by requiring trained preachers. This challenge represented a crisis for the young order that envisioned all of its members as preachers from the beginning. It seemed the church would restrict who could preach and, thus, change the nature of the order. Paragraphs 37–40a confirm numerous data about early chapters: Francis supported them; early chapters were held at the Portiuncula; the members discussed how to observe the rule better; Francis gave admonitions, reprimands, and prescriptions there; and preachers were appointed in each province.

The Legend of the Three Companions 57–60 confirms much of the same data. It also confirms that a second annual chapter was held in September near the Feast of Michael the Archangel; that friars were assigned to provinces during the chapters; and that lay friars, not only cleric friars, were appointed as preachers.

Celano's *The Remembrance* simply gives testimony that *The Earlier Rule* was functioning in the lives of the friars. Paragraph 66 portrays a brother quoting ER VIII 6 about trampling on coins. The admonitions in ER VII 16 to be joyful and not sad hypocrites is mentioned in 2C 128. Paragraph 143 highlights the responsibility of ministers for friars who fall into sin, as discussed in chapters four to six of the ER. Finally, the admonition in ER X 3–4 that sick brothers be patient is quoted in 2C 176.

Jordan of Giano documents Francis' visit to Syria, Palestine, and Egypt (1219–1220). During this time, Francis left Matthew of Narni and Gregory of Naples in charge of the order. During Francis' absence, the two vicars intensified the rule's regulations about fasting and abstinence. Individual friars began to seek papal privileges for their personal ministries. Francis returned to correct the situation. What is important throughout is to observe that Matthew, Gregory and Francis all worked through chapters to make their desired changes, testifying to the group process that developed the rule.

The Fourth Glimpse: The Earlier Rule (1221)

Source: The Earlier Rule

Starter suggestions

Scholars study *The Earlier Rule* from a variety of perspectives. I prefer a historical approach and believe such an approach establishes a firm foundation for a later theological or spiritual approach. Before I lead you through a historical study, read *The Earlier Rule* in its entirety to gain an overall familiarity with the text. Do that now.

Now that you have read the text at least once, we can turn our attention to the historical development of the rule. I have already mentioned that all scholars agree the Franciscan rule was a dynamic document that developed with time. The last section cited sources that verified that development and highlighted major church events that influenced the content of the developing rule.

The fact that scholars view the Franciscan rule as a single document with multiple moments at which we can view it has led many of them to assume that *The Primitive Rule* (1209/10) is buried somewhere within the rambling *Earlier Rule* (1221). The following works in English can help you understand this perspective.

- Hardick, Lothar, et al. *The Marrow of the Gospel: A Study of the Rule of Saint Francis of Assisi.* Trans. Ignatius Brady. Chicago: Franciscan Herald Press, 1958. 11–30.
- Flood, David, and Thadée Matura. *The Birth of a Movement: A Study of the First Rule of St. Francis.* Trans. Paul Schwartz and Paul Lachance. Chicago: Franciscan Herald Press, 1975. 3–56.
- ____. "The Early Writings." *The Cord* 60.3 (2010)329–338. This short work corrects a common misperception that Francis wrote the *Earlier Rule* upon his return from the Middle East, insisting that the *Earlier Rule* is a testimony to the ongoing development of the rule.
- Cuthbert Hess of Brighton. *Life of St. Francis of Assisi.* London: Longmans, 1921. 102–108, 465–476.
- Moorman, John. *Sources for the Life of St. Francis.* Manchester: Manchester University Press, 1940. 38–54.

I have found attempts to uncover *The Primitive Rule* within *The Earlier Rule* to be a very profitable exercise for my students. This practice helps students to better understand the organic nature of the rule as well as to reinforce their awareness of the order's history that contributed to the development of the rule. I recommend that you do the same, either alone or, preferably, with a group. More minds seem to make for a more rewarding study experience.

Let me begin by outlining the methods proposed for this task by two of the authors listed above. Cuthbert of Brighton says we can find *The Primitive Rule* by removing from *The Earlier Rule* the following elements:

1. All information that reflects the work of chapters (gatherings of friars to discuss observance of and changes to the rule, and to make appoint-

ments), which first began in 1217, well after the composition of *The Primitive Rule*.

2. All material reflecting papal injunctions occurring after 1209/10 and the decrees of the Fourth Lateran Council (1215).
3. All material that reflects situations not possible in 1209/1210. This would include material addressing juridical mandates or prophetic warnings.
4. All material reflecting the existence of ministers, provinces, or many clerics in the order. These were all realities that develop after *The Primitive Rule*.
5. All passages that presume the friars were widely scattered throughout Europe, the Middle East, or Northern Africa. At the time of *The Primitive Rule,* the friars rarely left the Italian province of Umbria in which Assisi is located.

Cuthbert assumes that the bulk of material left after removing that mentioned in points one through five will roughly approximate the content of *The Primitive Rule.*

David Flood outlines six elements he believes constituted the work we today call *The Earlier Rule*:

1. *The Primitive Rule* of 1209/1210;
2. Negative insertions responding to later experience;
3. Elaborations and clarifications responding to later experience;
   Flood believes these three elements comprised chapters one through seventeen of *The Earlier Rule* as we have the text today and were the parts of the document that ruled or guided the friars' life. He holds that the remaining three elements were tacked on to the first three to form *The Earlier Rule* as we find it in the manuscript tradition today.
4. A section reflecting relevant legislation from the Fourth Lateran Council (chapters 18–20);
5. Several independent texts that were sources of inspiration for the friars (chapters 21–23);
6. A letter of presentation that was tacked onto the end of the document in the manuscript tradition (chapter 24).

So that we can do the exercise of finding *The Primitive Rule* within *The Earlier Rule*, we can reorient Flood's list by saying that if we remove all the elements found in points two through six from *The Earlier Rule*, we will roughly be left with what originally constituted *The Primitive Rule*.

I would like to offer my own observation that scripture texts that appear to have a proof-texting purpose (support role for a previous statement) and that do not reflect the popular scriptures of the lay apostolic movement, which were part of the earliest development of the rule in 1208, should be likewise removed.

In the final analysis, I need to offer a precaution. It is easier to say which specifics were not part of *The Primitive Rule* than to say what was definitely part of it. Despite that warning, I still encourage you to engage in the exercise for the positive benefits I mentioned above.

I propose that your group proceed in this manner. Have a different member of your group slowly read each chapter of *The Earlier Rule*. Whenever a member of the study group believes he or she can identify something that must be or probably is of a later origin than 1209/1210, he or she should stop the reader, make the claim, and give a reason for the claim. As you read, pay careful attention to the footnotes. If you are ambitious, you may want someone to follow along in Flood, Moorman or Cuthbert's books to see how they assess things and if they provide additional data that might be helpful to you. As the leader of my groups, I have done this in advance and provide the information, as it may be helpful. This allows group members to concentrate on the text of *The Earlier Rule* itself.

I list below some points and guidelines that might be helpful in your study. I think it would be best if the group's leader were most aware of these points so that the group members can focus on the text itself. The leader can bring up these points as the group touches the relevant areas in *The Earlier Rule*.

1. The Sign of the Cross and the shorter formula, *in nomine domini* (in the name of the Lord), were common, popular ways to begin medieval church documents. In the opening of the prologue, its presence is normal. However, the use of this opening in ER IV 1 and XXIV 1 reveals that what follows was once part of an independent document that was later introduced into the current text. See the beginning of the first version of the *Letter to the Faithful* for another example of the phrase *in nomine domini*. The second version uses the longer version of the Sign of the Cross.

2. Pope Innocent III died in 1216. So the use of his name in the prologue indicates it was written before then. More probably, I suspect Roman officials added the prologue in some form during the visit that led to the approval of *The Primitive Rule* (1209/1210).

3. The evidence suggests that scripture quotes that were popular with lay apostolic groups are most likely part of *The Primitive Rule*. Four of these texts were already part of the rule after Francis heard the gospel on the feast honoring an apostle and Bernard of Quintavalle joined Francis

(1208). Other scriptures, especially if they are used to support positions of the rule, could well have been added close to 1221 when Caesar of Speyer was asked to embellish the rule with scripture (see Jordan 15).

4. Any talk of ministers, custodes (or custodians), custodies, provinces, or missionary activity should be dated after *The Primitive Rule* and probably after 1217.
5. Before the papal bull *Cum secundum concilium* (1220) a year of probation (novitiate) was not required of new entrants to religious orders.
6. Keep your eyes on the lookout for *layers* of development within the text. For instance, ER II 4 states that entrants should sell all their possessions and strive to give all the proceeds to the poor. The parenthetical comment, "if he wishes and is capable of doing so spiritually without any difficulty," appears to be a clarification added later because of experience. A possible example of such an impediment could have been the moral obligation of an entrant to care for aging or sick parents. This clarification would seem to allow entrants to give their worldly belongings to such needy parents. Verse 11 even further clarifies that if giving everything away to the poor is impossible, it suffices for the entrant to simply leave all material things behind. The text shows three levels of development intended to clarify the issue.

   Another example in the same chapter begins with verse two where the friars are admonished not to become involved in the temporal affairs of the entrants. (It is interesting to note that Francis himself was very involved in the disposition of Bernard of Quintavalle's wealth! See AP 12 and related texts). Verse five reiterates the ban, adding the ministers (not only the brothers in general) to the subject of the prohibition. Verse six further clarifies that money from entrants should not be accepted, either by the brothers or through intermediaries (people who could use the money for the brothers without the brothers themselves violating their rule). Finally, verse seven concludes that the brothers can accept some things from the entrants if the gift fills the bodily needs of the brothers like other poor people and if the gift is not in the form of money. Apparently, the point needed to be made more forcefully at some times and exceptions needed to be clarified at other times. This shows development arising from experience.

   A final example can be found in chapters four and five. ER IV 3–6 states a reciprocal set of responsibilities: brothers are to obey their ministers diligently; ministers are to treat the brothers compassionately, as they themselves would like to be treated. ER V 2 goes on the defense of brothers who have been commanded things that are in violation of their consciences. I am sure that opportunistic friars took advantage of that addition, for ER V 3 further clarifies that the brothers should "*reasonably and diligently* consider the action of the ministers." Once again, three levels of development are visible in the text.

7. No friars are known to have died before approval of *The Primitive Rule*.
8. Looking at many of Francis' writings, we find he often used run-on sentences and started sentences with *and*. While he used this style throughout his writings, it is pervasive in the second section of *The Letter to the Faithful* (either version) and *A Letter to a Minister*. This style is pervasive in chapters nine and eleven of *The Earlier Rule*, which leads me to wonder whether Francis had a direct hand in its composition. Some may think this indicates an early composition, if not back to *The Primitive Rule* itself. However, Francis was involved in the writing of the rule throughout its development. Stylistic evidence of his direct authorship cannot necessarily prove an early composition. However, the content of the writing might provide some clues. If the content is simple and positive in tone, it could be early. Content that appears to be reacting to an important experience is probably later. The scripture in these two sections would seem to reflect the work of Caesar of Speyer.
9. The issue of preaching, raised by the canons of the Fourth Lateran Council, is a delicate one in the rule. Chapter seventeen clearly reflects the provisions of the council document. It is problematic for the friars because their early identity included the charism of preaching by all the brothers, lay as well as cleric. Innocent III seems to have sanctioned this in stories about the approval of *The Primitive Rule*. However, the Fourth Lateran Council required dogmatic preachers to be trained. The concern is heightened in AP 18, which portrays the friars as worried about the lack of learned friars in the order. Francis predicted that learned, prudent and noble men would soon join their ranks in an apparent reference to the new restrictions on preaching issued by the council.
10. Many manuscripts of *The Earlier Rule* include an *Amen* at the end of chapter seventeen, prompting David Flood to speculate this was the end of the legal section of the rule and that the rest of the document represents add-on documents that became part of the manuscript tradition (pp. 39–40). I find his arguments persuasive.
11. Flood holds that chapters eighteen through twenty were a single unit concerning matters of the Fourth Lateran Council, which was added onto the rule. Considering the *Amen* at the end of chapter seventeen, the commonality of material in chapters eighteen through twenty, and the

odd positioning of this material at this point in the document, I find his argument persuasive. Read the text and decide for yourself.

12. Chapter twenty-one also appears to be an add-on. It is a second chapter on preaching. If it were part of the legal rule, it more likely would have been placed next to chapter seventeen. Furthermore, chapter twenty-one issues no legal prescriptions. Rather, it presents a model exhortation that any friar would be capable of delivering, even after the restrictions on preaching issued by the Fourth Lateran Council. This model exhortation is careful to avoid doctrinal topics and simply urges the listener to repentance. The chapter may have been an attempt to recoup part of the group's original identity as an order all of whose members were meant to preach.

13. Chapter twenty-two is more of a meditation than a rule. I believe someone thought this writing of Francis was an important testimony to his spiritual legacy and added it to the document. See Flood's work to examine his theory that chapter twenty-two was a testament written by Francis before going to the Near East.

14. Chapter twenty-three is a prayer of thanksgiving, not a rule. It strikes me as a celebration of the brothers' wonderful vocation and popularity with the people. Again, I believe someone thought this prayer of Francis needed to be preserved and attached it to the rule.

15. Chapter twenty-four appears to be an independent document for several reasons. First, it begins with the *in nomine domini* characteristic of beginning church documents of the time. Second, it talks *about* the rule as if it is not *part* of the rule. Flood believes this chapter was a letter originally presenting the rule. With time, he believes it was placed at the end of the manuscript, a position that eventually was secured by copyists who continued to insert it at the end.

16. When I use this approach with my students, we usually read *The Earlier Rule* in its entirety through chapter twenty-one, allowing anyone to comment as we proceed. I don't continue that practice with the remaining chapters. Rather, I explain some of the theories about these last chapters. Simple visual perusals of these sections make the points evident. For instance, the length of chapter twenty-two indicates it is a different type of literature. FA:ED's presentation of chapter twenty-three in verse form helps one to see that this chapter is a lengthy prayer of thanksgiving. Chapter twenty-four is worth examining in greater detail.

17. After the group has gone through the entire *Earlier Rule*, I usually have the group read John Moorman's reconstruction of *The Primitive Rule*.

The text is found on pages 52–54 of his work *The Sources for the Life of S. Francis of Assisi*. Manchester: Manchester University Press, 1940. After reading the text as a group, critique Moorman's attempt. With what do you agree and disagree as being part of *The Primitive Rule*. What might Moorman have excluded which you would include?

18. I conclude this historical study of *The Earlier Rule* by offering my students the chance to respond to the experience. I try to highlight their experience of seeing the various levels of development in the rule and the way it responded to experience and need. My students seldom need much prodding. The experience makes these and other impressions quite strong.

Suggested reading

- Anderson, C. Colt. "Clerics, Laity and Preaching the Gospel among the Early Franciscans." *Franciscan Evangelization: Striving to Preach the Gospel*. Ed. Elise Saggau. Washington Theological Union Symposium Papers 2007. St. Bonaventure NY: The Franciscan Institute, 2008. Pp.55–77.
- Chinnici, Joseph. "The Impact of Clericalization on Franciscan Evangelization." *Franciscan Evangelization: Striving to Preach the Gospel*. Ed. Elise Saggau. Washington Theological Union Symposium Papers 2007. St. Bonaventure NY: The Franciscan Institute, 2008. Pp.79–122.
- Flood, David. *The Daily Labor of the Early Franciscans*. St. Bonaventure NY: Franciscan Institute Publications, 2010.
- ____. "Franciscans at Work." *Franciscan Studies* 59 (2001) 21–62. A more recent rendition of Flood's ideas about the pivotal chapter seven of *The Earlier Rule*, showing development in the rule on the topic of work and Franciscan identity. A good follow-up to reading *The Birth of a Movement* listed above.
- ____. *Francis of Assisi and the Franciscan Movement*. Quezon City, Philippines: The Franciscan Institute of Asia Contact Publications, 1989. An earlier and longer work than "Franciscans at Work."
- ____. *Work for Every One: Francis of Assisi and the Ethic of Service*. Inter-Franciscan Center, Quezon City, Philippines: The CCFMC Office for Asia/Oceania, 1997. An earlier and longer work than "Franciscans at Work."
- Hoeberichts, J. *Francis and Islam*. Quincy IL: Franciscan Press, 1997. A superb study that uses the sixteenth chapter of *The Earlier Rule* to learn

about Francis' attitude toward Islam, and highlights its marked difference from the approach of Christian Church leadership of his day and Francis' portrayal in hagiography.

The Fifth and Sixth Glimpses: The Later Rule (1223)

Sources

Solet annuere (See the introduction to LR in FA:ED I 99.)
The Later Rule
The Testament
Quo elongati (See the summary found in the earlier chapter "The Fourth Lateran Council (1215).")
AP 44–45
L3C 62
LMj IV 11
Verba (AC 15–20; LP 111–115. See my commentary in the earlier chapter "*The Assisi Compilation* and Its Problems.")
Intentio regulae (AC 101–106; LP 66–77. See my commentary in the earlier chapter "*The Assisi Compilation* and Its Problems.")

Starter questions and suggestions

The story of *The Later Rule* involves two moments: the composition of a rule lost by Elias of Assisi and the composition of the document we today call *The Later Rule.* The events of the story are more important than any differences between the texts of these two moments. In fact, I am aware of no scholar who thinks the texts of these two moments differed in any significant way. The sources listed above support the idea that Francis simply rewrote the text after Elias apparently lost it.

Several aspects of the story create historical intrigue. The first involves Elias of Assisi (Francis' vicar general) representing the other ministers and trying to dissuade Francis from writing a rule difficult for the friars to observe. The account includes a theophany (manifestation of God's intervention), which has a chilling effect on any dissent. You will want to consider the fact that these elements of the story are only found in the Leonine tradition, which would favor a stricter observance. You will also want to consider the forces of hagiography in assessing the historicity of the theophany. Finally, if you conclude that large sections of the story are not true, you need to decide what you believe is true and what impact the truth might have on subsequent followers of Francis, including us.

A second fascinating story is how Elias of Assisi lost the original manuscript of *The Later Rule.* Since the integrity of the text is not an issue, our focus is on the loss and the possible motives of Elias. With its threatening theophany and portrait of a permissive Elias, the Leonine tradition imputes sinister motives to Elias. The other sources don't convey suspicion, but attest that the loss was probably historical. Given the bad end Elias eventually realized in the order, one has to be worried that the sources might be prone to vilify Elias unnecessarily. Elias is a difficult person to know in the sources. There are many concerns and questions that cloud our attempts to know him historically.

Beyond these soap-operaish stories, try to discover why this final version of the rule was written. Why was the development of the rule frozen at this moment? Despite the good reasons for freezing the development of the rule, what dangers or disadvantages do you see in doing this?

Read the text of *The Later Rule*. Compared to *The Earlier Rule*, the changes in style are major and obvious. List the stylistic changes you observe. On another level, can you find any significant changes in the ideas?

Which of the two written forms of the rule (ER or LR) do you prefer? Explain your preference. Describe the benefits and limits of each version.

One Last Review:
The Testament (1226)

Sources

The Testament
Quo elongati (A translation is found in FA:ED I 570–575)

Commentary

From many perspectives, *The Testament* should be allowed to stand on its own as a writing of Francis. However, controversy after its composition thrust it into the debates surrounding the story and content of *The Later Rule*.

After Francis' death, some friars began to approach *The Testament* as if it had the authority of the rule. Though *The Testament* did not present any new ideas not found in the rule, its tone attracted friars who strove for a more primitive observance of the rule. Apparently, *The Testament* became symbolic of that more primitive observance, and many felt it made requirements not found in the rule. In addition, some were arguing that because Franciscan life was focused on Gospel living, the friars were bound to observe all the precepts found in the Gospels, not only those explicitly found in the rule. Without our modern methods for studying scripture, these medieval friars tended to approach the Gospels in a fundamentalist manner. Focusing on passages dealing mostly with poverty, they postulated a more severe life than called for in *The Later Rule*.

Gregory IX addressed these issues in his bull *Quo elongati* (1230). Not all of his decisions resolved the issues that were plaguing the Franciscans. However, he generally assured the integrity of the rule by stating that the friars were only bound to those precepts explicitly found in the rule and that *The Testament* was not a legally binding document on the friars.

Gregory did not settle the issue of *The Testament*'s authority. Some groups within the order continued to consider it binding. Some groups were later chastised for their stubbornness. Centuries later, the Capuchins revisited the issue. They agreed that *The Testament* was not legally binding, but, publishing it with almost every edition of their constitutions through the centuries, they considered it the primary interpretation of the rule.

These issues are very interesting, but go beyond the scope of our study here. The important question is this: What exactly is *The Testament* if it is not a legally binding document?

Francis himself offers the most helpful answer in line 34 of *The Testament* where he clearly states his testament is not another rule, but a "remembrance (*recordatio*), admonition (*admonitio*), exhortation (*exhortatio*), and my testament…." In fact, an examination of the text reveals this is what *The Testament* is. Passages using the past tense are descriptive of the primitive life of the friars, a remembrance. Passages in the present tense admonish and exhort the friars to live up to the inspiration of those early days.

Perhaps the nostalgia and fervency of *The Testament* can be explained by the situation of Francis at its composition. Francis was sick and dying. Undoubtedly, some of what happened in his order discouraged him. He yearned for the good old days, that idealistic vision of the past that often captivates people when experiencing later troubles. He longed for the simplicity of the early days and the purity of vision shared by all the brothers.

Starter questions and suggestions

Begin by reading *The Testament* and noting which parts are a remembrance (*recordatio*), and which are an admonition (*admonitio*) or an exhortation (*exhortatio*). Try to find new ideas, values, or commands not found in the rule. Observe the tone and describe it. List the themes that are prominent. Relate Francis' lack of health to various points of the composition.

Suggested readings

- Mitchell, Daria, ed. *The Rule of the Friars Minor, 1209–2009: Historical Perspectives, Lived Realities*. Spirit and Life: Essays on Contemporary Franciscanism 14. Saint Bonaventure NY: Franciscan Institute Publications, 2010. Contains six articles on the History of the First Order Rule.

The Admonitions

References about The Admonitions

1C 82
AP 37b
L3C 57–59

Starter suggestions

1. Read the references about *The Admonitions.*
2. Read the introduction to *The Admonitions* found in FA:ED I 128–137.
3. Keep in mind the following information about The Admonitions:
   a. they are undated;
   b. were given at various times, often at chapters;
   c. were collected by an unknown person or group;
   d. reflect and confirm Francis' spirituality;
   e. are solidly in the manuscript traditions of Francis' writings;
   f. may or may not have a firm principle of organization.
4. Read *The Admonitions* themselves.

Suggested reading

- Armstrong, Regis J. *St. Francis of Assisi: Writings for a Gospel Life.* New York: Crossroad, 1994. Pages 136–176 present a synthesis of the spirituality found in *The Admonitions.*
- Esser, Cajetan. "Meditations on *The Admonitions* of St. Francis of Assisi." Trans. M. Belane Apel. *Greyfriars Review* 6.supplement (1992) 1–174. These retreat conferences provide reflections on each admonition. This article reflects the fruit of Esser's scholarly work in a non-academic style.
- Hardick, Lothar. *The Admonitions of St. Francis of Assisi.* Chicago: Franciscan Herald Press, 1982.
- Karris, Robert J. *The Admonitions of St. Francis: Sources and Meanings.* St. Bonaventure NY: The Franciscan Institute, 1999. This insightful study is challenging but not beyond a reader with a good general theological education. It might be difficult for an initiate into Franciscan life or a student with little theological background. Karris, who is trained as a biblicist, identifies Francis' patristic and (especially) monastic sources, explaining their common interpretation in his day. Karris then shows how Francis changed the traditional understanding to make his unique

statement. Thus, Karris shows how Francis used the tradition in a way that expressed his originality. The uniqueness of Francis' spiritual intuition is discovered in the process. Highly recommended.

Francis' Three Trips to the Moors

Sources:

General reference
ER XVI

Attempted trip to Syria
1C 55
LJS 34
LMj IX 5

Attempted trip to Morocco
1C 56
LJS 35
3C 34
LMj IX 6

Successful trip to Syria and Egypt
1C 57
LJS 36
2C 30
LMj IX: 7–9
Jordan 10
Jacques de Vitry's Letter #6 (Spring, 1220) found in FA:ED I 580–581.
Jacques de Vitry's *Historia Occidentalis* 14–15 (c. 1221/25) found in FA:ED I 584–585.
Chronicle of Ernoul (1227/1229) found in FA:ED I 605–607.
Chronicle of Bernard the Treasurer 1–3 (1229/1230) found in FA:ED I 608.
The History of the Emperor Eracles (1229/1231) found in FA:ED I 609.
The anonymous *Verba fr. Illuminati* found in Habig 1614–1615.

Starter questions and suggestions

1. Report on each of the trips (or attempted trips) and lay out the facts as much as possible. Where did Francis actually go? When did he do so? Whom did he meet there (if he got there)?
2. Explain Francis' motivation. What role did his desire to be a martyr play? What did Francis hope to prove by martyrdom? To whom did he hope to prove it? How influential were the crusades and the call of the

Fourth Lateran Council for the crusades in Francis' motivation? What was Francis' *personal* goal in making these trips?

3. Focus on the last successful trip to Egypt. What was Francis' relationship with the Christian army? Was he for or against the Christian army? Was Francis for or against the sultan? What was Francis' goal with the sultan? How did the goal of the Christian army differ from that of Francis? Did they differ? When Francis left the sultan, did he support the work of the Christian army? Is Francis portrayed here as a pacifist? Be very careful! Do not read into the sources! What do the *sources* tell us about Francis in this situation!

Suggested reading

- Cusato, Michael F. "Healing the Violence of the Contemporary World: A Franciscan Paradigm for Dialogue with Islam." *Daring to Embrace the Other: Franciscans and Muslims in Dialogue*. Ed. Daria Mitchell. Spirit and Life 12. Saint Bonaventure NY: Franciscan Institute Publications, 2008. 1–37.
- ____. "From Damietta to La Verna: The Impact on Francis of His Experience in Egypt." *Daring to Embrace the Other: Franciscans and Muslims in Dialogue*. Ed. Daria Mitchell. Spirit and Life 12. Saint Bonaventure NY: Franciscan Institute Publications, 2008. 81–112.
- Daniel, E. Randolph. *The Franciscan Concept of Mission in the High Middle Ages.* Lexington, Kentucky: University Press of Kentucky, 1975.
- de Beer, Francis. "St. Francis and Islam." *Francis of Assisi Today*. Eds. Christian Duquoc and Casiano Floristán. New York: Seabury, 1981. 11–20.
- Gallant, Laurent. "Francis of Assisi: Forerunner of Interreligious Dialogue—Chapter 16 of the Earlier Rule Revisited." *Franciscan Studies* 64 (2006) 53–82.
- Hoeberichts, J. *Francis and Islam.* Quincy IL: Franciscan Press, 1997. A superb study that uses the sixteenth chapter of *The Earlier Rule* to learn about Francis' attitude toward Islam, and highlights its marked difference from the approach of Christian Church leadership of his day and Francis' portrayal in hagiography. Highly recommended.
- ____. "Francis's View of Islam in the Mirror of God." *Mirroring One Another, Reflecting the Divine: The Franciscan-Muslim Journey into*

God." Ed. Daria Mitchell. Spirit and Life 13. Saint Bonaventure NY: Franciscan Institute Publications, 2009. 1–38.

- Muir, Fareed Z, "Sultan al-Malik Muhammad al-Kamil and Saint Francis: Interreligious Dialogue and the Meeting at Damietta." *The Cord* 60.3 (2010) 271–288.
- Moses, Paul. *The Saint and the Sultan: The Crusades, Islam, and Francis of Assisi's Mission of Peace.* New York: Doubleday, 2009. Though Moses is not a professional Franciscanologist, he has impressively mastered the primary Franciscan sources. His journalistic background provides an interesting presentation. I would consider this among the most valuable sources on this subject for the English-speaking beginner.
- Sumption, Jonathan. *The Age of Pilgrimage: The Medieval Journey to God.* Mahwah NJ: HiddenSpring, 2003. Originally published in 1975 under the title *Pilgrimage* by Faber and Faber. Explores the complex medieval experience of religious travel: crusades, pursuit of the miraculous, penance, and relics, among others.
- Tolan, John. *Saint Francis and the Sultan: The Curious History of a Christian–Muslim Encounter.* Oxford UP: Oxford, 2009. Not an account of the meeting between Francis and Sultan Malik al-Kamil, this commentary by a renown medievalist on various writings across 800 years and from many places shows how churchmen, politicians, military leaders, artists, Moslems, Christians, and historians understood this meeting.
- Warren, Kathleen A. *Daring to Cross the Threshold: Francis of Assisi Encounters Sultan Malek al-Kamil.* Rochester MN: Sisters of St. Francis, 2003. A readable master's thesis for the Franciscan Institute at St. Bonaventure University NY.

Francis' Return from the Holy Land: Problems Back Home

Sources

Francis' return from the East
Jordan 11–14

The request for a cardinal protector
1C 73–75, 100–101
LJS 65b–66, 73b
AP 42–45
L3C 61–66
2C 23–25
Jordan 14

Actions of Hugolino
1C 73–75, 99
AP 45
L3C 66
Jordan 14

Francis resigns as minister general
2C 143
AC 11, 39, 44 (LP 75–76, 103–104, 105)
2MP 39

Starter questions and suggestions

These citations cover a variety of events and realities that, while seemingly unrelated, all have a relationship to one another. Begin by defining what the immediate reasons for Francis' return were. Note specific people and what they were doing, as well as general trends that were developing in the order back in Italy.

As you continue to wade through these sources, try to identify more radical problems in the life of the rapidly growing order that demanded attention. Why did these problems exist? When did they begin to occur? What was different in the order between 1219 and the early days after the trip to Rome (1209)? Was Francis to blame for problems? Was the order departing from Francis' original vision? Was the order able to live Francis' vision? What judgments do you make about Francis' vision in light of what was already happening while Francis was still alive? Was Francis out of control? Was

Francis a weak, inept leader? Were his ideas inadequate for leading a group of several thousand people?

Identify what measures Francis took to address the problem(s). Were the measures called for in light of the problems? Were they effective?

Pay special attention to the texts that treat of Francis' resignation. Review what you know about the *Intentio regulae* from the chapter in this book on *The Assisi Compilation*. The *Intentio* presents a reason for Francis' resignation not found in 2C and continued in *The Mirror of Perfection*. Identify the difference. How do you account for the difference? Is someone twisting the truth? Why do you think Francis resigned?

Suggested reading

- Esser, Cajetan. *Origins of the Franciscan Order*. Chicago: Franciscan Herald Press, 1970. Chapter three is a good overall treatment of this period in the life of Francis and his order.
- Desbonnets, Théophile. *From Intuition to Institution: The Franciscans*. Trans. Paul Duggan and Jerry Du Charme. Chicago: Franciscan Herald Press, 1988. Chapter five deals with Francis' resignation.

Both books deal with the necessary historical and sociological forces that move groups beyond their founding charismatic leaders to institutionalization, which allows groups to survive with their values.

Christmas at Greccio

Sources

1C 84–87
LJS 53–55
AC 14c (LP 110c)
2C 199–200
LMj X 7
2MP 114

Starter questions and suggestions

The story of Christmas at Greccio is one of the most popular stories about Francis. It is the subject of TV game shows and magazine trivia columns. Many religious publications also discuss the story, especially near Christmas time.

Try to put the images and ideas you have received from those popular presentations to the side. Line up the accounts of the story side by side as you have done for numerous other worksheets. In red ink, write changes or additions to the original story that was found in 1C for easy identification.

Examine your chart and see how the traditions of the story differ. Do you believe anything miraculous occurred at Greccio? Why is there so much buildup to the story, especially in 1C? Many experts in Franciscan spirituality talk about that spirituality as focusing on the historical Jesus, i.e., an incarnational spirituality. What do you think were the benefits of that type of spirituality in Francis' time as evidenced in the Greccio story?

1C begins by describing Francis' desire to walk in the footsteps of Jesus. How does this story demonstrate that characteristic? Does Francis have a fundamentalist or literal approach to following Jesus?

What is your response to this story?

Commentary

LMj X 7 portrays Francis as seeking the pope's permission before arranging this Greccio celebration so as not to appear to be an innovator. This note, not found in the earlier sources, may try to avoid an embarrassing situation for Bonaventure and his goal to secure greater acceptance of the Franciscans by bishops.

Medievals were avid theatergoers, but perhaps in ways you would not expect. The troubadours provided regular entertainment in city squares. Besides performing music, they also recited poetry and short stories. Often, the stories were acted out. Biblical stories were frequently part of their repertories.

These biblical dramas were also common in churches. During the early 13th century, many of these dramas were thought to be buffoonery, and Pope Innocent III issued a statement forbidding them in church buildings.

At a time when Franciscans had to defend their existence within the church, Bonaventure could hardly afford to circulate a story about Francis that potentially portrayed him as disobedient. Some argue this is the reason Bonaventure included the comment that Francis asked for and received permission from the pope.

Francis' Stigmata: Interpretations of the First Thirty Years

Commentary

Perhaps this chapter is the most changed chapter in the revised edition of this workbook. The past ten years have seen many valuable studies about Francis' stigmata and the sources for knowing about them. Relevant important documents have been dated much later than previously believed. Hagiographic studies have repeatedly examined the story and its symbolism. Medical studies have raised questions about the substance of the stigmata.

The final state of scholarship on this topic is far from completed. Scholars need more time to thoroughly digest and evaluate all the new information. This has left the chapter on the stigmata in the first edition of this workbook unhelpful to the beginner. A different approach is needed to introduce new students to the various questions about the stigmata.

I also wish to make a comment about the word *stigmata*. It is a Greek *plural* noun. Its use most likely comes from Gal. 6:17b where Paul of Tarsus said, "I carry the marks (stigmata) of Jesus branded on my body." Thus, its original meaning referred to brands, marks, wounds, and physical evidence of suffering. As a plural noun, it takes a plural verb. Thus it is correct to say, "The stigmata *are*...." It is incorrect to say, "The stigmata *is*...."

Starter suggestions

The unanswered questions about the stigmata make it difficult for beginners to know the historical events surrounding Francis' religious experience on Mount La Verna in September of 1224. Thus, I find it best for beginning students to read some of the various studies that approach the subject in any number of ways. These familiarize beginners with the myriad questions. This study can be done alone, in groups reading the same studies that are then discussed, or in groups whose members report on different studies read by different members of the study group. The list of suggested readings that follows provides many resources for this type of study.

Another approach that can be done in conjunction with the first is to thoroughly read a single historical source and study its use of symbolism to *interpret* Francis' religious experience. This is a different type of study that does not hope to uncover the historical objectivity of the event. Placing historical questions to the side, this type of study seeks to comprehend how various authors at different times in the development of the stigmata tradition understood the importance of the event. Often, this interpretation is tied up with spirituality. Sometimes, the stigmata event is used to verify the validity of a Franciscan way of life and an endorsement of the Franciscan orders. Usually, this approach underscores how the event was/is a confirmation of Francis' personal holiness. Other times, the stigmata are seen as the climax of Francis' great spiritual journey that can be imitated by others. The stigmata are meant to encourage those attracted to walk down a similar path.

I encourage students of the stigmata to select a number of primary sources listed below and to explore their *interpretations* of Francis' stigmata. I suggest a minimum of three sources in order to benefit from the similarities and differences among the studied sources. Begin by clearly understanding the story of the stigmata as narrated in each of your chosen sources. Outlining the story can help you maintain clarity about the various presented stories. This is important because students often *assume* parts of one story version are also present in another version. Often, this is not true. Be careful and accurate. Next, examine the biblical, patristic, and monastic images used in each source. Sometimes, historical people will be mentioned by name. At other times, historical figures will be known by a reference to their story. Footnotes and marginal citations in the text will often help you identify these figures. Determine how references to these historical figures help the author to *interpret* Francis' stigmata.

Also pay attention to how each source links the stigmata experience to Francis' previous life. Notice that often the stigmata are portrayed as a testimony to something true about Francis' entire converted life. Pay attention to ways authors may present the story or parts of the story of the stigmata as a pattern of spiritual life for anyone. Finally, pay attention to any virtues associated with the stigmata. You will want to be aware of the dates of each source in order to see how the traditions about the stigmata developed over the early Franciscan years. A partial list of primary sources to study follows.

Sources

- The Parchment that Francis gave to Leo of Assisi, which contains *The Praises of God* on one side and *A Blessing for Brother Leo* on the other side, written in 1224, and marginal notes about the stigmata event added by Leo sometime later. (FA:ED I 108–112)
- 1C 91–96, 98b, 113–115, 118 (written between 1228–1229; see 2C 10 for Celano's comment in 1246)
- *The Divine Office of Saint Francis*, complete by Julian of Speyer between 1228–1232 (FA:ED I 327–345; see preceding introduction)
- LJS 36b, 59b–63, 71 (written between 1232–1235)
- Luke of Túy's Chronicle dated between 1231–1234 (FA:ED I 595–596)
- Roger of Wendover's Chronicle dated between 1225–1235 (sections 10–13 on FA:ED I 600–601)

- AP 46 (written between 1240–1241)
- L3C 69 (generally dated 1246)
- AC 118 (LP 93) (developing between 1246 and 1311)
- 3C 2–13 (completed by 1252)
- An anonymous letter purportedly announcing Francis' death and his stigmata that was formerly erroneously ascribed to Elias of Assisi but is now dated no earlier than 1253. (FA:ED II 485–491)
- *An Umbrian Choir Legend*, dated between 1253–1259 (FA:ED II 471–482
- LMj XIII 1–10 (completed in 1262). Pay attention to Bonaventure's scriptural allusions and his portrayal of Francis as another Christ.
- *The Divine Office of the Feast of the Stigmata,* dated around 1340 (FA:ED III 661–670)

Suggested reading

- Accrocca, Felice. "Is the 'Encyclical Letter of Brother Elias on the Transitus of St. Francis' Apocryphal?" Trans. Robert Stewart. *Greyfriars Review* 13.supplement (1999) 19–64.
- Armstrong, Regis. *The Spiritual Theology of the* Legenda major *of Saint Bonaventure*. Diss. Fordham University, 1978. Ann Arbor: University Microfilms International, 1978. 7814881. Describes Bonaventure's use of Francis' life as an illustration of his theology of the spiritual life.
- Cousins, Ewert. Introduction. *Bonaventure: The Soul's Journey into God, The Tree of Life, The Life of St. Francis*. By Bonaventure of Bagnoregio. Trans. Ewert Cousins. The Classics of Western Spirituality. New York: Paulist Press, 1978.
- Cusato, Michael F. "From Damietta to La Verna: The Impact on Francis of His Experience in Egypt." *Daring to Embrace the Other: Franciscans and Muslims in Dialogue*. Ed. Daria Mitchell. Spirit and Life 12. Saint Bonaventure NY: Franciscan Institute Publications, 2008. 81–112.
- Dalarun, Jacques, Michael F. Cusato, and Carla Salvati. *The Stigmata of Francis of Assisi: New Studies, New Perspectives*. St. Bonaventure NY: Franciscan Institute Publications, 2006
- Delio, Ilia. "Francis and the Body of Christ." *The Cord* 53.1 (2003) 26–35.
- Frugoni, Chiara. *Francis of Assisi: A Life*. New York: Continuum, 1999. Generally, a modern biography like many others. However, her chapter on the stigmata is unusual for popular biographies in that this University

of Rome historian lays out her suspicions about the historicity of the stigmata. This chapter is the best English treatment of the subject more thoroughly argued in the untranslated *Francesco e l'invenzione delle stimmate: Una storia per immagini e parole fino a Giotto ed a Bonaventura*. Turin: Einaudi, 1993.

- Hellmann, J. A. Wayne. "The Seraph in Thomas of Celano's *Vita Prima*, in *That Others May Know and Love: Essays in Honor of Zachary Hayes, OFM, Franciscan, Educator, Scholar*. Eds. Michael F. Cusato and F. Edward Coughlin. St. Bonaventure NY: The Franciscan Institute, 1997. 23–41.
- Krüger, Klaus. "A Saint to be Looked at: The Image of St. Francis in Thirteenth-Century Panel Paintings." *Greyfriars Review* 16.2 (2002) 119–143.
- Lapsanski, Duane. "The Autographs on the *Chartula* of St. Francis of Assisi." *Archivum Franciscanum Historicum* 67 (1974) 18–37.
- Schatzlein, Joanne and Daniel Sulmasy. "The Diagnosis of St. Francis: Evidence for Leprosy." Franciscan Studies 47 (1987) Annual XXV, 181–217.
- Schmucki, Octavian. *The Stigmata of St. Francis of Assisi: A Critical Investigation in the Light of Thirteenth-Century Sources*. Trans. Canisius F. Connors. Historical Series No. 6. St. Bonaventure, New York: Franciscan Institute Publications, 1991.
- Vauchez, André. "The Stigmata of Saint Francis and Its Medieval Detractors." Trans. Edward Hagman. *Greyfriars Review* 13.1 (1999) 61–89.

Francis' Illnesses

Commentary

This worksheet is another one vastly altered in this revised edition of the workbook. Previous lists of passages that described Francis' illnesses were difficult to manage. Considerable expertise is required to know the meaning of the various symptoms and diagnoses ascribed to Francis. To correct this situation, I now recommend that students simply read some of the available studies about Francis' illnesses. If particular students want to create a list of primary sources about his illnesses, that information can be gleaned from the various articles. I highly recommend the Schatzlein/Sulmasy study listed below.

Suggested reading

- Schmucki, Octavian. "The Illnesses of Saint Francis of Assisi before His Stigmatization." Trans. Sergius Wroblewski. *Greyfriars Review* 4.3 (1990) 31–61.
- Schmucki, Octavian. "The Illnesses of Francis During the Last Years of His Life." Trans. Edward Hagman. *Greyfriars Review* 13.1 (1999) 21–59.
- Schatzlein, Joanne and Daniel Sulmasy. "The Diagnosis of St. Francis: Evidence for Leprosy." *Franciscan Studies* 47 (1987) Annual XXV, 181–217.

Registered nurse Joanne Schatzlein, who also holds a masters degree in Franciscan studies, and medical doctor Daniel Sulmasy present the only paper I know of in English on Francis' illnesses by a team whose combined expertises cover both medical and Franciscan fields. While bold in their investigations, they are conservative in making claims to certainty. They conclude that Francis *probably* died with leprosy, but hold a definitive conclusion is impossible.

While many might accept their most basic suggestions, some will be shocked by the possibility they raise that Francis' stigmata (wounds) could be external manifestations of leprosy. Because the stigmata are the symbolic crowning event in Francis' life, some might think a non-miraculous interpretation of the stigmata threatens the entire meaning of Francis' life.

I don't believe this has to be true. One of Schatzlein and Sulmasy's reasons for suggesting this possibility is Francis' close and prolonged contact with lepers. Certainly, if Francis did indeed share their disease, I cannot think of anything more compelling through which to see in Francis the same self-emptying (kenosis) we celebrate in Jesus. This self-emptying is the very spiritual height we celebrate in Francis through the stigmata.

Read the paper and decide for yourself.

The Parchment Given to Leo

Sources

The Praises of God
A Blessing Given to Brother Leo
2C 49
LMj XI 9

Starter questions and suggestions

Begin by reading the introduction and footnotes in FA:ED I 108–112.

What does the blessing reveal about the relationship between Francis and Leo? Why does Francis give it to Leo? Note that the majority of this writing comes directly from scripture and is not the words of Francis.

How does *The Praises of God* strike you as different or unique from other prayers? What type of prayer is this? Remember that the setting for the composition of this text is the spiritual experience Francis had on La Verna. Can you find any connection between the experience and this prayer? What images of God does this prayer portray?

Suggested reading

- Accrocca, Felice. "The 'Unlettered One' and His Witness: Footnotes to a Recent Volume on the Autographs of Brother Francis and Brother Leo." Trans. Edward Hagman. *Greyfriars Review* 16.3 (2002) 265–282. A challenging article, not for the beginner, that gives a view into the world of textual criticism.
- Lapsanski, Duane. "The Autograph on the *Chartula* of St. Francis of Assisi." *Archivum Franciscanum Historicum* 67 (1974) 18–37. Lapsanski provides a critical edition of the parchment. While some general information is of interest to most readers, this article will mostly interest those wishing to see how a technical critical edition is produced.

The Canticle of the Creatures

Sources

The Canticle of the Creatures
1C 81
AC 7, 83 (esp. I–q), 84 (LP 43, 44, 100)
2C 172, 213
LMj VIII 6; IX 4
2MP 100, 101, 122–123

Commentary

The Canticle of the Creatures (sometimes called *The Canticle of Brother Sun*) was composed at three distinct moments, all after Francis had his religious experience on La Verna in 1224 (the stigmata). The first two parts were probably written in 1225 and the final section shortly before his death in 1226.

The original canticle comprises verses one through nine and celebrates the wonderfulness of God's creation. The notion of sister-brotherhood among all creatures, including us, is very strong. Francis added the second section (verses ten and eleven) shortly thereafter in an attempt to bring strong and destructive rifts between the bishop and podestà (mayor) of Assisi to an end. Unity is its goal. The final section (verses twelve and thirteen) goes so far as to embrace death within the community of creatures. Francis befriends death and sees it as something that serves us like the rest of creation. Some theorize that the final verse was an antiphon, possibly sung after each verse. Thus, the prayer emphasizes the themes of praising God, humility, unity, reconciliation, and, in a strong way, community (sister-brotherhood).

Many scholars of Italian literature consider this canticle to be the beginning of Italian literature. It was later translated into Latin.

Starter questions and suggestions

Begin by reading the introduction and text found in FA:ED I 113–114. Then read the medieval hagiography that is listed. Describe the conditions under which Francis composed the canticle. Are the two additions consistent with the content of the original canticle? How does it fit together as a whole?

Note the spiritual attitudes revealed in the canticle. Reflect on the importance of the titles: brother, sister, mother, and sir. How does relationality fit into Francis' vision expressed in the canticle? Relate the canticle to other aspects of Francis' spiritual vision.

The hermeneutics (modern retrieval) of Francis' relationship with nature has undergone major changes since the 1950's. In that earlier period, Francis' popular image was very romantic, portraying him often through animal stories, particularly from *The Little Flowers*. That retrieval of Francis began to wane after the 1950's so that Francis' relationship with nature was in serious danger of being ignored. Things changed when the environmental movement became popular in the late 1960's and early 1970's. John Paul II proclaimed Francis the patron saint of the environment. Significantly, the popular retrieval of Francis as the nature saint reemerged. However, this time it focused not on animal stories, but on *The Canticle of the Creatures*.

What spiritual images and values about our environment does this canticle bring to believers' attention? What is the impact of Francis' physical suffering and illnesses on this composition?

Suggested reading

- Doyle, Eric. *St. Francis and The Song of Brotherhood*. New York: Seabury Press, 1981.
- Fumagalli, Edoardo. "Saint Francis, the Canticle, the Our Father." Trans. Edward Hagman. *Greyfriars Review* 19.supplement (2005) 1–87. A literary study of the canticle leading to conclusions about its proper interpretation. Not an easy article to read, but worthwhile for the reader who wants a current summary of research about *The Canticle of the Creatures*. Fumagalli takes many positions that are on the cutting edge of research and might shock new students and veterans who haven't been reading the more scholarly research on Francis' poem. When asked whether the *Canticle* was written at three moments toward the end of Francis' life as many have held, Fumagalli argues for a one-time composition. He doesn't believe the strophe on forgiveness is about a conflict between the podestà and the bishop of Assisi as indicated in the Leonine sources; rather it's about his own coming to terms with conflict between himself and his growing community of lesser brothers. The story of menacing mice from the Leonine Tradition is a tribulation sent by the devil to tempt Francis. After the tribulation, Francis has a strong experience of consolation that he is right with God, and composes the *Canticle* to praise God for this healing experience. Essentially, the *Canticle* and the story around its composition are about obedience to the will of God, and this sets Fumagalli up to assert that it is derived more from the *Our Father* than either the *Canticle of the Three Young Men* in the *Book of Daniel* or *Psalm 148*, which traditionally have been considered its primary sources.

This article is another in a growing number of studies which asserts that Francis was much more literate than previously thought because of mistakes Cajetan Esser is purported to have made in his critical editions of Francis' writings. The cursus present in this *Canticle* is too complicated to be the work of a barely literate Francis. Several times, Fumagalli reviews the studies of *The Canticle* about use of the Umbrian (vernacular dialect) preposition *per*, which has been given as many as six meanings by different authors. This article is unique in that it might be the only English article that reviews so much of the thinking about *The Canticle of the Creatures* whose studies have been dominated by Italian-speakers. While most entries are in languages other than English, the bibliography available through the footnotes is enormous and cites all the most important studies of the past and recent times.

- Leclerc, Eloi. *The Canticle of Creatures: Symbols of Union*. Chicago: Franciscan Herald Press, 1978.
- Nothwehr, Dawn M., ed. *Franciscan Theology of the Environment: An Introductory Reader.* Quincy IL: Franciscan Press, 2002. A collection of reprints and original articles with original introductions. It lays scriptural and Franciscan foundations for a theology of the environment and then more specifically explores Bonaventure of Bagnoregio and John Duns Scotus' contributions. The anthology concludes with a section of articles describing a Franciscan praxis for peace, justice, and the integrity of creation.
- Ühlein, Gabriele. "Creation: A Franciscan Conversion Conversation." *In Solitude and Dialogue: Contemporary Franciscans Theologize*. Ed. Anthony M. Carrozzo. St. Bonaventure NY: The Franciscan Institute, 2000. 47–72. Ühlein begins her article with a reflection on *The Canticle of the Creatures*.

Francis' Death and Burial

Sources

1C 88, 108–118
L3C 68 (a later addition from 2C or LMj)
AC 5–8, 12–14a, 22, 99–100 (LP 64–65, 99–101, 107–110a, 117)
2C 214–221
LMj XIV 3–6; XV 1–6
2MP 112

Starter questions and suggestions

Read this entire worksheet before you begin working. There is a great deal of material to read, and you will want to have several things in mind while you read the sources. You may have the energy to read the sources only once.

Outline the events of Francis' death. Quite a few stories are related here, so you may not want to become too detailed. Go for the broad strokes.

Of all the values and ideals that the hagiographers have regarding Francis, which ones stand out in their accounts of Francis' death? How do the purposes of the various accounts show themselves in the different ways of portraying Francis' death? Pay attention to the hagiographers' images, especially the biblical images. List the biblical characters compared to Francis in the sources. You will have to keep your awareness up because the sources will not always give you the names of the biblical characters. Often, the sources simply tell a story that parallels a biblical story. Find out for what the biblical figure is known, and what about him or her applies to Francis. Evaluate the desired impact of such biblical comparisons on the reader.

Describe the different ways the various accounts portray Francis' relationship with Elias of Assisi at the time of Francis' death. It is important to remember that Elias was Francis' "vicar general" at the time of Francis' death. Shortly thereafter, Elias left office and devoted himself to building the Basilica of St. Francis in Assisi. Elias was elected general of the order again in 1232. His generalate ended in disgrace in 1239 when Pope Gregory IX presided over a chapter to elect a new general. Some, like Moorman, believe Elias' later fall from grace affected the way later authors portrayed him or totally ignored him. Note which accounts have changed or deleted sections that deal with Elias. Try to summarize what you think was Elias' true relationship with Francis.

Today, many people interested in Francis' relationships focus on his relationship with Clare of Assisi. These stories suggest Jacoba also had a relationship with Francis. Describe the nature of the relationship. To read more in the sources about Jacoba, see 3C 37–39 and LMj VIII 7.

Suggested reading

- Barone, Giulia. "Brother Elias Revisited." Trans. Giles Bello. *Greyfriars Review* 13.supplement (1999) 1–18.
- Dalarun Jacques. "The Death of Holy Founders from Martin to Francis." Trans. Edward Hagman. *Greyfriars Review* 14.1 (2000) 1–19. Dalarun shows how the hagiographic descriptions of Francis' death demonstrate Francis' holiness by following the established patterns of saints' deaths.
- Iriarte, Lázaro. *Franciscan History: The Three Orders of St. Francis of Assisi.* Chicago: Franciscan Herald Press, 1983. Pages 33–35.
- Moorman, John. *A History of the Franciscan Order: From Its Origins to 1517.* Oxford: Clarendon Press, 1968. Pages 96–104.
- Odoardi, Giovanni. "St. Francis and His Basilica, Brother Elias, Gregory IX and the Transfer of 1230." Trans. Edward Hagman. *Greyfriars Review* 13.supplement (1999) 65–89.
- Wood, Joseph. "Living in the Shadow of Brother Elias." *The Cord* 53.1 (2003) 17–20.

A final word

This is the last worksheet in this book. Hopefully, by using the worksheets you have learned skills and techniques to study Francis of Assisi. Now that you have the skills, you should be able to study other topics about Francis and the movement he began.

When I conclude my guided study, I invite my students to engage in one more reflection period by answering these questions. How would you summarize the mission of Francis? What do you believe are the most important truths about Francis? How are you different now that you have completed this course?

Beyond History

I frequently admit my preference for beginning a study of Francis through a historical-critical approach. I believe our spirituality and theology are only as good as the history on which they rest.

However, I also firmly believe the historical approach is only the first step. If our study of Francis is to have any importance, it has to help us to live *today*. The process of interpreting texts like the scriptures or a person like Francis for people today is called *hermeneutics*. It is the ultimate reason for which I engage in a historical study of Francis.

The skills needed for doing hermeneutics are different than those needed for a historical-critical study. The techniques used differ as well. It is beyond the scope of this book to explore hermeneutics. Furthermore, different people may best implement the two processes.

However, many of the worksheets invite you into an informal process of hermeneutics. The starter questions that ask you to reflect on your own experiences in light of Francis' experiences begin the hermeneutical process.

As we end this educational journey, I only hope to point to the unfinished work: making Francis' vision meaningfully alive today. A fundamentalistic transference of Francis' words and deeds will not be enough for us. I want to be a modern person in a modern church. I hope others in the church and Franciscan movement desire the same. To bring Francis alive today requires us to understand our modern culture(s). We need to understand what our church and world need.

A key concept in approaching this process is *adequacy*. Does the way we understand Francis and present him to others address the real yearnings and needs of people today? If it does not, people will ignore us and much of what the Franciscan spirit has to offer will be lost. However, if our modern presentations of Francis can tap into the experiences and cultures of modern people, Francis' spirit will continue to live in others and us.

It isn't necessary that Francis' spirit continue to live in our church and world. God's spirit, not Francis', is what every age and place needs. This is further illustrated by the hundreds of religious orders and movements that have died over the centuries of Christian faith. However, I would hate to see Francis' spirit die only because we lacked the vision to embody it today. Francis has a lot to offer our church.

With that, I bid you goodbye. I hope you have been changed by this study. I pray your new knowledge will change others as well. Peace and goodness.

Index